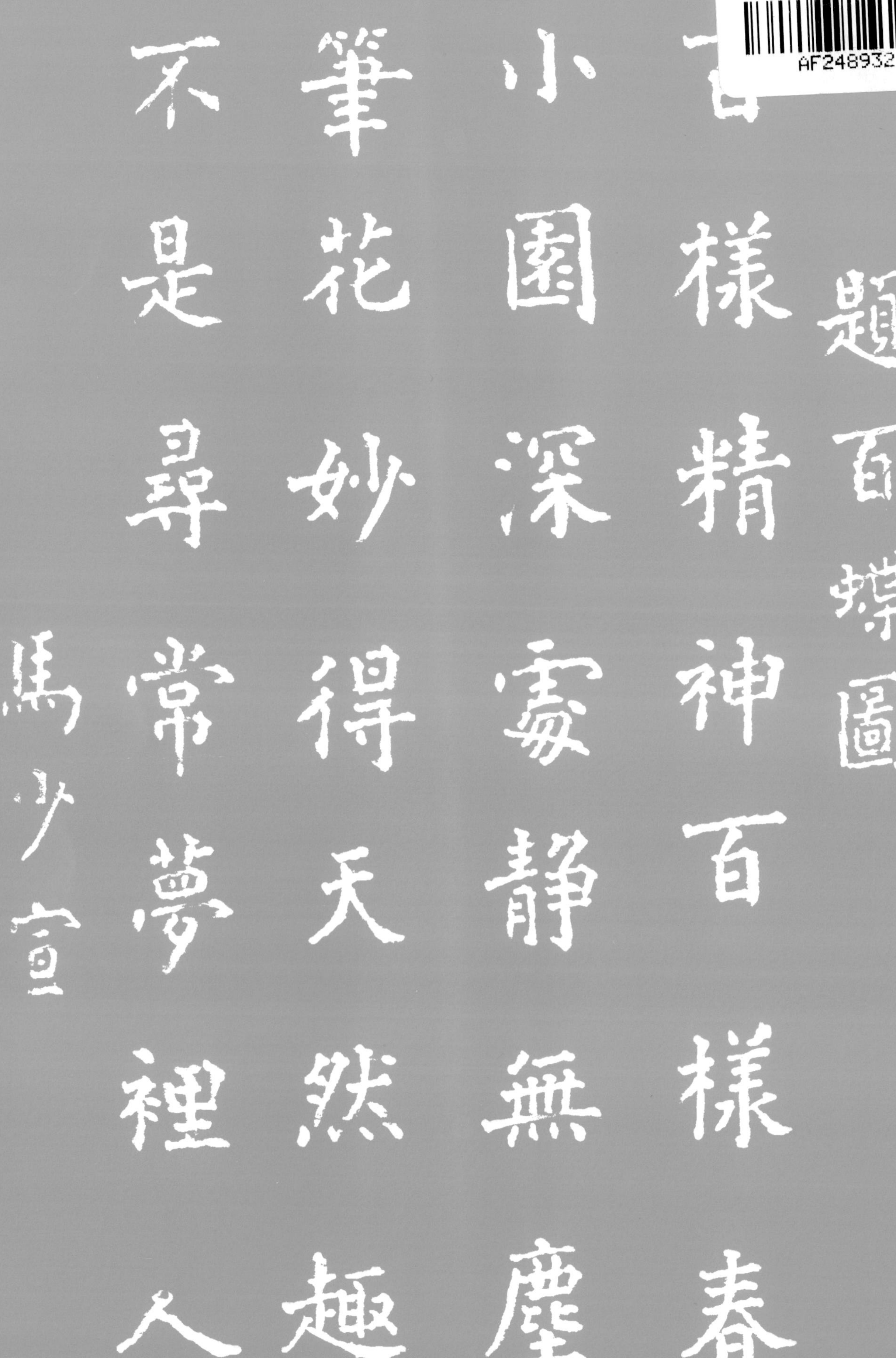

題百蝶圖
春樣精神百樣春
小園深靄靜無塵
筆花妙得天然趣
不是尋常夢裡人
馬少宣

Inside-Painted Snuff Bottle Artist

Ma Shaoxuan (1867–1939)

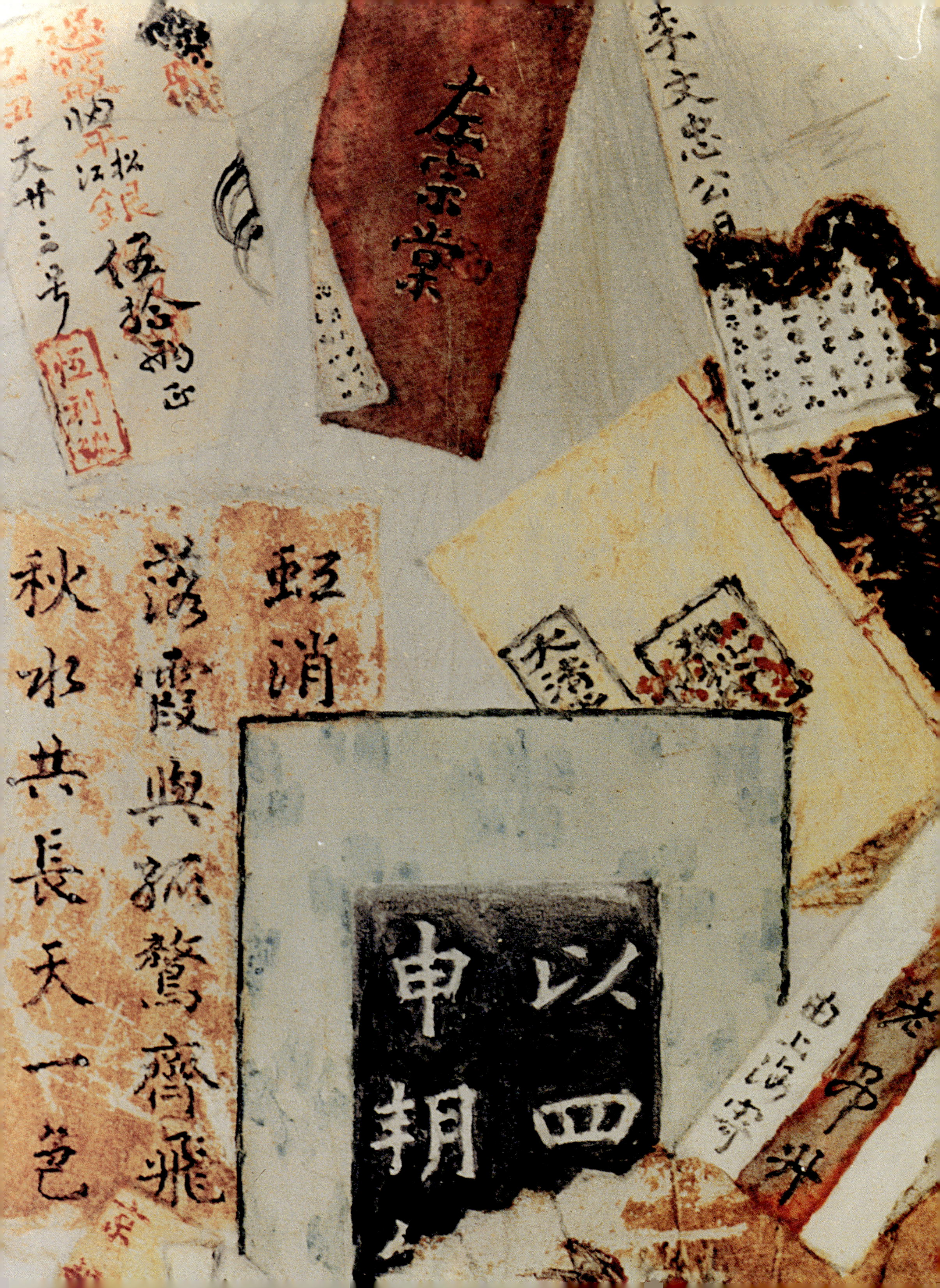

左宗棠
李文忠公日
天井三年 松江銀 伍拾兩正
恒利
虹消
落霞與孤鶩齊飛
秋水共長天一色
以四申朔
大灘

Inside-Painted Snuff Bottle Artist

Ma Shaoxuan (1867–1939)

A Biography and Study by Ma Zengshan
Translated and Annotated by Ka Bo Tsang

The International Chinese Snuff Bottle Society

Frontispiece
Portrait of Ma Shaoxuan by Ma Zengquan made in 1996 (Ma Family Collection)

Cover
Portrait of Ma Shaoxuan by Liu Shouben from a photograph taken in 1925 when
Ma was 59 years old, dated 1992 (The Collection of Mary and George Bloch)

Back Cover
The reverse of the bottle illustrated on the cover

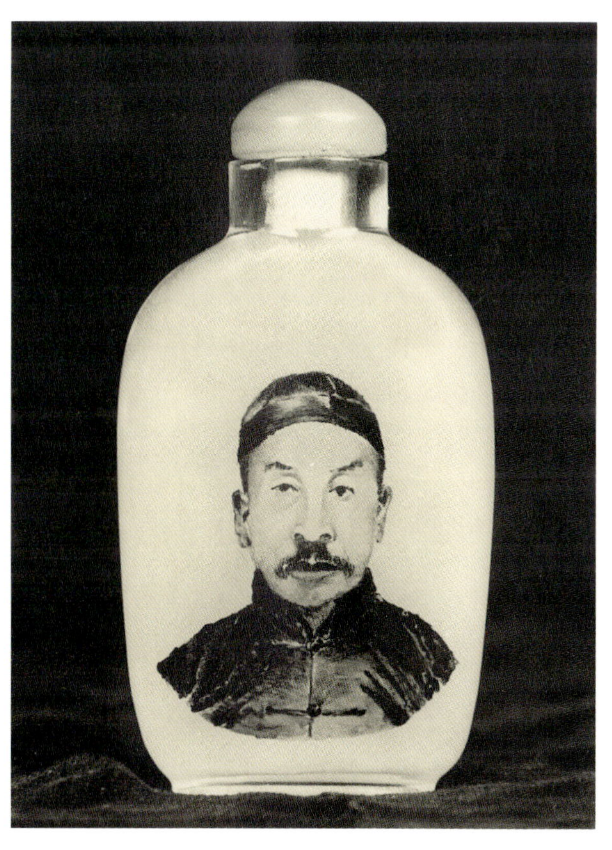

Published by The International Chinese Snuff Bottle Society
2601 North Charles Street, Baltimore, Maryland 21218.

Designed by Rosanne Chan
Produced by C A Design (Communication Art Design & Printing Ltd), Hong Kong

ISBN 962-7502-30-8

Contents

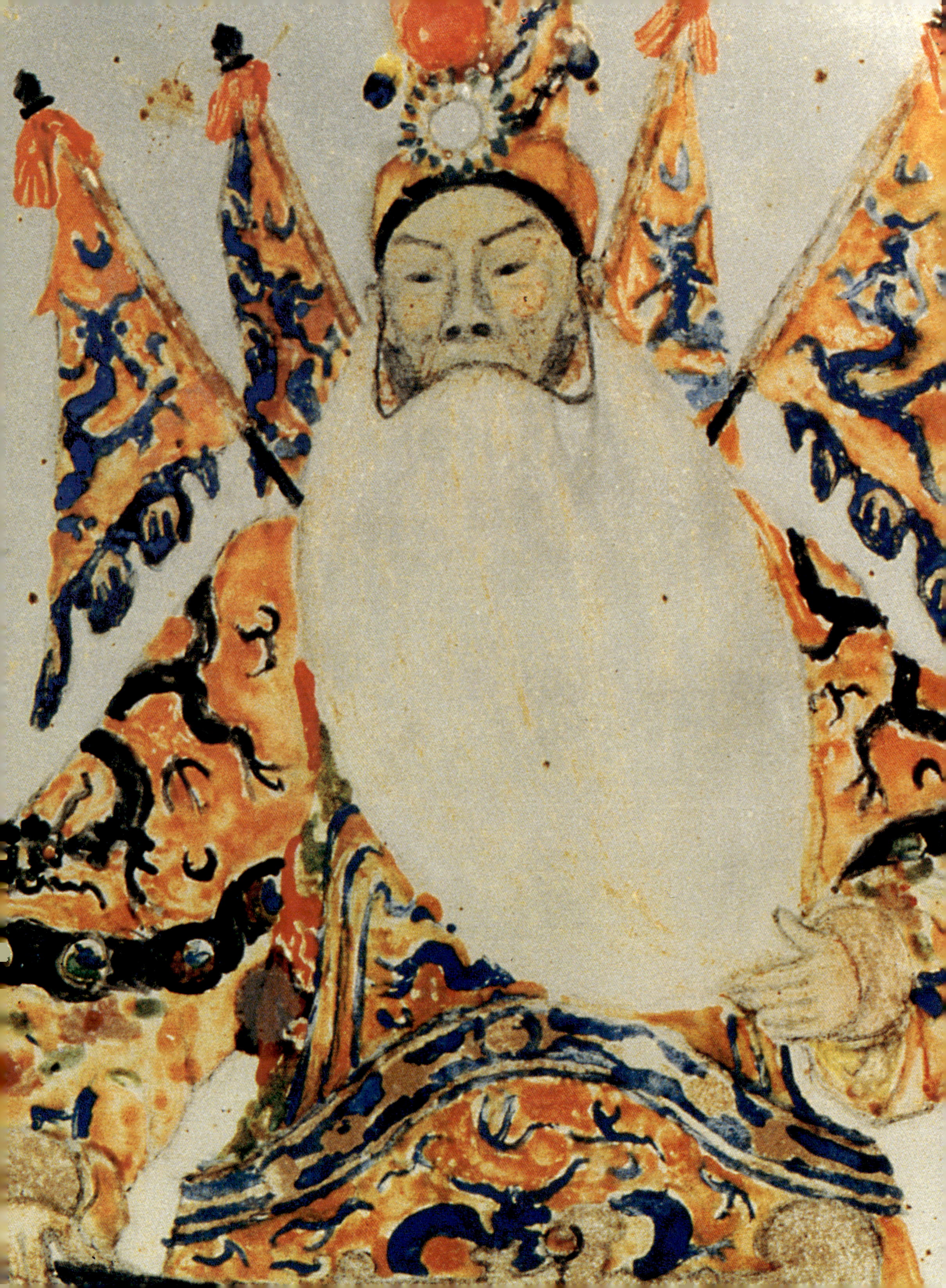

Foreword

The International Chinese Snuff Bottle Society is proud to present this important document which is the first publication to be subsidized by the Society's Educational Fund—the biography of Ma Shaoxuan (1867–1939) by his grandson, Ma Zhengshan, translated and annotated by Ka Bo Tsang. It is not a definitive study of Ma Shaoxuan but an important personal narrative recounting his life and career by a grandson who provides details about his background, date of birth, training and education, the origin of his art name and the seals he used, his attraction to inside-painted portrait bottles and the choice of calligraphic texts that appear on the reverse of so many different types of bottles.

The biography is written in a lively and informal style. Critical scholarly commentary has been kept to a minimum, providing only essential explanations and minor corrections derived from other sources, where necessary. A very important element in the narrative was the choice of illustrations to fit the dates and descriptions of subjects as given in the text. The author, Ma Zhengshan, supplied a certain number from the Ma family archives and most of the other illustrations in the text have come from the private collections of members of the International Chinese Snuff Bottle Society.

Hugh Moss very generously made available his complete files on Ma Shaoxuan, and both Emily Byrne Curtis and Virginia Mead provided invaluable information on the personalities depicted in the portrait bottles. The only examples of this genre which have been illustrated, however, are those showing individuals mentioned in the text where slides or transparenices were available from the current owners or their immediate sources.

Ma Shaoxuan painted many examples of certain well-known subjects—the two Qiao sisters, the celebrated actor Tan Xinpei in the role of General Huang Zhong, the scholar Ouyang Xiu in his study, the "Eight Brokens". It was often necessary in the text to illustrate some of these more than once but great caution had to be exercised because many of these popular subjects were copied by other artists, including Ma Shaoxian who worked closely with Ma Shaoxuan.

The author of this biography tends to be repetitious and the rather colloquial style was at times difficult to translate. This exacting task was accomplished with great skill by Dr. Ka Bo Tsang of the Far Eastern Section of Royal Ontario Museum. She has been a frequent contributor to the *Journal of the International Chinese Snuff Bottle Society* and her highly professional skills in translating and annotating have already been amply demonstrated in two major catalogues, *The Art of the Chinese Snuff Bottle. The J and J Collection* (1993) and *A Treasury of Chinese Snuff Bottles. The Collection of Mary and George Bloch*, vol. 1, Jade (1995), in which she collaborated with Hugh Moss and Victor Graham.

Dr. Graham provided endless editorial assistance with the Ma Shaoxuan biography. He also took charge of the extensive search for the ideal illustrations which proved to be a very complex and exacting task.

Last but not least, we are deeply indebted to Rosanne Chan of Communication Art Design & Printing Ltd. Her dedication to the task of coordinating the many arts and crafts necessary for this publication is exemplary. Readers will note that Ms. Chan recommended the format of our Journal so that the biography can be filed on shelves which house them. This volume is yet another testimony to Ms. Chan's growing number of publications elegantly designed and devoted to snuff bottle literature.

John Gilmore Ford, President
The International Chinese Snuff Bottle Society
Baltimore, Maryland
July 1997

Acknowledgments

Many friends assisted me generously during the course of writing this book. They include Wang Xisan, an inside-painted bottle artist and President of the Chinese Snuff Bottle Society, Li Kechang, Liu Shouben, Zhu Peichu of the Head Office of Chinese Arts and Crafts Import and Export Company, and Xia Gengqi of the Palace Museum, also Beijing Library, Xuanwu Library, Beijing Municipal Cultural Bureau, Beijing Cultural Relics Company, Administrative Office of the Yonghe Palace, and the Director and staff at the Chinese Islamic Association with which I am affiliated. Special thanks are due to my colleagues in the editorial department of the Chinese Muslims magazine. To facilitate the completion of this book, they have given me continuous support.

John G. Ford, President of the International Chinese Snuff Bottle Society, Ka Bo Tsang, translator, and Victor Graham, a snuff bottle expert, have been instrumental in making possible the publication of this book in English.

I am grateful to all who have given me encouragement in this project. I will always think fondly of them.

Ma Zengshan
Beijing
January 1994

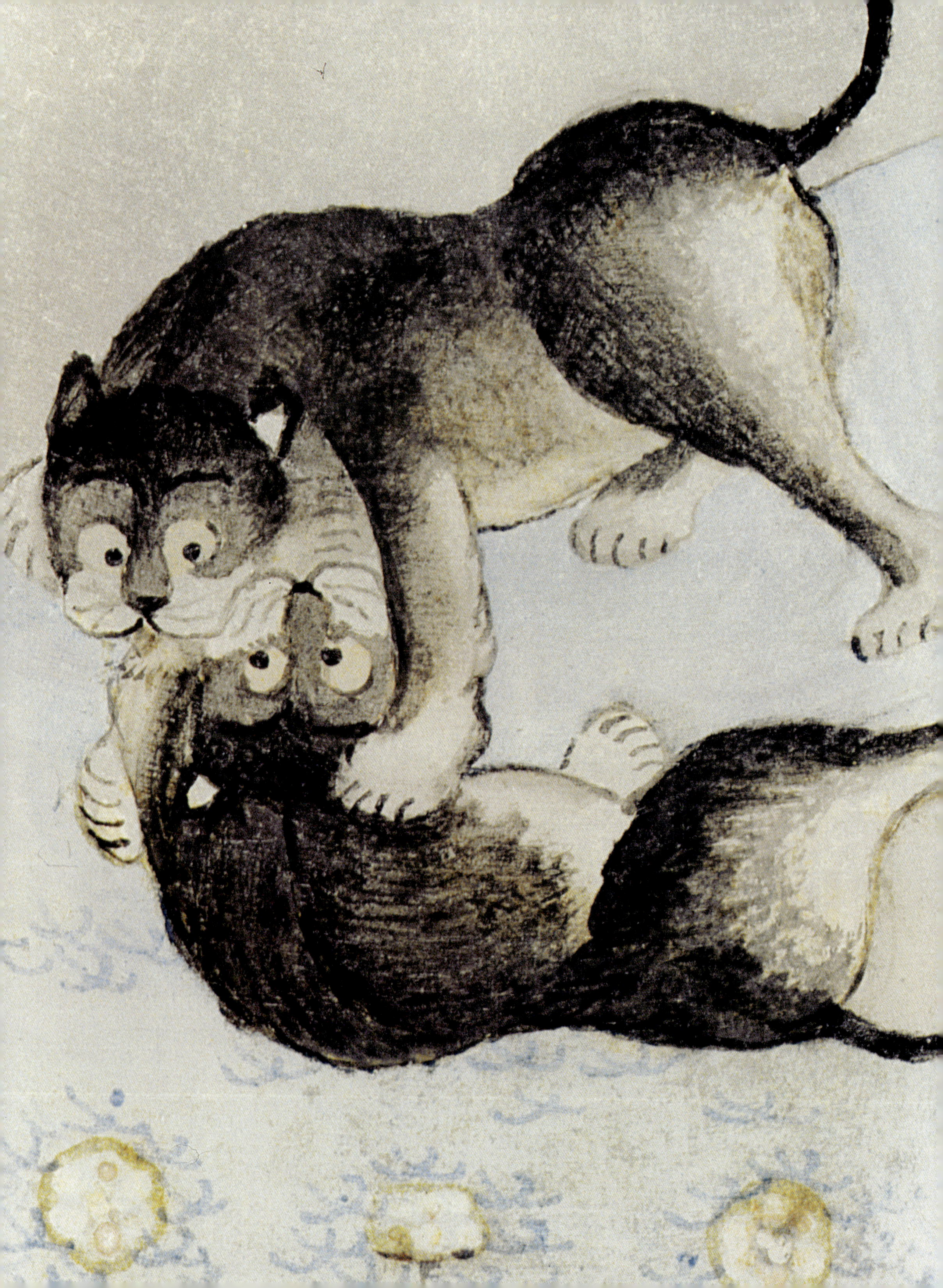

Introduction

Ma Shaoxuan (1867–1939), an inside-painted snuff bottle artist, lived during an era that extended from the late Qing dynasty to the early Republic. For forty-eight of his seventy-three years, from the time he was eighteen until he was sixty-six, he concentrated all his energies and talents in the art of painting snuff bottles. He had attained great achievements and his many outstanding works now hold places of honor in museums and private collections throughout the world. As his works spread, his reputation as a great artist grew both in China and abroad. During the 1930s and 1940s both the eminent Chinese ethnologist, Jin Shoushen, and the connoisseur of antiquities, Zhao Ruzhen, praised Ma's inside-painted snuff bottle art in their writings. While Jin declared that Ma was the most famous among the inside-painted snuff bottle artists, Zhao proclaimed his work "a manifestation of supernatural workmanship."[1] Bob C. Stevens, in his *The Collector's Book of Snuff Bottles*, extolled Ma Shaoxuan as "the Picasso of inside-painted snuff bottle artists," adding that, "Picasso's style is not as agreeable to my own taste as is that of Ma Shao-hsüan."[2] Monographs written on inside-painted snuff bottles, both Chinese and foreign, all rank the art of Ma Shaoxuan extremely highly.

While people passionately appreciate Ma's art and collect and treasure his works, they know very little about his life and artistic career. Some even are ignorant of his studio names, nationality, place of origin, or birth and death dates. This ignorance of Ma's artistic ambitions, training and development, the many forgeries of his works, with the authentic and fake often mixed, has left a fog about the man and his works that makes difficult the study and appreciation of his art. For years, scholars have eagerly hoped to discover research materials on Ma Shaoxuan, but, since the flow of information was cut off during this period, few have been found.

For the past several decades, Ma's descendants have been too preoccupied with their own responsibilities to release materials about Ma. However, we now are duty-bound to publish everything about him.

1. See Jin Shoushen, *Lao Beijing de shenghuo*, p. 226 and Zhao Ruzhen, *Guwan zhinan xubian*, ch. 20, p. 13.

2. Bob C. Stevens, *The Collector's Book of Snuff Bottles*, p. 250.

I, the author, am Ma Shaoxuan's grandson, and I wrote this biography and study of him to honor the warm memories I have of him and to express my profound admiration and respect for him. I also consider it as a gift presented to grandfather's spirit, now residing in heaven. At the same time, I present this book to all members of the older generation and other friends, in China and abroad, who cherished him, collected his works, and conducted research on his art of inside-painted snuff bottles.

My father's generation consisted of two brothers whose deaths followed closely in 1949 and 1953. Of the five members of my generation, the two eldest—my father's older brother's eldest son, Ma Zengxiang, and my own elder brother, Ma Zengrui — died respectively in 1990 and 1992. Even recounting these events makes sad and painful feelings well up in my heart. Of the survivors, I am the eldest and, at sixty-five, in the sunset years of life. If I were not to take careful advantage of the time remaining to me and gather the materials our family controls, compile a book, and make it available to the public, many circumstances concerning Ma Shaoxuan would remain unknown to everyone, and many questions about him would forever remain a riddle. It would be futile to try to understand Ma Shaoxuan and his art, learn the history of the art of inside-painted snuff bottles, or encourage its further development. Consequently, I resolved to put aside many important matters of my own in the past few years, so that I might overcome all difficulties and devote myself completely to writing this volume.

Its composition is based upon materials left behind by my grandfather and members of my father's generation, what things I had seen with my own eyes and heard with my own ears, and materials contributed by my two older brothers, other brothers and sisters, cousins, and other relatives and friends, and accounts of what they had seen and heard. The work is the product of the joint effort of three generations of our family, from grandfather to grandchildren.

Writing about the achievements of an ancestor runs an obvious risk: if one does not maintain careful control, emotions can be so overwhelming as to lead to undeserved praise of one's subject. I recognize the damage caused by undeserved praise: if slight, it diminishes the work's credibility, and, if severe, it robs the work of all value. Therefore, I guarded absolutely against it. Before beginning to write I took this as my guiding principle: seek truth from facts and write only what they support. While writing, this principle should be in force from start to finish. For example, the narration of Ma Shaoxuan's life must be based on facts, and, lacking sufficient evidence, it would be better to omit material and refrain from groundless assertion. Discussions of the creation of his inside-painted snuff bottle art must be based on his actual works. It is necessary first to set out the works and then subject them to analysis, avoiding vague and general opinion. When discussing his artistic achievements and contributions, one should as far as possible present the judgments of earlier critics, and, when lacking such judgments uphold absolutely strict standards, and, if in doubt, err on the side of understatement. Exaggeration should be avoided absolutely.

Although the Introduction precedes the main text, I composed it only after the main text was complete. In it I clarify the grandfather-grandson relationship that exists between Ma Shaoxuan and myself. However, in the main text I use a third-person narrative throughout, since over the several years of writing, I thought that adopting an objective approach to Ma's biography, one in which there is no hint of the family tie between artist and author, would best help me hold to the guiding principle. For Ma's descendant to refer to him simply by name may be considered disrespectful, but I hope to be forgiven for doing so since respecting the facts is a way of showing respect for the reader, my grandfather, and myself.

As a biography, this work is an account of things that really happened and not at all a work of fiction. It contains no fabricated circumstances, fantastic stories, or garish exaggerations. I have made every effort to write in a plain, carefully crafted, direct, and lucid manner. However, the reader may feel such writing is dull and insipid, which would also result in failure. How could this be avoided? Here, my grandfather gave me all the help I needed. As his entire life is filled with fascinating stories, accounts of them would be sure to engage the reader's interest. The only problem might be that I, with my reserved personality and clumsy writing, might not be up to telling these stories with all the passion and force they deserve, which would be a great pity.

A biography of this inside-painted snuff bottle artist must, of course, include everything of significance during his life but should also emphasize the history of his art and its development. I have presented his story as occurring in a series of stages and treat the crises he faced, the contradictions that emerged, his artistic development and achievements, and their essential features stage by stage. Considered as a whole, they allow one to discern the main trends that constitute the development of Ma's art and make clear representative works—bright pearls—that are scattered throughout his artistic creation. For a number of the important works, I present accounts of their background, the processes through which their designs took shape, and descriptions of their essential artistic characteristics and value. The reader will encounter most of Ma's key works, many introduced here for the first time. To represent each period of artistic development and place works in their rightful historical position it is essential, of course, that the works considered be indisputably authentic.

I have spent a few years on the writing of this book. After revising my manuscript several times the task is finally completed. Although it is now ready to go to press, I fully realize that there must still be omissions and mistakes and hope that such deficiencies will be pointed out to me by the experts so that further revisions may be made in the future.

Ma Zengshan
Beijing
January 1994

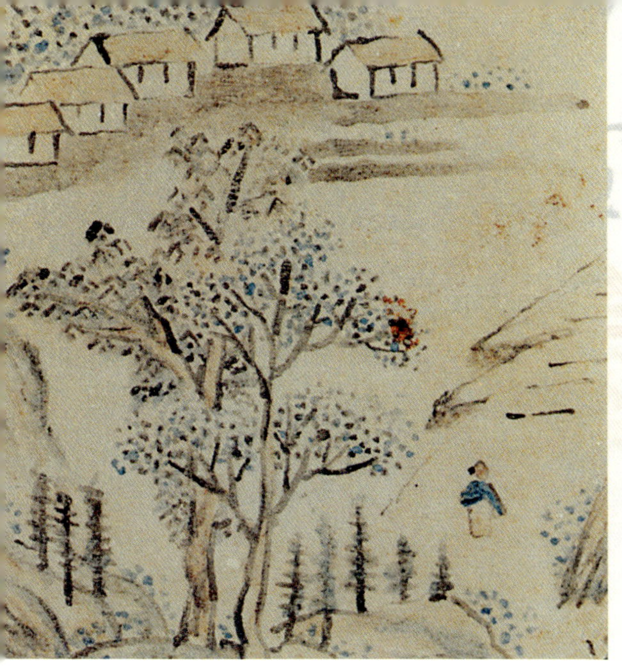

CHAPTER ONE

Youth

Ma Shaoxuan, the inside-painted snuff bottle artist who practised his art from the last years of the Qing dynasty (1644–1911) until the time of the early Republic, was born in the sixth year of the Tongzhi period (1867). During his early years he was educated at home, and at the age of seven he started school. He was eighteen when he embarked on his career of painting inside snuff bottles, to which he remained devoted body and soul. In the course of this career, he managed to paint inside tiny snuff bottles an entirely new world. Not until 1932, when he was sixty-six, did he finally set down his brushes. In the autumn of 1939 he fell ill and died at the age of seventy-three.[3]

Throughout his life Ma ardently loved China's traditional culture, especially the arts of calligraphy and painting. He absorbed and further developed the accomplishments of earlier inside-painted snuff bottle artists, remaining deeply engaged for fifty years in intense study and constant practice. His accomplishments were tremendous: he greatly extended and enriched the range of subject matter for snuff bottle painting, significantly advanced the technique of painting inside snuff bottles, immensely expanded the horizons of the art form, and produced an enormous number of exquisite snuff bottle paintings profoundly imbued with both the traditional characteristics of Chinese national art and his own individual style. He has immensely enriched the cultural holdings of China, winning high praise at home and abroad. For many years, his works have been continuously displayed in important Chinese and foreign exhibitions where they have been received with the greatest

3. In the past the Chinese calculated a person's age like this: a child was considered one year old when he was born. From then on a year was added to his age as a year passed by. This was quite different from the current method of calculating age as beginning at birth. For the sake of distinguishing one from the other, the age calculated by the earlier method is called "false age." Ma Shaoxuan's ages were all calculated according to the "false age" system by the author.

enthusiasm and interest. He has garnered glory for the art of inside-painted snuff bottles and for China. Together with his colleagues, their brilliant contributions to the development of this art form elevated the world of the inside-painted snuff bottle to a new height of achievement.

ENVIRONMENT

One's life, whether long or short, whether his accomplishments be many or few, is played out on history's stage. Ma Shaoxuan's ancestors, hailing from Eastern Turkestan, were Muslims. Their descendants for dozens of generations lived in the Niujie (Ox Street) district of Beijing. Ma Shaoxuan was born in Ox Street district and grew up and lived his entire life there. Since Ox Street had a great influence on his life, what was it like?

Southwest of Xuanwu Men (Promulgate Military Prowess Gate), Ox Street district before liberation was an out-of-the-way, lower-income area where Muslims (the Hui minority in China) crowded together to live. It was an insignificant odd corner of the old imperial capital of Beijing. Similar to Beijing and other areas in China, it had maintained the long-lasting bloodline of Chinese culture, at the same time being nourished by the Han Chinese culture. Nevertheless, one special feature sets it apart from other districts in Beijing. Since the tenth century, it had been infused with the culture of Islam, brought into China by the Arabs. Over many centuries its people were influenced by both Chinese and Islamic cultural forces, which in time fused into a single, synthetic culture which uniquely affected how these Chinese Muslims thought and felt, conducted human relations, practised religious faith, and developed folklore and customs. Without such background knowledge, it would be hard to understand the inhabitants of this district.

Ox Street is a major north-south thoroughfare, somewhat more than a *li* long, lined with about a thousand Chinese Muslim households. Their ethnic features are quite obvious. East of Ox Street, there are three Muslim mosques in less than a *li*: the Dong Si (Eastern Mosque), the Jiaozihutong Libaisi (Disciple Alley Temple of Prayer); the Xi Si (Western Mosque), the Niujie Libaisi (Ox Street Temple of Prayer); and the Nü Si (Women's Mosque), which provides a place for ablution and worship for the female inhabitants. Early every morning before daybreak, when everything is absolutely quiet, calls to prayer simultaneously come from the minarets, the muezzins crying out in Arabic the *adhân* in resounding voices, carrying to each of the thousand Muslim households. As soon as these people open their eyes, they feel the gentle breeze of Islam waft over them; they then quickly make their way to the mosques for ablution and prayer. According to custom, this call is repeated five times each day. After morning prayer shopkeepers, workers, laborers, farmers, and others who follow sundry occupations all start making their day's living as Muslims. Once the day's work is done, at nine or ten o'clock, they perform evening rituals and retire for the night. In all their religious and secular dimensions, these activities give order to life, day by day, year after year. Passed down from generation to generation, they permeate people's lives from beginning to end.

Especially exciting are the great annual Islamic festivals. The Chinese Muslims of Ox Street district, male and female, young and old, all join in celebrating together as a people. On such occasions, although the Muslim communities distributed in Beijing and other regions in China all observe the traditions with fervor, inhabitants of Ox Street district showed unparallelled zeal. Bright and early, people put on clean clothes, don sparkling white ceremonial caps, and go to mosques to perform ablution. At nine o'clock, worship begins. From every direction Muslims assemble near the mosques, and, whether involved in worship or in performing services, fill the entire street from one end to the other. Everywhere you turn there are people; all you can see is an ocean of white caps. The street is also filled with the sound of people greeting one another in Arabic, and clouds of sandalwood incense everywhere give off wafts of fresh fragrance.

Any member of the Hui minority living under these circumstances so permeated with Islam is sure to be deeply affected by them. From earliest childhood, one is imperceptibly influenced by what he hears and sees, and, with time, these influences deeply penetrate his very spirit. Islam's religious doctrines are profound and complex, but lying at the center of all Muslim thought and behavior the most generally known is a simple axiom—"We are commanded to do good and forbidden to do evil." Ma Shaoxuan was born into this environment.

He was shaped simultaneously by Confucian thought, exemplified by the *Four Books* and *Five Classics*,[4] and the rules and doctrines of Islam.

The special character of Ox Street district, a fusion of Han Chinese and Islamic cultures, was deeply pervasive. The Ox Street Mosque itself embodies this fusion, with a hall of classical Chinese architecture—a large and lofty octagonal-shaped pavilion, a wooden ceremonial gateway, a great hall of tiles with a high ridged roof, carved wooden support blocks at the corners, and multi-colored painted decorations—yet flowing through these old-fashioned Chinese architectural forms and shapes is a strong undercurrent of Islamic form and content. The two traditions merge into one style without the least flaw or inconsistency. The very ways in which Islam is propagated are also apparent in this kind of cultural fusion. In both verbal proselytizing and the publication of religious materials, the Chinese and Arabic languages are used in combination, the one interspersed with the other, or the same text appearing in both languages on facing pages. Even in everyday language, members of the Hui minority developed a way of speaking that combines both languages. This combination of cultures accounts for a major historical phenomenon: China, with a dominant Han majority culture, has long permitted the propagation of Islam, and Islam, as propagated among the Hui minority, does not deprecate Chinese culture. Significantly, the Hui minority advocates that Muslims should nourish themselves by assimilating both Chinese and Islamic cultures simultaneously. By so doing, one brought up among the Hui people is steeped not only in Chinese culture but also in the Islamic tradition. This approach encouraged the development of a significant number of talented Hui minority people whose level of sophistication with Chinese culture is matched by that of Islam.

This fusion of Chinese and Islamic cultures in Ox Street district goes back one thousand years. Testifying to this is the Ox Street Temple of Prayer, generally recognized as first built during the Liao dynasty (907–1125), probably toward the end of the tenth century. In the east courtyard, the memorial steles of two ancient graves preserve old Arabic inscriptions recording that two

4. The *Four Books* are *Daxue* (Great Learning), *Zhongyong* (Doctrine of the Mean), *Lunyu* (The Analects of Confucius), and *Mengzi* (Mencius). The *Five Classics* are *Shijing* (Book of Odes), *Shangshu* (Book of Documents), *Sanli* (Three Classics on Etiquette—*Zhouli*, *Yili* and *Liji*), *Yijing* (Book of Change), and *Chunqiu* (Annals of the Spring and Autumn Period).

learned men from Western Asia who came to preach the Islamic faith are buried there. One grave, of Ahmad Burdani of Ghazna, buried in 679 of the Islamic calendar (1280 A.D.), refers to Ghaznî, the capital city of the Ghaznavid empire (the first Muslim dynasty of Afghanistan), within the borders of present-day Afghanistan. The other grave, of Ali, the son of the Bokharan Arwa Junaydi, buried in 682 of the Islamic calendar (1283 A.D.), refers to Bokhara in present-day Uzbekistan. These two learned men went to the trouble of travelling thousands of miles to spread the Islamic faith in Ox Street district, and both were buried there in proper graves within the precincts of a mosque, proving that a considerable number of Muslims were living there at that time.

With the arrival of the Islamic religion and Muslim inhabitants of Western Asia came Arabic incense and perfumes, jewelry and jade, pharmaceuticals and medical arts. Henceforth, many people in Ox Street district made their living dealing in antiques, jewelry and jade, and practised medicine or owned incense and perfume shops. Even today, there are many following such occupations throughout the district. Ma Shaoxuan's father, for example, practised medicine and many of his friends and relatives dealt in antiques and jade. They had expert knowledge of snuff bottles and great familiarity with inside-painted snuff bottles, and they both greatly eased Ma's way to becoming a snuff bottle painter and supported him in his chosen career. Ox Street was Ma's cradle, and it was from Ox Street that he took his first steps on the road of his life. His honors and accomplishments and the kind of man he became all can be traced back to Ox Street.

CRADLE YEARS

Number 3, Menlou Hutong (Archway Alley), which runs off the east side of Ox Street, is a compound consisting of some ten rooms about a courtyard. Here Ma Shaoxuan was born. His father was a practitioner of traditional Chinese medicine, an excellent doctor, also very learned in both classical Chinese studies and Islam, and an ardent lover of calligraphy and painting. The family was well-to-do and enjoyed a quiet and

comfortable existence. Of the three sons and two daughters, Ma
Shaoxuan was the youngest. A handsome, bright little boy, he had
a broad forehead, dark black hair, and sparkling, inquisitive eyes.
His older relatives became very fond of him. His father gave him
the name of Guangjia (Brilliant First-place), which derives from
the phrase *guangyao jiadi* (the brilliant first-place examination
candidate). When Ma was five or six, his father began to teach
him how to write characters with a brush. Imitating his father, his
little hand picked up the brush and made the character *ren*
(man), which thoroughly delighted his father. Traditionally,
Chinese medicine has emphasized the use of classical Chinese
language in its treatises, prescriptions, and other writings, and it
placed equal emphasis on fine calligraphy. Since all Chinese
medicinal literature and pharmacopoeia were published in
classical Chinese, it was impossible to study these fields without
knowing the language. Prescriptions had to be written out in
calligraphy with a brush; if a doctor did not have good
handwriting, his prescriptions would not be respected. It is not
surprising, then, that Ma Shaoxuan's father was very fond of
classical poetry and prose, calligraphy and painting, and also
attached great importance to his children's learning how to read
and write at an early age. The very first time Ma held a brush to
write a character convinced his father that the boy was an
intelligent child, and he began to make plans how to nurture this
talent. From then on Ma progressed from tracing models to
imitating examples free-hand, and, as he grew older, to copying
the *Jiuchenggong liquan ming* (An Account of the Sweet Spring at
the Palace of Nine Accomplishments) by Ouyang Xun
(557–641).[5] Ma's development was so steady and sure as to dispel
all his father's worries about him.

ENTERING SCHOOL

At seven, Ma Shaoxuan entered a traditional private school.
The curriculum consisted of studying the *Sanzijing* (Trisyllabic
Classic), *Baijiaxing* (Book of One Hundred Family Names), and
Qianziwen (Thousand Characters Classic).[6] After Ma turned ten,
his father found him the best teacher in the southern part of the
city, and the boy took instruction under this new mentor.

5. Ouyang Xun, who lived at the end of
    the Sui and beginning of the Tang
    dynasties, is one of China's great
    calligraphers. One of his most famous
    pieces was inscribed on a stone tablet
    erected in the sixth year of the
    Zhenguan period (632) in the Tang
    summer palace northwest of Chang'an
    (present-day Xi'an), a text arranged in
    24 columns of 50 characters of a
    composition by the imperial counselor,
    Wei Zheng (580–643), which records
    the event of Emperor Taizong of Tang
    (r. 627–649) discovering a gushing
    spring at the time when he stayed at his
    summer resort, the Palace of Nine
    Accomplishments. Many ink rubbings
    were made of it over the centuries, and
    it became, through published
    reproductions, one of the principal
    models for aspiring calligraphers. See
    Jean François Billeter, *The Chinese Art of
    Writing*, pp. 35–37, 44, note 7; partial
    reproductions of a rubbing appear on
    pp. 36-37.

6. *Sanzijing*, *Baijiaxing*, and *Qianziwen*
    were among the most popular primers
    used in traditional China. Because their
    texts were composed of short sentences
    with rhymes, they were generally
    regarded as ideal educational tools for
    aiding children to memorize many of
    the commonly used characters in the
    Chinese language. *Sanzijing* is believed
    to have been written by Wang Yinglin
    (1223–1296) of the Southern Song
    period (1127–1279). *Baijiaxing* is a
    Northern Song (960–1127) work; its
    author, however, is not known.
    Qianziwen was composed by Zhou
    Xingsi (d. 521) of the Liang dynasty
    (502–556) who selected one thousand
    different characters from the calligraphic
    works of Wang Xizhi (321–379) to
    make up the text, its content touching
    on the natural, social, historical, ethical,
    and educational aspects of the Chinese
    culture.

7. Zhong You and Wang Xizhi are credited with the development of the regular script (*kaishu*). Ouyang Xun also did much to give this style of calligraphy a strong, enduring form. See Jean François Billeter, *The Chinese Art of Writing*, p. 76.

8. *Jieziyuan huazhuan*, since it first appeared in 1679, has been the most famous and widely used manual of traditional Chinese painting. For that first edition, the well-known essayist and playwright Li Yu (1611–1680) wrote a preface. The work, in fact, was named after his villa, which included a bookstore/publishing house, called the "Mustard Seed Garden," located near the South Gate of old Nanjing. The illustrations and most of the text were prepared by three brothers, Wang Shi, Wang Nie, and Wang Gai (dates unknown). Wang Gai was the principal contributor and general editor, and Li Yu's son-in-law, Shen Xinyou, who managed the bookstore, was the publisher. There is an English version, which includes reproductions of all the illustrations, translated and edited by Mai-mai Sze, *The Mustard Seed Garden Manual of Painting*.

9. Ma Zengshan makes no mention of his grandfather prior to this of having prepared for or taken the district or county examination (*xianshi*), prefectural examination (*fushi*), or other qualifying examinations offered at the prefectural level, which were the prerequisite for admittance to the provincial examination. Strict regulations governed candidacy and, at the end of the Qing, the quota by province was fixed at about 100 candidates per province who, every three years, were allowed to compete for *juren* status, the basic qualification either to enter lower officialdom or subsequently compete for the *jinshi* (admitted scholar) degree in the triennial palace examinations, the route to higher officialdom. It would have been impossible for someone simply to "enter the imperial examination hall," as Ma Zengshan states, without having had success in the earlier examinations, but such examinations were held every three years, and one was held in 1884, when Ma Shaoxuan was eighteen, exactly the right age. However, it seems strange that Ma Zengshan says nothing about all the hard work that would have gone into preparing for these preliminary examinations, not to speak of the grueling experience of sitting for them, which suggests that the family legend of Ma Shaoxuan's experience with the examinations may be exaggerated— he might have sat for only one of the preliminary examinations in 1884. A detailed account of the traditional civil service examination system as it existed at the end of the Qing era can be found in Ichisada Miyazaki, *China's Examination Hell: The Civil Service Examinations of Imperial China*.

He then studied the *Four Books* and *Five Classics*, began to attend lectures, and read other classical writings. Although the course of study was old-fashioned, the teacher was superb. Ma possessed an excellent memory and great powers of comprehension. After his school day was over, he received additional instruction at home, which was also very strict. During the evening he practised calligraphy, working his way through books of model calligraphy containing examples by Zhong You (151–230), Wang Xizhi (321–379), and Ouyang Xun.[7] Ma also liked to paint, so he often took his father's copy of the *Jieziyuan huazhuan*[8] (The Mustard Seed Garden Manual of Painting) and looked at or imitated the models in it, always with the greatest enthusiasm. At fifteen or sixteen, he was already quite proficient in painting and calligraphy. His small regular script was especially fine, imparting an air of dignity.

Ma's family was not financially pressed, so there was no hurry for the three brothers to seek jobs, and they often stayed home studying poetry, calligraphy, and painting and reciting famous pieces of classical literature. The days passed pleasantly.

The year Ma turned eighteen happened to be a year when the triennial provincial examination (*xiangshi*) was held for the *juren* (elevated scholar) degree. Encouraged by his father, Ma entered the imperial examination hall and took the examination, writing essays on assigned topics. However, he failed to pass and never again competed in the civil service examinations.[9] For the rest of his life he devoted himself to calligraphy and painting.

GOOD FORTUNE

Failing the provincial examination did not trouble the young man, for Ma Shaoxuan never wanted an official career. However, now what was he to do? It seemed as if he were standing at a crossroads waiting to choose the way to go. His father had not tried to train him in the arts of healing, nor did he have any interest in this profession. What career could develop his particular talents and allow him to continue to work with his beloved calligraphy, painting, and classical poetry and prose? The whole family pondered this and explored possibilities.

One day, several of his father's friends and relatives assembled at the Ma house. Among them was a relative who ran an antique shop, and he brought out several inside-painted snuff bottles to show to everybody. The paintings of flowers, birds, and landscapes painted inside the tiny glass bottles were exquisitely executed, gorgeous works, which amazed and delighted everyone.

During the 1880s only a very few people could execute paintings inside snuff bottles, so when Ma's relative happened upon such bottles, he was struck by their rarity and, when possible, brought them to gatherings so that family and friends could enjoy them and talk about them. The bottles enhanced the party mood. Although Ma Shaoxuan was then still quite a young fellow, as his father was extremely fond of him, he was allowed to take part in such adult gatherings, which gave him the opportunity to see the painted snuff bottles. These so enthralled him that he fondled them incessantly and could not let them go. He begged his elders to explain how the paintings were done and was eager to try his hand at it. When Ma's father saw how absorbed his son had become, he said, "Don't you love to do calligraphy and painting? Do you think that you could paint and write inside snuff bottles?" Ma Shaoxuan realized that he and his father had arrived at exactly the same thought and immediately replied, "Of course!" All the family friends and relatives present encouraged him to pursue this career, since it seemed to promise so much opportunity for success and satisfaction.

This happened quite by chance, and, for all their enthusiasm, no one realized the significance of the occasion. Yet it determined the course of a man's entire life's work, for it was then that Ma decided to become an inside-painted snuff bottle artist.

FIRST STEPS

Ma Shaoxuan together with his two older brothers began studying how to paint inside snuff bottles. All were very enthusiastic. The brothers visited relatives and experts who knew a lot about inside-painted snuff bottles. They tried to discover what kind of brushes were used, what methods of painting were involved, how to buy blank snuff bottles, where to find steel balls (*tieshazi*), how to frost the inside surface of the bottle cavity, and so on. They found out all that could be found out and bought everything that could be had. They learned to split bamboo into slender pens, with which they used to experiment, trying to discover how to paint and write inside snuff bottles. As the saying goes, "Everything is difficult at first," and this was no exception. Although in theory the art of painting inside snuff bottles can be described in a few sentences and might seem very simple, in actual practice it involved numerous difficulties. The brothers had many setbacks. Ma Shaoxuan never became the disciple of a master painter nor did he systematically learn the art of painting inside snuff bottles from a single painter of the previous generation. He had no opportunity to study at any length or in any detail bottles painted by older artists. All he could do was to make inquiries about painting methods through his relative who ran an antique shop and to rely on his relative's connections for introductions, which allowed him to meet older and more recently established painters. Ma would visit them and observe, ask questions, and, after having been exposed to all sorts of unsystematic and incomplete materials, would then go home to try to fabricate his own pens and practise painting and calligraphy inside snuff bottles.

Using a brush to paint on paper and using a bamboo pen to sketch inside snuff bottles require two completely different actions. Brush painting follows the traditional way of doing calligraphy: the hand grasps the brush and writes downwards on the paper. Painting inside snuff bottles requires the hand to grasp the bamboo pen, insert it through the tiny mouth opening of the bottle, and, with upward strokes, sketch the picture on the inside surface. The tip of the bamboo pen is sharpened with a knife and is so smooth and hard that it cannot contain any ink, so one must catch a tiny bit on the tip by dipping it slightly into a little ink; then, with extreme caution, insert it into the bottle mouth; and at the precise place bring it into contact with the glass surface—by this time the ink is almost dry. Often the stroke is hardly carried through to the finish and the ink has dried out. Moreover, the bamboo pen is very difficult to manipulate inside the bottle. Horizontal and vertical strokes will not keep straight and tend to go astray; stroke thickness cannot be controlled; and ink density cannot be maintained. It's all so terribly difficult! Ma Shaoxuan had an excellent command of small regular script on paper, but when it came to calligraphy inside a snuff bottle, it was almost as if he were starting all over again. Every step he took was fraught with difficulty. Just as the common expression says, "Different trades are separated as by mountains," it is truly not easy to climb over a mountain.

A succession of difficulties can block progress, destroy morale and shatter confidence. For someone of great resolve, however, difficulties can actually strengthen the resolve to succeed, and, for the very intelligent, can inspire strategies for their solution, turning obstacles into advantages. It was advantageous that the three brothers were studying snuff bottle painting together: they could focus three good minds at once on each problem as it arose; with such combined intelligence, problems dwindled. One brother would come up with part of the solution, immediately present it to the others, then another would contribute something more, and all three would move ahead together. It was as if three people shared a pole in carrying a load, each would feel the weight a little lighter and keep up a faster pace when they got on the road. Especially important was their father's advice and help from family members and friends. The brothers may never have paid their respects to an expert and become disciples, but many master craftsmen came to their home to give advice and assistance. After several months of intense effort, real progress began to show: all three brothers could execute simple characters and paintings inside snuff bottles. This was an extraordinary breakthrough.

"AS IF HIS HEART WERE BOUND FAST"

To do calligraphy and painting well inside snuff bottles means overcoming many unusual difficulties. The road to mastery is long and tortuous, taxing not only one's physical strength, an ordeal to be endured, but also involving a whole series of skills to be honed, understood, and made one's own. Some skills practically defy acquisition, though their acquisition is essential. Most people never solve some problems involving the coordination of mind and hand, no matter how positively they apply themselves, no matter how long they work at them. During the years that he studied painting inside snuff bottles, Ma Shaoxuan remained preoccupied with such perplexing problems, which he pondered, experimented with, failed at, and despaired over, but finally conquered, enjoying the exhilaration of achievement. Ma threw himself body and soul into painting snuff bottles and became so absorbed and fascinated with them that he relinquished most of the pleasures, interests, and unique opportunities of youth.

"Neglecting food and sleep," a phrase often used to praise devotion to one's career, literally described Ma Shaoxuan. He habitually let his food grow cold; only upon his mother's constant urging would he eat a few bites indifferently and then return to work, bent over his table painting bottles, utterly oblivious to time, unaware whether it were morning or afternoon, and still at it late into the night.

The expression "like a madman or an idiot" is often used to describe obsession, and Ma was clearly obsessed. People came to regard him as being obsessed, and even he acknowledged his obsession. A poem he composed in 1903, eighteen years after he had begun to paint bottles at the age of eighteen, reflects this awareness. The pentasyllabic quatrain is fittingly inscribed inside a snuff bottle:

> *I exhausted all my powers of concentration,*
> *Turned into a madman for painting and*
> * calligraphy.*
> *But worthies of the past would surely laugh at me,*
> *For I know my results are but trivial and*
> * incomplete.*[10]

Ma Shaoxuan was so crazy for painting and calligraphy that he even forgot completely about getting married! In those days, young men married about the age of eighteen, but he was already well past twenty and still unmarried. Ma was a brilliant and handsome fellow, and his family circumstances were beyond reproach. His two older brothers had been married for some time and already had children. Matchmakers often knocked on the Ma compound gate trying to arrange a marriage for him; his parents also kept urging him to get married. However, because he had not yet established himself in his career, Ma was unwilling to start a family.

---

10. For illustration, see fig. 93; for more on this poem and the circumstances of its composition, see the detailed presentation in Chapter 5.

It is said in the poem entitled "The Turtle Dove" in the "Airs of Cao" (*Caofeng*) section of *The Book of Songs* (*Shijing*):

> *The noble man, with his goodness and refinement,*
> *Keeps his demeanor one and unchanging.*
> *He keeps his demeanor one and unchanging,*
> *As if his heart were bound fast.[11]*

Just as the noble man upholding his principle steadfastly, Ma focused his existence on snuff bottle painting. He was passionately in love with his art, was married to it, and inseparable from it for the rest of his life.

In 1891, however, when he was twenty-five, he did finally marry a young woman from the Wang clan of the Haidian district of Beijing.[12] She was two years younger than he, a wholesome, honest woman, very intelligent, magnanimous, and absolutely sincere. She was understanding and gave complete support to her husband's career and kept him loyal company throughout their happy married life.

Talking about careers, only those who were willing to give up many privileges in life for the sake of their career could hope to attain accomplishments in their endeavors.

SPRING BREEZE

A famous axiom in the chapter "Exhortation to Learning" in *Xunzi* (The Sayings of Master Xun) goes:

> *If there is no dark obscurity of purpose, there will*
> *be no reputation for brilliance; if there is no*
> *hidden secretiveness in the performance of duties,*
> *there will be no awe-inspiring majesty in*
> *achievement.[13]*

This observation applies to Ma's artistry. "Dark and obscure" and "hidden and secret" describe the inner processes that must have been at work as he came to understand the principles of painting inside snuff bottles and acquired the many facets of its technical skills.

When Ma was twenty-five, just before he got married, he had already been painting inside bottles for seven or eight years, years of hard, painstaking study and effort. It was then that he brought together his best works, products of his most meticulous efforts, and took them to his father to look over and criticize. His father

11. See Zhu Xi, *Shijing jizhu, juan* 3, p. 69.

12. The Haidian (Sea of Ponds) district is located in the northwestern suburbs of Beijing.

13. Master Xun was Xun Qing (ca.300–210 B.C.), the early Confucian thinker known for his pragmatic, systematic, and rigorous approach to moral and social issues. The translation is that of John Knoblock, *Xunzi: A Translation and Study of the Complete Works*, vol. 1, p. 138. The passage quoted here is taken from a section devoted to the ideas that "achievement consists in not giving up," "the mind must be fixed on a constant end," and "inner cultivation is the key to outer success."

was delighted: a young fledgling with so much promise had finally learned to soar! The father cast his mind back to when his son had embarked on his arduous and demanding career and knew that what he had achieved had not come easily. Now hopeful that Ma Shaoxuan could become a truly great artist but still fearful of difficulties and dangers ahead, he thought of these lines to serve as a motto for his son's hard days to come:

> *Pursue essential truths with steady, deep resolve,*
> *And place no value on ornate and showy effect.*

Then, he called his son in and shared his thoughts: snuff bottle painting is a meticulous and demanding art form, one that requires the utmost dedication and effort. Although remarkable results had been accomplished in the last few years, with which he was thoroughly delighted, his son's calligraphy and painting both still had a long way to go before they met the standards of true excellence. If he wanted to have a successful life-long career in snuff bottle painting, Ma would have to make the most sincere commitment to it and never give up, never be satisfied, always work to approach closer and closer to absolute perfection, and spend his entire life refining his art. He also warned Ma against the temptation of settling for superficial showiness. Instead, he must be resolved to achieve what no one had ever been able to do

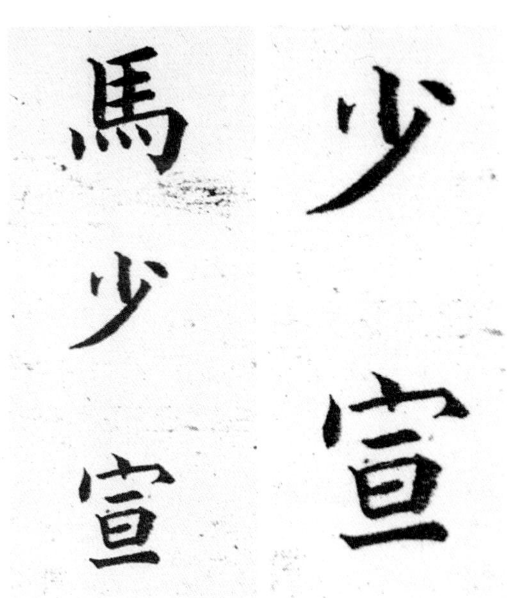

Fig. 1. Characters forming the name Ma Shaoxuan, sometimes shortened to Shaoxuan (Ma Family Collection)

before. Then, the father went on to lecture his son on the characteristics of inscriptions on traditional Chinese painting and calligraphy and their artistic requirements. He suggested that henceforth Ma sign each piece of completed work with a distinctive studio name, Shaoxuan, meaning "a young man (*shaonian*) whose reputation spreads (*xuan*) both near and far," a name in harmony with the one his father had given him as a child, Guangjia (Brilliant First-place). "Shaoxuan" was not only elegant and cultured, it also consisted of characters that were easy and convenient to write (fig. 1).

This interview with his father greatly influenced Ma Shaoxuan throughout his life. What the old man had to say to his son came across to him like a warm spring breeze, filled with the hope of success to come and a stimulant to the growth that lay within him. His father's words extended his vision and encouraged him to reach out for the artistic and cultural riches the tradition offered, to make them his own, and to enrich them.

Upon hearing his father's new name for him, Shaoxuan, Ma immediately thought of the lines in Qu Yuan's (ca. 340–278 B.C.) *Lisao* (Encountering Sorrow):

> *My father, seeing the aspect of my nativity,*
> *Took omens to give me an auspicious name.*[14]

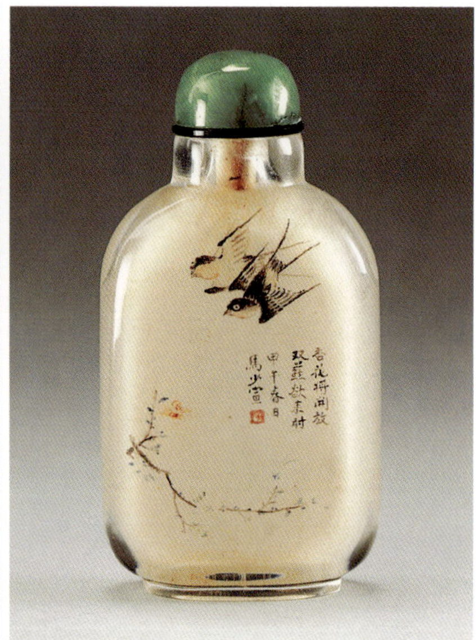

Figs. 2 and 3. Landscape, with two swallows on the reverse, dated 1894 (The Collection of Mary and George Bloch)

Ma Shaoxuan was deeply moved by his father's concern and encouragement and resolved never to forget his hopes and warning. Thereafter, for the rest of his life, whenever he signed a piece of his work, Ma remembered his father's teachings and admonished himself to "pursue essential truths with steady, deep resolve and place no value on ornate and showy effect." These words, constant companions to the end of his days, set the standards for Ma's art and the sign-posts for his journey through life.

EARLY WORKS

Of all those works that Ma Shaoxuan had shown his father in 1891, not a single one survived. So if we wish to speak of the works of 1895 and earlier as belonging to a "first period," it means that this period consists for the most part of works that date only from 1894 and 1895 (figs. 2 and 3).

In 1895 Ma Shaoxuan produced several pieces entitled *Huantian xidi* (Boundless Joy, fig. 4), and these are preserved in collections and considered extremely valuable both as the earliest surviving significant works testifying to all those years of training, dedication, and hard work and as the forerunners of the fifty years of mature works that follow.[15]

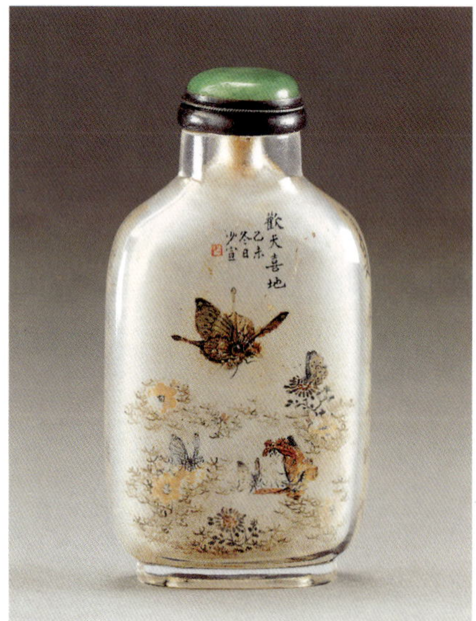

Fig. 4. "Boundless Joy" (*Huantian xidi*), dated 1895 (The Collection of Mary and George Bloch)

14. The translation is by David Hawkes. See *Ch'u Tz'u: The Songs of the South*, p. 22.

15. One of these "Boundless Joy" pieces of 1895 is compared to a work with the same title done in 1925 in Chapter 7, "Art Has No Boundaries," and as a detailed analysis is provided there, nothing more will be said about these pieces here.

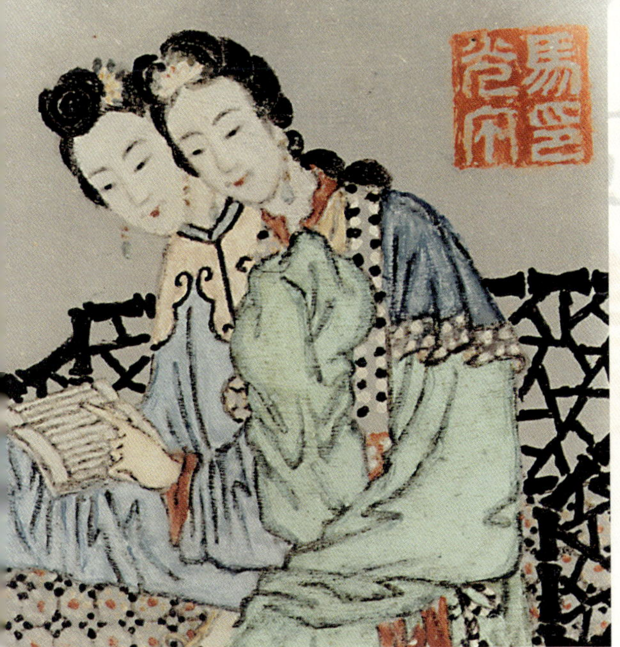

CHAPTER TWO

"At Thirty I Established Myself"— Works of the Early Period

In 1896 Ma Shaoxuan was thirty years old by Chinese count. In the chapter "To Govern" (*Weizheng*) in *Lunyu* (The Analects) is recorded a statement made by Confucius: "At fifteen, I set my heart on learning; at thirty, I established myself; at forty, I no longer had doubts; at fifty, I understood the pronouncements of Heaven; at sixty, my ear was compliant; and at seventy, I followed my heart's desires without transgressing rules or standards."[16] When Ma reached the age when one should "establish himself," he did so. At home were kind and amiable parents and a good and wise wife. He had some success in selling his own works and enjoyed a sufficient income of his own. The works of his first period, his inside-painted snuff bottles up to 1895, attest to an artistic career headed at full gallop in the right direction. He had begun to receive public recognition. These circumstances yielded Ma a rich harvest between 1896 and 1900 when he produced many works that circulated widely and reached the turning point in his career with pictures of General Huang Zhong,[17] which brought him fame throughout Beijing.

In this chapter some of the works that Ma Shaoxuan produced between 1896 and 1900 will be examined. Emphasis will be placed in particular on the development of Ma's art of painting inside snuff bottles, and the range of subject matter and his individual characteristics in painting and calligraphy embodied in his early works, in order to, step by step, gain a better understanding of his early productions.

16. The translation is by Arthur Waley. See *The Analects of Confucius*, p. 88.

17. Tan Xinpei (1847–1917) was one of the most famous Beijing opera stars of his day, and one of his best known roles was that of Huang Zhong (d. 220), the aged general who greatly assisted Liu Bei (161–223) in establishing the kingdom of Shu-Han in Sichuan upon the breakup of the Han dynasty (206 B.C.– A.D. 220). Huang's biography can be found in *Sanguo zhi* (Chronicle of the Three Kingdoms), *juan* 36, p. 948. Huang Zhong is also a major character in the novel *Sanguo yanyi* (Romance of the Three Kingdoms), attributed to Luo Guanzhong (14th century), and is also often portrayed in the many opera-dramas about the episodes and heroes of the Three Kingdoms period (220–265).

"THE TWO QIAO SISTERS"

During 1896 and 1897 Ma Shaoxuan many times painted "The Two Qiao Sisters," a subject he also returned to in later years (fig. 5). The motif has its origin in a story that took place during the last years of Eastern Han (AD 25–220). According to the "Biography of Zhou Yu" in *Sanguo zhi* (Chronicle of the Three Kingdoms) *juan* 54, Zhou Yu was twenty-four years old in the third year of the Jian'an period (198).[18] At the time the Marquis of Wu, Sun Ce,[19] was offered Lord Qiao's (Qiaogong) two daughters, both charming beauties. Sun Ce took the Elder Qiao (Da Qiao) for his own wife, and Zhou Yu made the Younger Qiao (Xiao Qiao) his wife. Their marriages won public approval. In *Jiangbiao zhuan* (Chronicle of the Area Outside [Southeast of] the Yangzi River [Wu]) it is recorded that "Sun Ce casually jested with Zhou Yu, saying, 'Although Lord Qiao's two daughters are gems that gleam and sparkle, to gain both of us as sons-in-law should be enough to make him happy!'"[20]

Writers and artists throughout the ages have often retold the story of the two Qiao sisters. In Ma Shaoxuan's version the sisters sit together reading a book. The composition is economical, dominated by the remarkable figures of the women. Many colors are meticulously applied in complicated and gorgeous combinations, yet the result is soft and elegant. Easy flowing lines define the two seated figures in natural poses. The figures have a real sense of life, and their facial expressions, calm and relaxed, suggest leisure and comfort—all of which creates an impression of proper grooming, gentleness, and beauty.

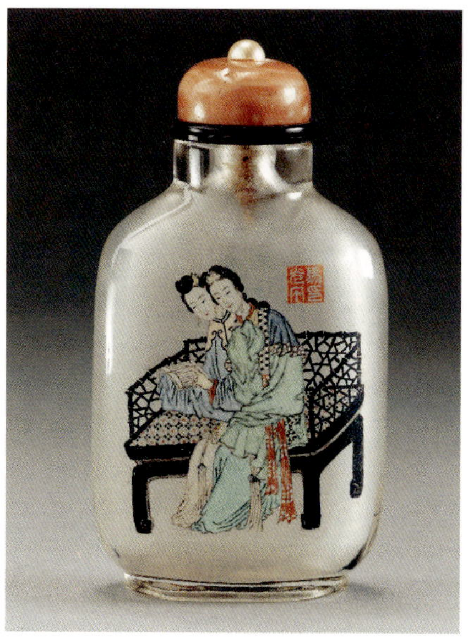

Fig. 5. "The Two Qiao Sisters," dated 1896 (The Collection of Mary and George Bloch)

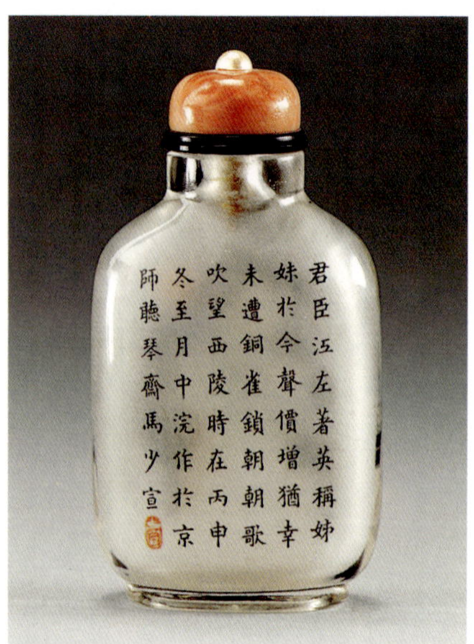

Fig. 6. The reverse of fig. 5, with the poem quoted in the text, dated 1896 (The Collection of Mary and George Bloch)

18. Zhou Yu (175–210) was a renowned general of the state of Wu during the Three Kingdoms period. Born to a gentry family, he befriended Sun Ce at a very young age and later helped him to establish the state of Wu.

19. Sun Ce (175–200) was the founder of the state of Wu, located on the south side of the lower Yangzi River.

20. Quoted in *Sanguo zhi*, *juan* 54, p. 1260, note 2. *Jiangbiao zhuan* has been lost for centuries and survives only in fragments quoted in other works such as *Sanguo zhi*. Pei Songzhi's (372–451) commentary on *Sanguo zhi* has become an integral part of that work and is included in all modern editions.

Ma Shaoxuan painted several versions of the "Two Qiao Sisters," but the color combinations and the seal legends differ. Some have poems inscribed on the opposite face (fig. 6), while others depicted "Picture of Antiquities" (*Bogu tu*) or "Picture of Longevity" (*Baisui tu*) (figs. 7 and 8).[21] The poems complementing the pictures also differ from work to work, for example, the one illustrated reads as follows:

> *Sovereign and minister are known as great heroes*
> *from Left of the Yangzi River,*[22]
> *And till now the reputation of the two sisters has*
> *continued to grow.*
> *Fortunately they have been spared confinement in*
> *Bronze Bird Tower,*
> *Where, morning after morning, they'd have sung*
> *and played the flute, gazing toward Xiling.*[23]

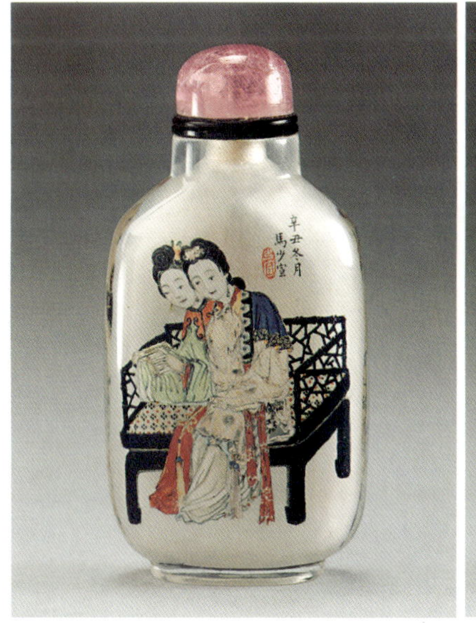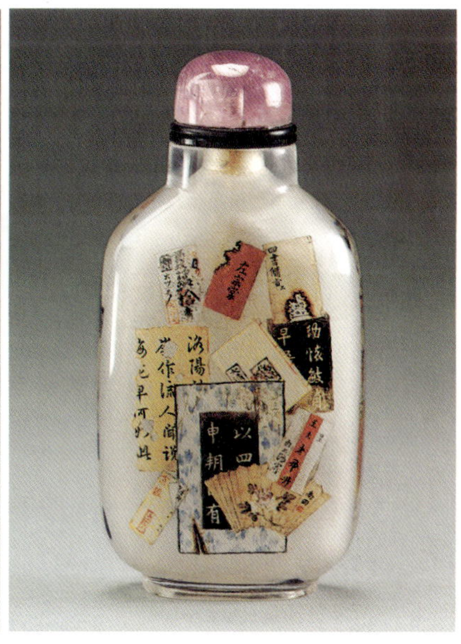

Figs. 7 and 8. "The Two Qiao Sisters," with the motif of "Picture of Longevity" (*Baisui tu*) on the reverse, dated 1901 (The Collection of Mary and George Bloch)

Ma's poem echoes a well-known quatrain by the late Tang poet Du Mu (803–852) entitled "The Red Cliff" (*Chibi*):

> *The broken halberd sunk in sand, the iron not yet*
> *rusted away,*
> *Once I take it up, scrape and wash it off,*
> *I recognize it's from a former dynasty.*
> *Had the east wind not worked to the advantage of*
> *Young Gentleman Zhou,*
> *When springtime lay deep at Bronze Bird Tower,*
> *there the Qiao sisters would have been confined.*[24]

21. This is actually a pictorial pun represented by a variety of (suggesting the idea of many, *bai*) broken (*sui*) objects of antiquity.

22. "Sovereign and minister" refers to Sun Quan (not Sun Ce!) and Zhou Yu, respectively. "Left of the Yangzi River" means the south side (facing upstream), the domain of Wu.

23. Xiling is the first of the three great gorges on the Yangzi River in Hubei, the entrance from the northwest into Wu territory.

24. Du Mu, *Fanchuan wenji, juan* 4, p. 47. There is no historical evidence that the Elder Qiao, who had been the wife of Sun Ce and become his widow in 200, eight years before the Battle of Red Cliff, ever subsequently became his younger brother Sun Quan's wife, though this seems to be a popular misconception, implicit in both Ma Shaoxuan's and Du Mu's poems. Or, perhaps simple confusion surrounds the question of whose wife the Elder Qiao had been—Sun Ce's or Sun Quan's, confusion perpetuated even by respected modern scholars of Chinese literature. See Stephen Owen, *Remembrances: The Experience of the Past in Classical Chinese Literature*, pp. 51–55. In this detailed analysis of Du Mu's poem, Owen identifies the Elder Qiao as "the wife of the king" of Wu, Sun Quan (p. 51). Also, the long, fictionalized version of the Three Kingdoms period, *Sanguo yanyi*, makes no mention of the Elder Qiao sister ever becoming the wife of Sun Quan.

The Bronze Bird Tower, named for the great bronze figure of a sparrow at the top, was built in the fifteenth year of the Jian'an period (210) by Cao Cao (155–220) in the city of Ye.[25] Here, using a relic associated with the battle fought at Red Cliff and salvaged from the bottom of the Yangzi River as a point of departure, the poet reminisces about the past, sighing over the fact that had the states of Wu and Shu not joined forces and had the east wind not arrived in time, the two Qiao sisters would have been captured by Cao Cao and confined in the Bronze Bird Tower.[26] The gist of the poem inscribed on the inside-painted bottle echoes that of Du Mu's composition. Yet, viewed from another perspective, it may be interpreted thus: both sovereign and minister of the state of Wu deserved to be known as great heroes; the two Qiao sisters enjoyed high esteem; and the battle won at Red Cliff was to be rejoiced at, all the more because as a result of this outcome the two Qiao sisters escaped the fate of being captured by Cao Cao. Otherwise, husbands and wives would be separated and could only gaze at each other, singing songs of sorrow. As to the name Xiling, since the Yellow Emperor took a woman native to that place as his consort, here it is used to stand for the two Qiao sisters.[27]

Another heptasyllabic quatrain by Ma Shaoxuan that accompanies a painting of the two Qiao sisters on a different bottle reads:

> *Here are the two sisters from the house of Qiao*
> *   together looking at a book,*
> *Both married to handsome husbands,*
> *   great martial heroes, too.*
> *On a fine night like this, they're sleepy but*
> *   would rather not go to bed—*
> *Their husbands' darlings also love to read the*
>   Book of the Hidden Concord![28]

Since the husbands are military leaders, naturally their wives should also share similar interests. The two Qiao sisters enjoy books about military strategy so much that they would go on reading in the wee hours of the night, forsaking sleep. How virtuous and sagacious they are! What perfect companions they make with their spouses and how wonderful their married lives

25. The city of Ye was Cao Cao's stronghold, located about 40 *li* west of present-day Linzhang district in Henan province.

26. In the autumn of 208 Zhou Yu destroyed Cao Cao's great invasion fleet moored at Red Cliff on the Yangzi River in Hubei province, releasing fire ships against it, which were driven by a long-awaited east wind. Luckily, this finally arrived, saving Wu from sure defeat, preserving its independence, and ensuring that the two Qiao sisters would not be taken north into Cao Cao's harem.

27. The Yellow Emperor (Huangdi) is a legendary figure credited with many inventions, such as raising silkworms, construction of boats and vehicles, writing and the art of medicine. Tribes indigenous to central China revered him as their common ancestor.

28. See John Gilmore Ford, *Chinese Snuff Bottles: The Edward Choate O'Dell Collection*, p. 70, no. 188. The *Book of the Hidden Concord* (*Yinfu jing*) is attributed to various ancient figures, including the mythological Yellow Emperor of remote antiquity, and seems to have referred at various times to different texts, of which some may have been quite different from the only work of that title preserved in *Daozang* (Daoist Canon, no. 31), a work largely concerned with the mysterious and secret correspondences that supposedly exist throughout the universe. However, in some historical bibliographies, the *Yinfu jing* is attributed to Taigong, the counselor of King Wen and King Wu of the early Zhou period (11th century–256 B.C.), whom he helped to overthrow the Shang (16th–11th century B.C.) and is listed under "Military Strategy" (*Bingfa*).

must have been! These poems by Ma are essentially conventional literary pieces designed to complement the paintings on the front of the bottles; poems and paintings are meant to enhance each other, a device that Ma worked to perfection. However, his success with the subject of the two Qiao sisters subsequently inspired many forgeries. One must exercise considerable care to distinguish the authentic from the spurious.

"THE ESSENTIAL HUMAN RELATIONSHIPS REPRESENTED BY FIVE SPECIES OF BIRDS"

In 1897, the 23rd year of the Guangxu period, Ma Shaoxuan produced a very significant work, a bottle that has never been made known to the public. Entitled "The Essential Human Relationships Represented by Five Species of Birds" (*Wuniao xulun*),[29] this is a rock crystal bottle 6.5 cm high and 4.5 cm wide (fig. 9). On the face is painted a *Wuniao tu* (Picture of Five Species of Birds): a pair of mandarin ducks play in the water with harmony and delight; a pair of red-crowned cranes stand in shallows at the water's edge, their neat, trim figures relaxed and at ease; two pied wagtails are on the bank, one fallen down on the ground, the other quickly comes up to help it; beneath a great *wutong* (paulownia) tree stand a pair of phoenixes in their gorgeous, variegated plumage; and a pair of orioles perch up in the foliage of the tree. The gleam of the water below extends and is lost in the distance, merging with the sky, where a round, red sun shines down on the scene. At the far left is a four-character vertical inscription: "*Wuniao xulun*" (The Essential Human Relationships Represented by Five Species of Birds). Though the tiny composition is filled with many elements on such a small bottle, there is not the least sense of overcrowding; each figure has its own distinct place, its own particular charm, and the elements form one harmonious whole, precise in detail and bright in overall effect.

In the pre-modern imperial era, these five species of birds represented the five principal human relationships (*wulun*) as defined by Confucianism: that between sovereign and minister, father and son, husband and wife, older and younger brother, and friends. This subject had been in use for a long time. Ma's

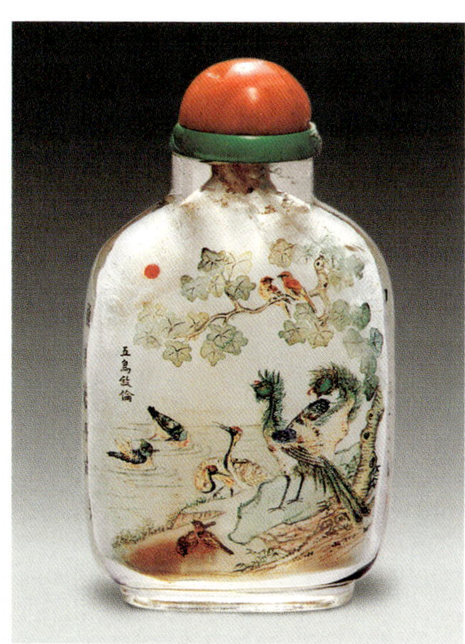

Fig. 9. *"The Essential Human Relationships Represented by Five Species of Birds" (Wuniao xulun),* dated 1897 (Ma Family Collection)

29. This particular bottle may not have been exhibited publicly or ever published, but a similar painting by Ma of "The Essential Human Relationships Represented by Five Species of Birds" (*Wuniao xulun*), also dated 1897, appears on one side of a bottle published in Hugh Moss, Victor Graham, and Ka Bo Tsang, *The Art of the Chinese Snuff Bottle: The J & J Collection*, vol. 2, p. 689. The theme of the *Wuniao xulun* can be traced to paintings on hanging scrolls, which date from the Ming dynasty and perhaps earlier. One such painting by an anonymous Ming artist, in the collection of the Honolulu Academy of Arts, is reproduced in Stephen Little and Joseph B. Silver, *The World in a Bottle, Chinese Inside-painted Snuff Bottles from the Collection of Joseph Baruch Silver and Traditional Chinese Paintings*, p. 56, where it is used to provide background for a *Wulun* (The Five Essential Relationships) inside-painted picture of five pairs of birds (a composition very different from Ma's) on a bottle by Tang Zichuan, painted probably during 1892–1896 (p. 55).

picture, painted in 1897 toward the end of the Qing dynasty and the demise of the traditional era, is a reflection of the social code essential to the old order, alluded to by the formula, *sangang wuchang*, the three cardinal guides (ruler guides subject, father guides son, and husband guides wife) and the five constant virtues (benevolence, righteousness, propriety, wisdom, and fidelity).

The phoenix represents the emperor or sovereign. As *Kongzi jiayu* (Sayings of Confucius Pertaining to Family Rituals) says, "There are three hundred and sixty species of birds, and the phoenix is lord of them all."[30] In the old days the crane was regarded as a divine bird having a long life. "A crane can live to a thousand years old" was a popular belief. For this reason the crane has been likened to an elderly person and with reference to the precedence of the elder over the younger, it serves to represent the relationship between father and son. Mandarin ducks live as mated pairs that never part and so represent the relationship between husband and wife. Pied wagtails usually search for food along the margins of waterways. Their association with brothers comes from the poem "The Cherry Tree" in the "Lesser Elegentiae" (*Xiaoya*) section of *The Book of Songs*:

> *Pied wagtails on the plain:*
> *When brothers are hard pressed and in danger,*
> *There are always good friends about,*
> *But all they can do is heave long sighs.*[31]

That is, when hard pressed, brothers can only depend on each other for help. Pied wagtails are supposed to be very helpful and caring toward each other: when one is in trouble, another is sure to come to its assistance. This is why a pair of them represent the relationship between elder and younger brother. The song of the oriole is very sweet and agreeable but also extremely moving. The association of orioles with friends may originate in another poem, "Cutting Trees," also in the "Lesser Elegentiae" section of *The Book of Songs*:

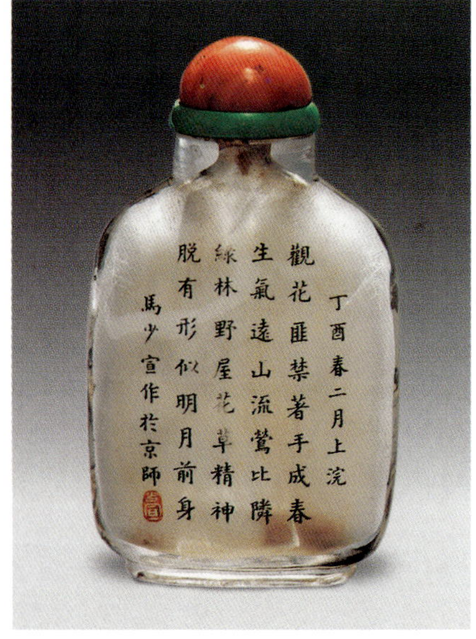

Fig. 10. The reverse of fig. 9, with a poetic inscription, dated 1897 (Ma Family Collection)

30. The date and authorship of *Kongzi jiayu* are in doubt, but this work, which purports to be a collection of questions and answers exchanged between Confucius and his disciples, is probably the invention of the later Confucian exegete Wang Su (195–256). The passage quoted here appears in *juan* 6, p. 257.

31. Zhu Xi, *Shijing jizhu*, juan 4, p. 80.

32. *Ibid.*, p. 81.

33. These lines are not originally from an integral poem but were taken from eight different poems and patched together to form a new poem. The practice of assembling poems out of pieces of other poems, either by the same author or by different authors, is called *jiju* (collecting lines) and is said to have begun with the famous statesman, poet, and literatus Wang Anshi (1021–1086). The lines assembled here are taken from eight different poems in the series *Ershisi shipin* (Twenty-four Categories of Poetry) by Sikong Tu (837–908): line 1 is poem 12, line 1 (p. 7); line 2 is poem 10, line 4 (p. 6); line 3 is poem 13, line 9 (p. 7); line 4 is poem 3, line 8 (p. 2); line 5 is poem 4, line 1 (p. 3); line 6 is poem 20, line 6 (p. 11); line 7 is poem 2, line 11 (p. 2); and line 8 is poem 7, line 12 (p. 4).

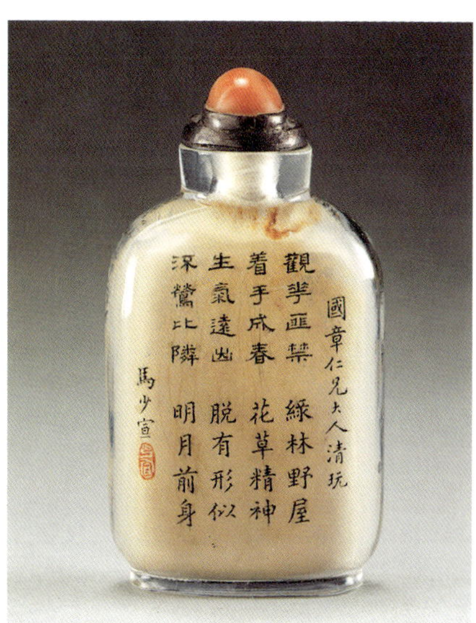

Fig. 11. *Jiju* (collecting lines). The text of this poem, which does not appear on the reverse of the bottle shown in fig. 9, is reproduced from another bottle painted by Ma Shaoxuan at about the same time (The Collection of Mary and George Bloch)

34. Deng Shiru was a celebrated seal carver and calligrapher of the mid-Qing period. He was known particularly for his rustic and powerful brushwork inspired by the seal script engraved on Han steles.

35. For example, in the third line the character *shan* (mountain) is replaced by *chu* (go out), a word used in the original line (poem 13, line 9) which reads: "The breath *(qi)* of life extends/goes out far." The last line in its original context (poem 7, line 12) seems to refer to how the moon appears reflected in water, that is, once removed (less resolution, some distortion, etc.) from its actual appearance. The pastiche cleverly enlists it to state how the imagery carried by these lines of poetry corresponds to the scene it describes.

Trees are cut–ding, ding;
Birds cry–ying, ying.
They leave the dark valley
And move into high trees.
Ying *is their cry,*
As they seek their companions' voices.
Behold how it is that even birds
Seek their companions' voices—
Should men any the less
Seek to find their friends![32]

It is customary to identify these birds as orioles and to use these lines of poetry on the occasion of a friend's promotion to higher office or his moving to a new place to live, as a way of expressing mutual goodwill. This is how orioles come to represent the relationship between friends.

Nowadays, except for the sovereign-subject relationship, the other four relationships still exist. When handled correctly, such themes represent people's felicitous blessings; likewise, they also reflect the painter's good wishes.

On the opposite side of the bottle are written in regular script the painter's inscription and eight lines of poetry, each line made up of four characters (fig. 10):

Viewing blossoms is not prohibited,
When, with a touch of the hand, springtime
* occurs,*
And the breath of life extends to distant
* mountains,*
And brings gliding orioles as close neighbors.
[Like] a rustic cottage in a luxuriant grove,
[Or] the essence of flowers and foliage,
[If one] discards [the notion of] outward
* resemblance,*
The bright moon [could well have been these] in
* its former lives.*[33]

This particular collection of lines can be seen among the calligraphic specimens of Deng Shiru (1743–1805).[34] Ma Shaoxuan also inscribed it on quite a number of inside-painted bottles, occasionally with minor changes in wording (fig. 11).[35]

The painting and calligraphy exemplified by this bottle display a high degree of technical finesse. It is a masterpiece among Ma Shaoxuan's early works, representative of his excellent artistic skills.

"RHAPSODY ON THE SOUNDS OF AUTUMN"

Qiusheng fu (Rhapsody on the Sounds of Autumn) is a well-known work by the great Song writer Ouyang Xiu (1007–1072). Ma Shaoxuan was extremely fond of this particular piece of prose. The beginning of the summer of 1898 was unbearably hot and Ma found relief by chanting this work; his mind quieted down as he went along. When he reached these lines:

> *At first it was a pitter-patter and a soughing,*
> *Then there was surging and crashing.*
> *It resembled waves breaking on a quiet night,*
> *Or a rainstorm striking all at once.*[36]

the hot weather seemed to break, as if an autumn breeze had sprung up. All of a sudden Ma felt cool and comfortable, the imaginative power of Ouyang Xiu's rhapsody, working the same way as "talking about plums slakes one's thirst." The experience inspired Ma to create a picture of "Rhapsody on the Sounds of Autumn" on a snuff bottle. However, since much of Ouyang's rhapsody is concerned with the desolation, ruin, and chill and dread of autumn, Ma did not copy the full text. Instead, he transcribed only a small fragment, lines 20–28 (fig. 12):

> *The boy reported:*
> *"The stars and moon shine brightly,*
> *The Milky Way is in the sky.*
> *There are no people about,*
> *The sounds are in the trees."*
> *I responded,*
> *"Oh, how sad!*
> *These are the sounds of autumn.*
> *Why have they come?"*[37]

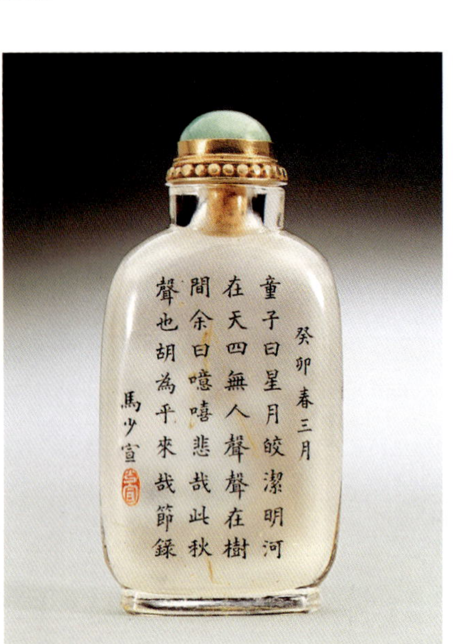

Fig. 12. "Rhapsody on the Sounds of Autumn" by Ouyang Xiu, an extract, dated 1903. The quotation is identical to that inscribed on the 1898 bottle described in the text (The Collection of Rachelle R. Holden)

36. This rhapsody was composed in the fourth year of the Jiayou period (1059). It is recorded in Ouyang Xiu, *Ouyang Wenzhonggong wenji, juan* 15, pp. 139–140. The translation is by Ronald Egan, *The Literary Works of Ouyang Hsiu (1007–72)*, pp. 127–128.

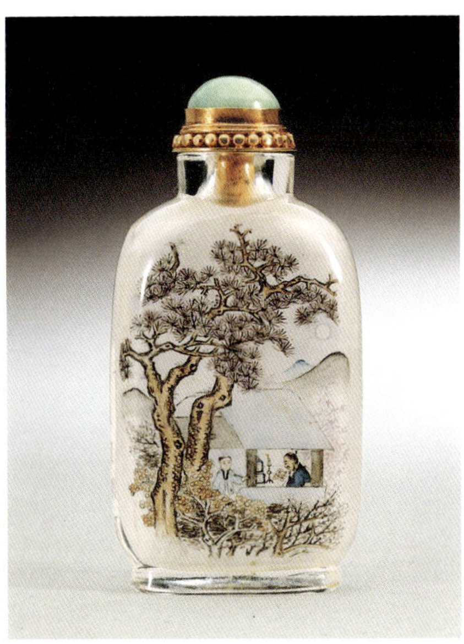

Fig. 13. Ouyang Xiu depicted in his candlelit studio with his houseboy, dated 1903 (The Collection of Rachelle R. Holden)

37. *Ibid.*, p. 127. The whereabouts of this 1898 bottle is unknown. However, existing evidence shows that Ma already did this theme a year before. On this earlier bottle, now in the collection of Charles V. Swain, Ma quoted the same lines from Ouyang Xiu's prose, but his inscription reads, "Made in the capital in the year *dingyou* (1897)." The example illustrated here was produced several years later, "in the third month, the spring of the year *kuimao* (1903)." It is included here because the arrangement of the characters in the quotation is exactly the same as that of the example (1898) described by the author.

38. *Ibid.*

39. An extensive biography of Tan Xinpei is included in Colin Mackerras, *The Chinese Theatre in Modern Times: From 1840 to the Present Day*, pp. 43–49.

These lines consist of thirty-four characters in the original, to which Ma added the two characters *jielu* (extracted). He divided these thirty-six characters into four columns of nine characters each. At the side, he inscribed the phrase *Wuxu chuxia* (First month of summer of the year *wuxu* (1898)) and signed and added his seal at the end.

On the reverse is a painting based on the general description given in Ouyang Xiu's rhapsody (fig. 13). The scene depicts Master Ouyang studying in his bright, candlelit studio; outside shadowy trees obscuring part of the sky, where a bright moon shines, and the sound of the wind resembling

> *Soldiers moving against the enemy,*
> *Running with gags in their mouths.*
> *No shouting of orders,*
> *Just the rumbling of horses and men.*[38]

The painting captures the moment just after Ouyang had interrupted his reading to ask his houseboy about the sound and the boy has just returned from outdoors to report. His answer is recorded on the other side of the bottle. The scene convincingly illustrates the text; both complement each other and fuse into an integral work of art.

HUANG ZHONG

Towards the end of the last century Ma Shaoxuan's inside-painted snuff bottle illustrations of the famous actor Tan Xinpei (1847–1917) in the role of General Huang Zhong (d. 220) constituted perhaps the most significant achievement of his early career. They signaled the culmination of the first period of his artistic development and anticipated his later series of snuff bottle portraits. They marked an important stage in his personal history of painting inside snuff bottles.

Tan Xinpei, twenty years Ma's senior, was a famous Beijing opera star.[39] When Ma Shaoxuan had barely reached thirty years of age, Tan was already giving command performances in the imperial palace, and his popularity had spread throughout Chinese society, among the scholar-gentry, peasants, artisans and merchants to high officials and aristocrats, even reaching the most exalted sphere of the Manchu court, where members of the imperial family, including court ladies, even the Empress Dowager Cixi (1835–1908), loved to see him perform. He had been appointed a *gongfeng* (Palace Attendant-Actor) by the emperor and was widely known to the public as *lingjie dawang* (Great King of the World of Acting). Opera fans not only loved to hear him sing but also imitated his singing style. In tea houses and wine shops, in alleys and lanes throughout the capital, everyone either copied him or spoke of him, calling him Jiaotian'er (Little Caller-on-Heaven). Tan's father, Tan Zhidao (active in the 1850s; died in 1877), also an actor, had sung his roles in an extremely sharp and high-pitched voice, which people said could "reach Heaven," so fans had given him the nickname Tan Jiaotian (Caller-on-Heaven Tan). In honor of his father, Tan Xinpei took for himself the stage name Xiao Jiaotian (The Younger Caller-on-Heaven). The great statesman and man of letters Liang Qichao (1873–1929) immortalized Tan in a poetic couplet: "Within the four seas there is only one Tan Xinpei / Whose reputation for twenty years has boomed like thunder."

Ma Shaoxuan was not only very fond of Beijing opera, he could himself also sing opera rather well. Tan Xinpei's stagecraft moved Ma profoundly, so much that he decided to make an inside-painted snuff bottle portrait of Tan performing an opera role. No one had previously done inside-painted portraits of actors in costume, so this appears to have been entirely Ma's original idea. However, Ma had some trouble deciding which of Tan's many roles to portray. A number of operas were currently being performed, all sure to play to full houses if Tan appeared in them: *Li Ling bei* (Li Ling's Gravestone),[40] *Maima* (Selling the Horse) (fig. 14), *Dingjun Shan* (Mount Dingjun),[41] and *Dayu shajia* (The Fisherman Kills off an Entire Household),[42] among others. However, most of Tan's roles in these were inappropriate for snuff bottle paintings: for example, the character of the Song general Yang Jiye (late 10th century), his dashing himself to death on the front of Li Ling's (d. 74 B.C.) gravestone;[43] "Selling the Horse" depicts the character of the early Tang general and statesman Qin Qiong (late 7th–early 8th centuries) as a young man caught in the depths of despair at being forced to sell his fine horse to pay for his lodging and food at an inn where he was

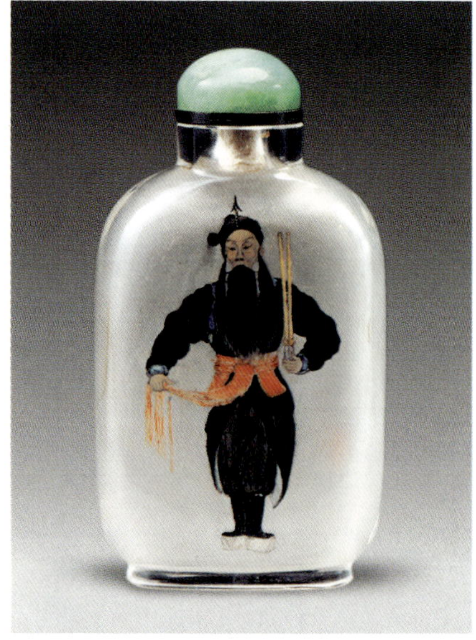

Fig. 14. Tan Xinpei in the role of Qin Qiong in "Selling the Horse" *(Maima)*, dated 1900 (J & J Collection)

40. Li Ling (d. 74 B.C.) was a Han general sent by Emperor Wudi to quell the Xiongnu (Central Asia Huns) nobles. He failed in his mission, surrendered to the enemy and eventually died in their territory.

41. This Beijing opera is also known by the titles *Laojiang desheng* (The Old General Won a Victory) and *Qu Dongchuan* (Taking Eastern Sichuan) and is an adaptation of Chapter 71 of Luo Guanzhong's *Sanguo yanyi*, pp. 425–431.

42. This Beijing opera has been translated into English by Yang Hsien-yi and Gladys Yang as *The Fisherman's Revenge.*

43. Yang Jiye committed suicide after he had failed to win a battle against the Liao invaders: his starving and frozen army was hopelessly trapped in the Tartar Liao territory in the far north.

trapped by a crooked local official who would not provide him with papers; Xiao En, the reformed bandit-turned-fisherman, gets revenge upon a local bully who tries to extort a "fishing fee" in "The Fisherman Kills off an Entire Household." The only suitable role was that of the old general Huang Zhong as portrayed in the opera "Mount Dingjun," as he leads an army to victory over Cao Cao's great general, Xiahou Yuan, whom he defeats in single combat, cutting off his head. Here, Huang Zhong is an awe-inspiring warrior, brilliant commander, and conquering hero: a perfect subject for a painting, one that could lift a viewer's spirits, delight the general public, represent well the stage image of Tan Xinpei, and when tackled with great enthusiasm and confidence, would yield wonderful results.

There was, however, one aspect of a Huang Zhong painting that would be problematic. Though Ma Shaoxuan had painted human figures many times before, in such works as "The Two Qiao Sisters" (fig. 7) and *Maihua tu* (Picture of a Flower Peddler) (fig. 15),[44] these were imaginary people and did not need to conform to the appearance of actual individuals. To paint Tan Xinpei in the role of Huang Zhong would be an entirely different matter, for Tan was a well-known actor whom countless people had seen on stage; his features had to be rendered true to life. If Ma failed to capture a likeness, he would be ridiculed, his reputation suffer irreparable harm, and his career be ruined. Therefore, Ma decided that if he were to paint this subject, he must do it extremely well; otherwise, it would be better not to attempt it.

When Ma made up his mind to do something, he always accomplished his goal. In this case, he spent a lot of time on preparation. After much deliberation, he

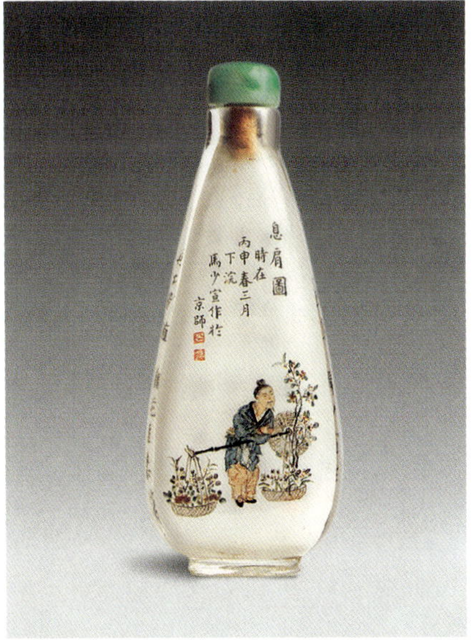

Fig. 15. "Picture of a Flower Peddler" (*Maihua tu*), dated 1896 (Monimar Collection)

44. Ma Shaoxuan also gave the title *Xijian tu* (Picture of Resting the Shoulders) to these works; they were completed 1896–1899; see Moss, Graham, and Tsang, *The Art of the Chinese Snuff Bottle*, vol.2, p. 691.

started to make sketches of Huang Zhong, based on which he eventually finished the portrait (fig. 16).

Here was Tan in the role of Huang Zhong, natural and poised, of strikingly martial appearance, bold yet magnanimous, capped with his general's helmet decorated with a crimson puff ball which seems to quiver ever so slightly. He wears an apricot-yellow coat of mail, with four ornamental banners attached at his back. Here is martial prowess at its most stern and awe-inspiring! A long, pure-white beard waves across his chest which he strokes with his left hand. In his right hand he grasps a sword. Indeed, he looks exactly like a hero of indomitable spirit, a great commander-in-chief of the combined armies!

Ma's picture of Tan in the role of Huang Zhong was a sensation with Beijing opera fans. These "Huang Zhong" bottles were passed from hand to hand, winning sweeping acclaim. When viewing Ma's portrait of Huang Zhong, fans would recall with great enthusiasm Tan's acting and individual singing style. They were equally fascinated by the play and the snuff bottle. Many were unwilling to let go when they fondled it. Some were amazed at the high degree of verisimilitude of the portrait, while others wondered how Ma painted the portrait inside the bottle. As word spread, Ma's reputation as a painter grew to a new height.

At the time, Ma composed a poem describing this situation. In response to a request by a client, he inscribed this pentasyllabic quatrain on the opposite side of a bottle illustrated with Tan as General Huang Zhong, thus providing for posterity an important piece of information (fig. 17). The poem reads:

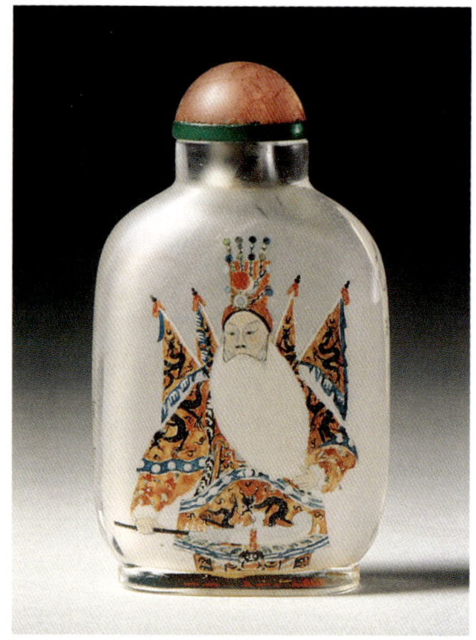

Fig. 16. Tan Xinpei in the role of General Huang Zhong, dated 1899 (Ma Family Collection)

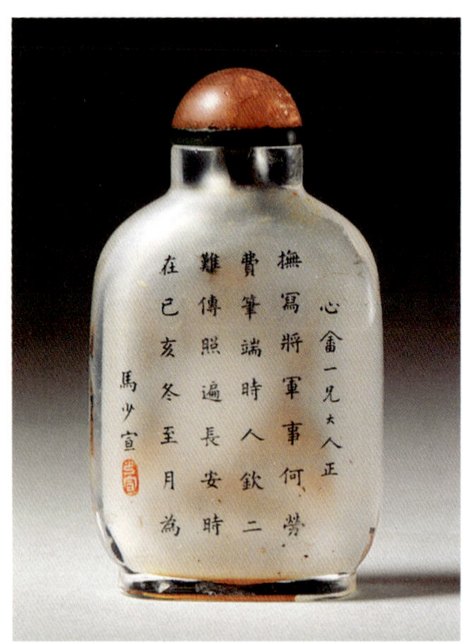

Fig. 17. The reverse of fig. 16, with a poetic inscription, dated 1899 (Ma Family Collection)

The "two exceptional feats" are Tan Xinpei's vivid portrayal of General Huang Zhong on the stage and Ma's own realistic depiction on snuff bottles of Tan's portrayal of the General. Chang'an was the imperial capital of the Tang dynasty (618–907). Here, it is a metaphor for Beijing. This particular bottle was painted and inscribed on the day of the winter solstice in the year *jihai* (1899).

As the fame of the Huang Zhong bottle portraits grew, the demand for them increased until Ma faced the problem of how to maintain his high artistic standards. Were he to simplify the portraits, he could more quickly satisfy the market demand and, of course, make much more money. But this would mean succumbing to vulgarization and lowering standards. This he refused to do, for he remembered how his father had admonished him to "pursue essential truths with steady, deep resolve and place no value on ornate and showy effect." So in spite of the fact that more and more people put in requests, he still upheld high artistic ideals and approached each new Huang Zhong portrait with the

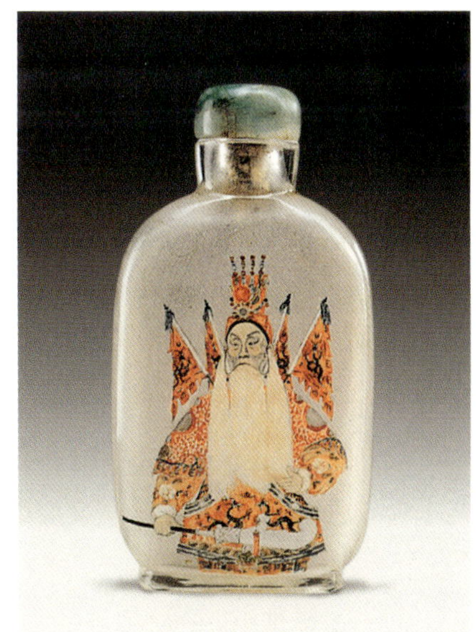

Fig. 18. Tan Xinpei in the role of General Huang Zhong, undated (formerly in the collection of Bernice Straus Hasterlik)

utmost seriousness and dedication. Examples of these works known today bear witness to this (fig. 18). All these portraits are not only meticulously executed, but most also differ slightly in composition and effect, and their complementary poems also differ. Evidently each time Ma worked on a new piece, he spent time to carefully plan out the compositional content.

---

45. Chang'an is the ancient name of present-day Xi'an in Shaanxi province.

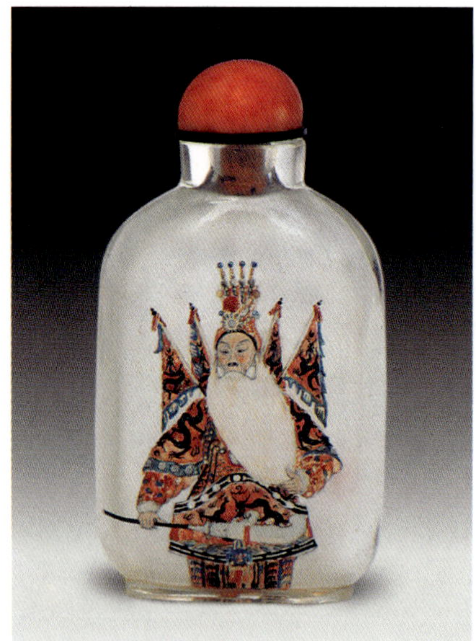

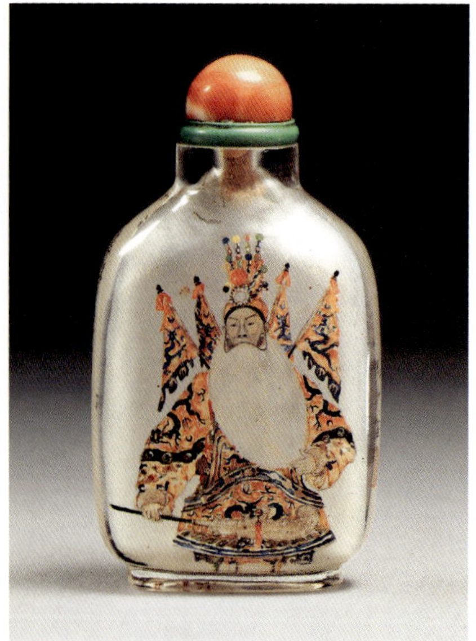

Fig. 19. Tan Xinpei in the role of General Huang Zhong, dated 1900 (The Collection of Susan B. Hacker)

Fig. 20. Tan Xinpei in the role of General Huang Zhong, dated 1899 (J & J Collection)

There seem, however, to be two broad categories of Huang Zhong portraits: one type clearly captures Tan Xinpei's actual features, with his thin face (fig. 19). Although these portray a hale elder warrior and have a real sense of spirit and life, the face depicted is not sufficiently full to satisfy the canons of traditional taste. The other type of portrait depicts a full, round face that departs from Tan Xinpei's actual appearance and obviously is the product of artistic modification and embellishment (fig. 20).

In addition, distinctions can also be detected in a number of details, such as the suit of armor which may differ in color, and, in some versions, the left hand strokes the beard from the left side downward, while in others, the hand strokes it from right to left, at the same time lifting it up, and in still other examples, the figure does not stroke the beard at all, and the beard may be divided.

As to the poem inscribed on the other side of the bottle, it also appears in several forms: pentasyllabic and heptasyllabic quatrains, as well as the pentasyllabic ancient style (*wuyan gushi*), an example of which is cited below (fig. 21):

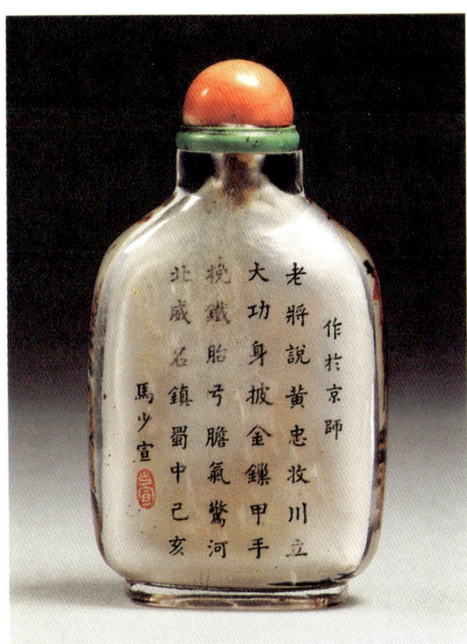

Fig. 21. Poem describing General Huang Zhong, the reverse of fig. 20, dated 1899 (J & J Collection)

Of veteran generals [in ages past], it is Huang Zhong [that is worth] mentioning.

He achieved great merit in recovering Sichuan.

Wearing metal chain,
Grasping an iron-clad bow,
His courage shocked all north of the Yellow River,
And his mighty military reputation made Shu tremble.[46]

A heptasyllabic quatrain on the same subject will be discussed in Chapter 5.

Ma's effort to introduce elements of variety into the same composition attests to the seriousness of his approach to art: each work was to be special. Because of this unique quality, today, in examining and comparing specimens that can be assembled together, one might find it to be a most enjoyable experience.

In addition to the well-known works just treated, the following can also be assigned to the same period 1896–1900:

1897: various works entitled "Picture of Longevity" (*Baisui tu*) (fig. 22) and "Picture of a Happy Pair" (*Shuanghuan tu*) (fig. 23), among others.

46. Shu is the ancient name of Sichuan province where Liu Bei established his stronghold during the Three Kingdoms period.

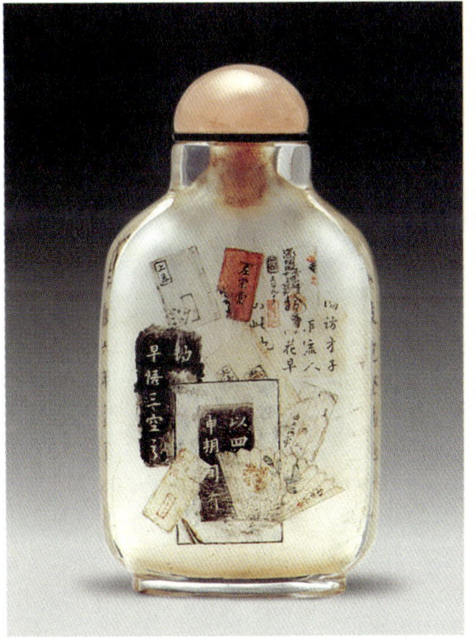

Fig. 22. "Picture of Longevity" (*Baisui tu*), dated 1897 (The Collection of Christopher Sin)

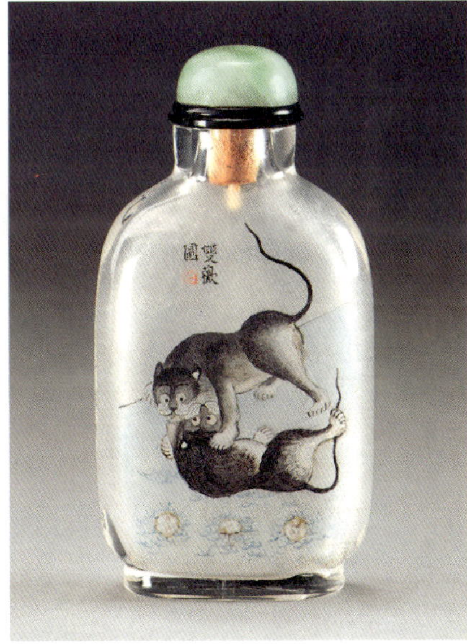

Fig. 23. "Picture of a Happy Pair" (*Shuanghuan tu*), dated 1897 (The Collection of Mary and George Bloch)

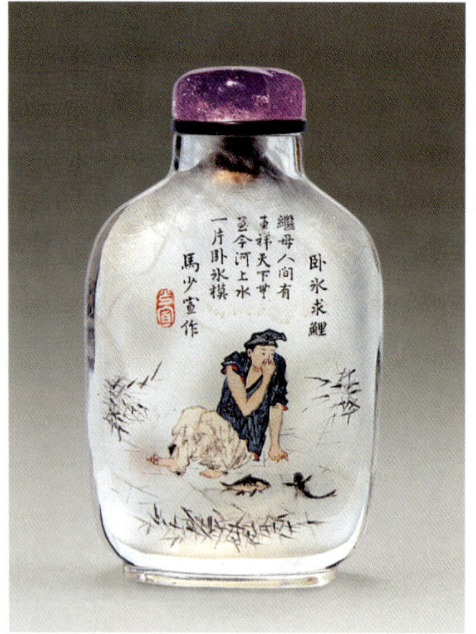

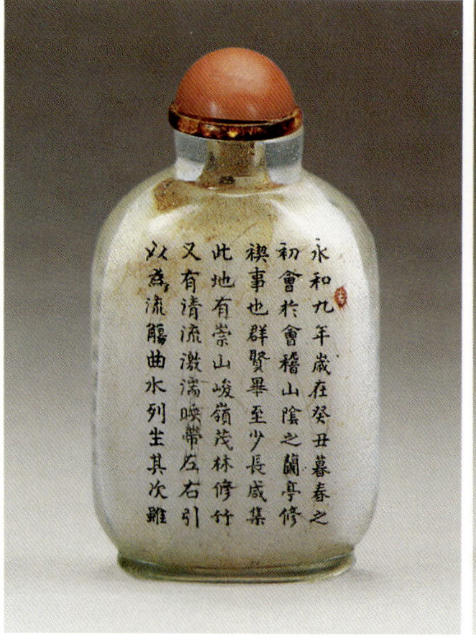

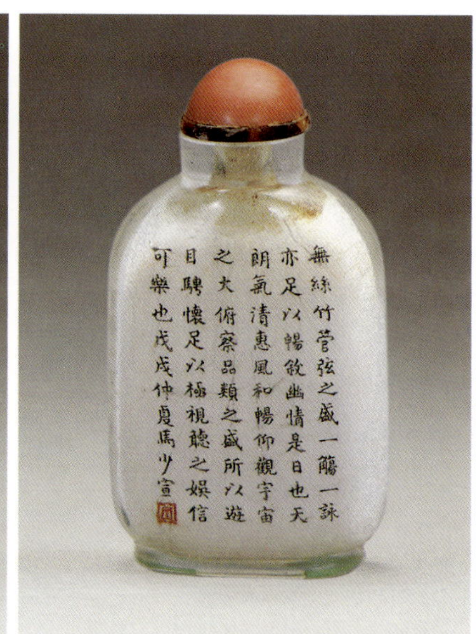

Fig. 24. "Lying on the Ice to Seek a Carp" (*Wobing qiuli*), dated 1898 (Private Hawaiian Collection)

Figs. 25 and 26. "The Lanting Preface" (*Lanting xu*), an extract, dated 1898 (The Collection of Charles V. Swain)

1898: "Lying on the Ice to Seek a Carp" (*Wobing qiuli*) (fig. 24);[47] an abridged inscription of the "Lanting Preface" (*Lanting xu*) (figs. 25 and 26);[48] and various landscapes and pictures of fish and insects, etc.

1899: "Boy Catching a Butterfly" (*Tongzi pudie*); "Picture of a Flower Peddler" (*Maihua tu*); and various landscapes and pictures of birds and flowers, etc.

1900: Landscapes (fig. 27), and portraits of Beijing opera performers in costume, etc.

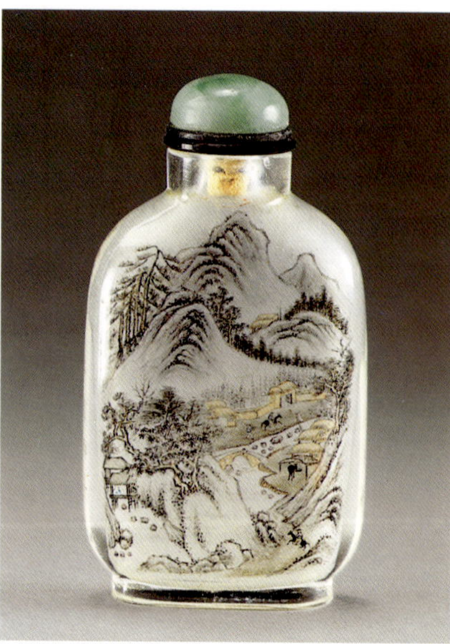

Fig. 27. Landscape, dated 1900 (The Collection of Mary and George Bloch)

47. "Lying on the Ice to Seek a Carp" illustrates the story of Wang Xiang (184–268), one of the "Twenty-four Paragons of Filial Piety," as given, for instance, in the work of that title, *Ershisi xiao*, compiled by Guo Jujing of the Yuan dynasty (1279–1368): One winter, Wang Xiang's stepmother, who had always treated him badly, had a sudden urge to eat carp, but, since the ponds were covered with ice, none were to be had. On his own initiative, Wang went out and lay down on the ice so that his body warmth would melt a hole. When the ice parted, two big carp leapt out, which he then carried home to his stepmother.

48. The "Lanting Preface" was written by Wang Xizhi on the occasion of a springtime gathering of a group of famous literati who assembled at a stream-side spot outside Guiji (southwest of Shaoxing, Zhejiang province) to celebrate the *Shangsi* (Lustration Festival) of 353, which fell on the third day of the third month. Wine cups were floated down the stream, and the guests were to compose a poem before the cups passed their seats or else drink a cup in forfeit. Twenty-six poems were composed and gathered in a volume to which Wang Xizhi wrote a preface that became famous both for its literary value and, in its original draft form, as an exemplary piece of running script (*xingshu*) calligraphy.

CHARACTERISTICS OF EARLY WORKS

In reviewing Ma Shaoxuan's early works, the following characteristics are discernible:

1. Based on a survey of extant works from the 1896–1900 period, the range of subject matter is quite extensive. It includes human figures (figs. 28, 29, 30), landscapes (fig. 31), flowers (fig. 32), birds (fig. 33), insects (fig. 32), fish (fig. 34), and animals (fig. 35).

2. Calligraphic works all display a distinct style. By this time, Ma had already become an outstanding calligrapher. His characters written with a bamboo pen inside glass snuff bottles look just like regular script in small characters (*xiaokai*) written with a brush on paper. Strokes are crisp and clean. Their beginning, turning, and ending points are articulated in exactly the same way as though they were written out with a brushtip infused with energy, conforming perfectly with the rules set down for the execution of this particular script. The structure of each character is tightly knit, producing images charged with spirit and elegance. Also, the spacing between the characters and the lines is well coordinated, so that the whole piece looks balanced, neat and attractive. Ma's calligraphy in these works has a strong sense of the style of the great master Ouyang Xun, whom he had begun to emulate as a child. That he could now execute such calligraphy in tiny characters inside snuff bottles was an amazing feat.

3. Works completed during this period are strongly imbued with a dimension of cultural refinement and literati taste, and their content often draws upon some of the most significant works in the Chinese literary tradition. For example, one piece of calligraphy is an abridgment of Wang Xizhi's "Lanting Preface," and another consists of excerpts from Ouyang Xiu's "Rhapsody on the Sounds of Autumn." Other works embellished with poetic compositions written in regular script or the theme of "Picture of Antiquities" are also characterized by an air of refinement and simplicity which in turn reflects the artist's literary cultivation.

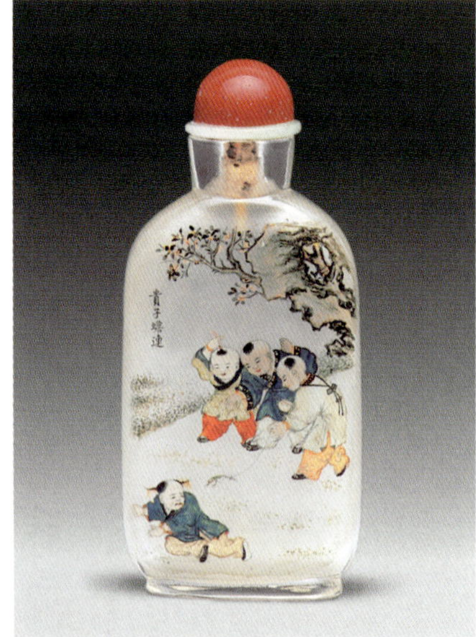

Fig. 28. "A Succession of Noble Sons" (*Guizi chanlian*), c. 1900 (The Collection of Christopher Sin)

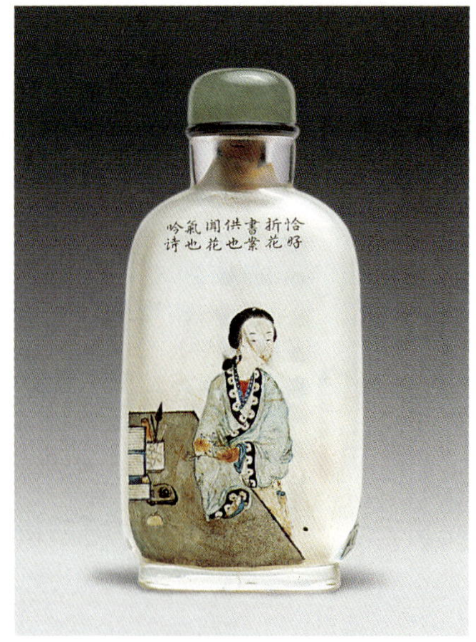

Fig. 29. "Lady at Table Holding a Flower Twig," undated (Monimar Collection)

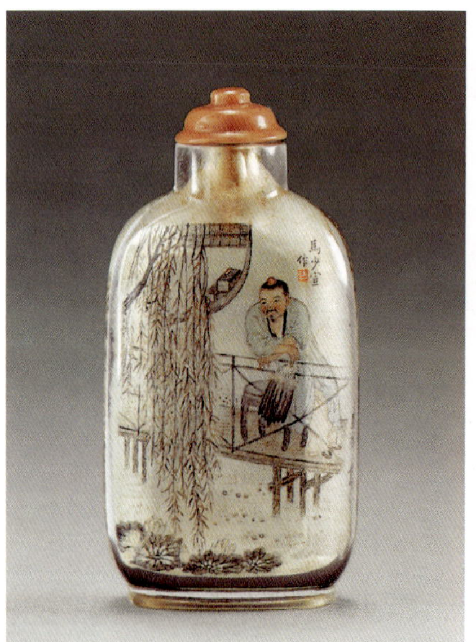

Fig. 30. "A Gentleman Admiring Lotus Blooms," c. 1900 (The Collection of Mary and George Bloch)

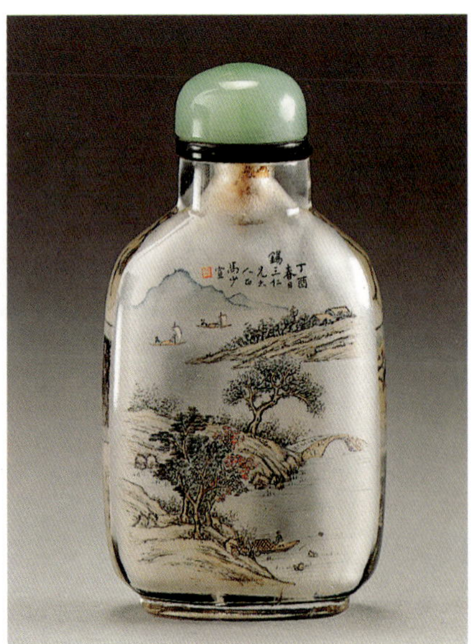

Fig. 31. Landscape, dated 1897 (The Collection of Mary and George Bloch)

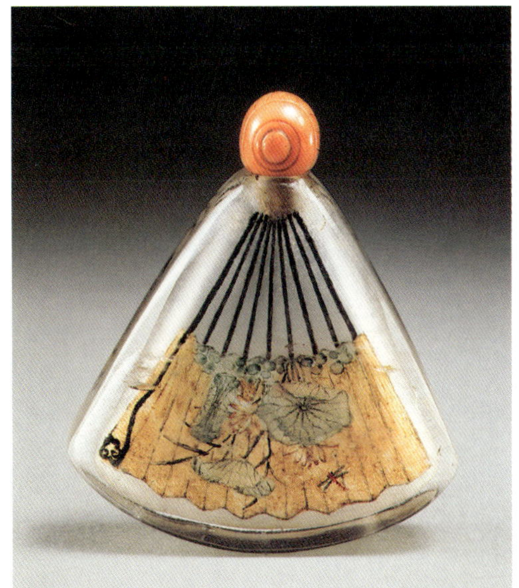

Fig. 32. "Lotuses and a Dragonfly," undated
(J & J Collection)

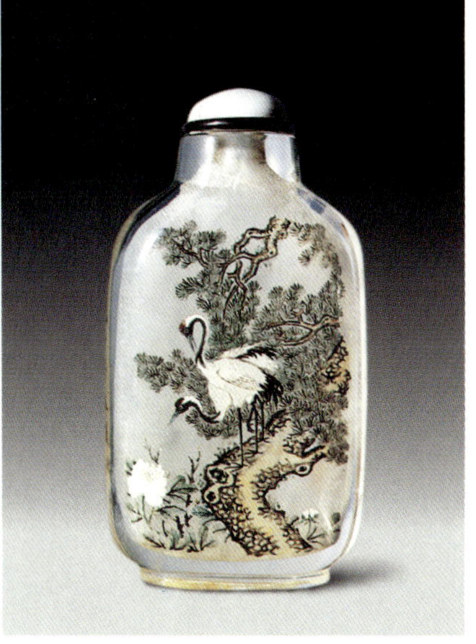

Fig. 33. "Cranes on a Pine Tree," dated
1897 (The Collection of Ann Kreuger)

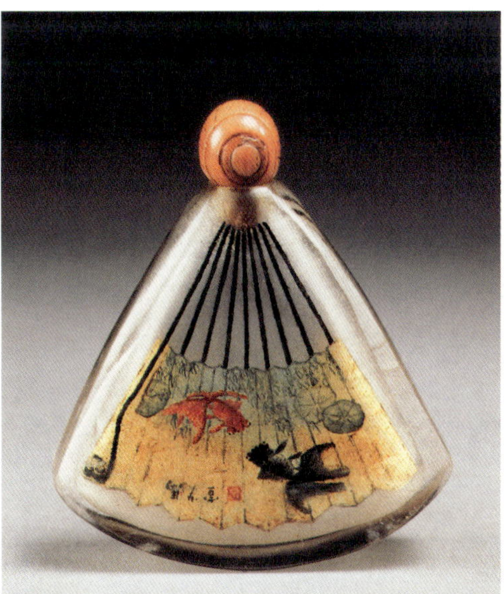

Fig. 34. "Goldfish," the reverse of fig. 32,
undated (J & J Collection)

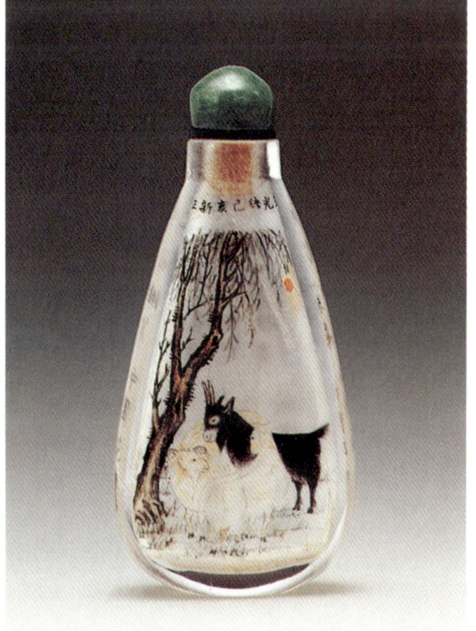

Fig. 35. "Three Goats on a Bright Spring
Day," dated 1899 (The Collection of
Humphrey Hui)

4. However, Ma Shaoxuan had to select the themes and contents of his works to appeal also to the prominent and well-to-do merchants and businessmen, military men, and political figures of the day. Works with literati content could appeal only to part of his potential source of patronage; to reach a wider audience, he had to create works with a more robust and popular appeal. Nothing could have served this aim better than his portrayal on snuff bottles of social figures enjoying wide esteem, such as Beijing opera stars. Ma's portraits of Tan Xinpei brought inside-painted snuff bottle art to the attention of popular audiences as had done no other previous effort in this genre. Art can neither be confined to an ivory tower, nor mass-produced rashly. To be able to make use of themes that appeal to a broad spectrum of audience and execute these with the highest degree of perfection is another characteristic of Ma's early works.

5. The great majority of works produced during this early period consist of paintings on one side of a bottle and a piece of calligraphy on the other. This approach already establishes the basic format of Ma's inside-painted snuff bottles. In placing equal emphasis on painting and calligraphy, he let them complement each other.

After studying Ma Shaoxuan's early works one may reach the following conclusion: from the time Ma produced inside-painted snuff bottles for sale, he was already well-equipped with better-than-average knowledge of literature and art. As well, his inside-painting skill had already attained a relatively high level of perfection. It was to be expected, therefore, that within a short time he would climb new heights and win even greater acclaim.

A special problem associated with this early period is the great number of forgeries purporting to have been done by Ma. These forgeries have greatly interfered with an accurate understanding and appreciation of Ma's artistic development. All illustrations in this book are of authentic works, and reference to them enhances our appreciation of the true state of his art at that time. They serve as guidelines for identification and authentication.

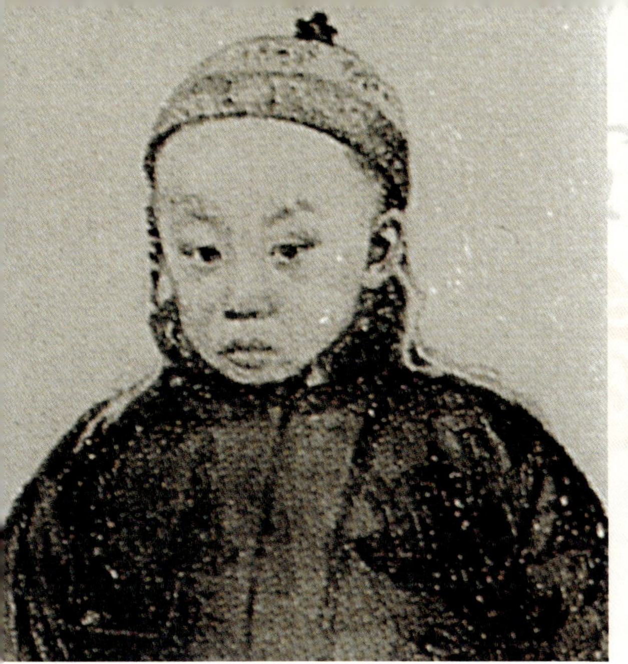

C H A P T E R   T H R E E

"At Forty, I No Longer Had Doubts"—
Snuff Bottle Portraits [49]

In the first decade or so of the twentieth century, Ma Shaoxuan was in his forties. If his career as an inside-painted snuff bottle artist is likened to scaling Mount Tai,[50] at this point, after spending half of his life on strenuous climbing, he had already reached Zhongtian Men (Gateway to Mid-sky). Still vigorous and full of creative power, he could look back to the path he had followed and reminisce over the lush, beautiful scenery; he could also look forward to a promising future, envisioning a mountain track that wound its way through thick green vegetation, like a ladder reaching up to the sky. He was determined not to be deterred by difficulties; he must conquer Shiba Pan (Eighteen Curves) and push for Yuhuang Ding (Jade Emperor Peak).[51]

SCALING THE PINNACLE OF SUCCESS

By the last years of the nineteenth century, friends had begun to ask Ma to paint their portraits on snuff bottles. Since he had been so successful in portraying Tan Xinpei in the role of General Huang Zhong, they argued, Ma could do portraits of anyone. They did not, however, take into account that painting an actor in costume and portraying an individual as he actually appeared in daily life involved different problems, demanding different solutions. The portrait of Tan Xinpei, with his colorful armor, gorgeous trappings, and makeup that exaggerated facial features, preserved only general aspects of his individual appearance, and only vague attention was paid to details. It was easier to achieve satisfying results in this kind of painting than to portray people in a way that captured the precise detail of their individual

49. For a general survey of Chinese inside-painted snuff bottle portraits, see Emily Byrne Curtis, *Reflected Glory in a Bottle: Chinese Snuff Bottle Portraits.*

50. Mount Tai (Tai Shan) is located in the middle of Shandong province. For centuries it has been given the most important place among the five major mountains in China, the others being Heng Shan in Hunan, Hua Shan in Shaanxi, Heng Shan in Shanxi, and Song Shan in Henan.

51. Yuhuang Ding is the main peak of Mount Tai. It was commonly referred to as East Peak in ancient times.

expression and actual physical appearance. Dressed usually in blue or black, with no gorgeous costume to dazzle and distract the eye, no makeup, and a familiar, unexaggerated facial expression, the subject expected a convincing and detailed likeness, usually with the clarity and detail of a photograph. This would please himself, his family, and friends.

Realistic portrait painting required new and demanding skills that seriously challenged Ma's talent. Were he to fail, his reputation as an innovative and creative artist would be damaged, and he would be consigned to the ranks of conventional snuff bottle painters, from whom he had always tried so hard to distance himself. Ma's aged father, whose counsel Ma always sought, again advised his son at this new juncture of his career: before accepting commissions for bottle portraits, Ma must develop the necessary skills, however much time and effort it required. If he did not, this new artistic direction would end in disaster, destroying the reputation Ma had worked so hard and long to achieve. Ma agreed and over the next few years he concentrated his energy on the study of inside-painted snuff bottle portraiture, forsaking social life and reducing the output of bottles painted with other subjects.

Ma already possessed a good grounding in Chinese figure painting and had experience in painting human figures inside bottles. Now, almost daily, he devoted part of his working hours to sketching people from life, including family members, servants, and other people with whom he came into contact. Some of these practice paintings were done on paper and some inside bottles.

The most important requirements of inside-painted snuff bottle portraits are that they be small, usually less than one square inch, and that they display a wealth of precise detail. An accomplished portraitist, Ma discovered, could not deal in broad outlines and general concepts but had to develop compositions that were methodically arranged, detailed in all parts, satisfying as a whole, yet emphasizing salient features of the subject. Drawing, brush handling, and application of ink all had to be directed to solving three basic problems:

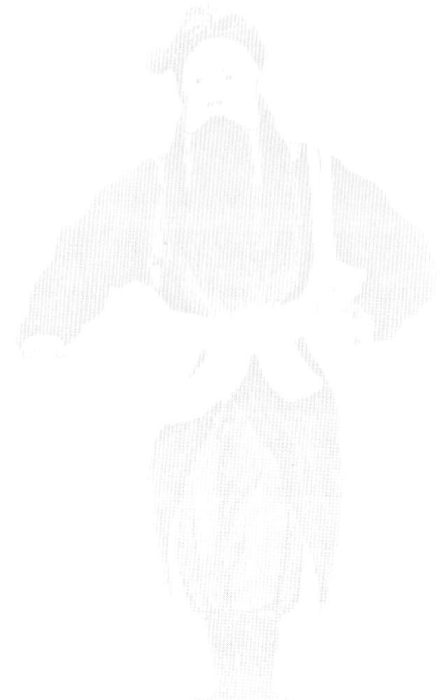

(1) To depict a multi-faceted, three-dimensional, living human figure on a flat, lifeless, two-dimensional surface.

(2) To create the illusion of differing textures for hair, skin, clothing, and other material aspects of human figures.

(3) To impart a sense of light. Only when there is light can one distinguish objects, colors, shading, distance, depth, size, and the convexity or concavity of shapes, which contribute to the perception of three-dimensional reality.

To achieve these three basic objectives, Ma studied both the tradition of figure painting and formal portraiture in China and the theory and practice of Western painting. This combined approach, in time, resulted in his own unique synthetic portrait style.

Chinese figure painting has a long and rich history. As it developed, it enjoyed considerable success at solving various problems associated with portraiture. At its best, Chinese portraiture achieved realistic arrangement and proportion of body and head elements and unity of physical depiction and expression of personality. It was, however, deficient in several other aspects. These included paying insufficient attention to the structure of the body and the failure to integrate the pose and attitude of subjects into comprehensive pictorial compositions. Also, little attention was paid to creating a sense of light, plasticity, or texture. Ma Shaoxuan was well aware of these deficiencies, and, while trying to work out his own new solutions, sought guidance from the works of Giuseppe Castiglione (Lang Shining 1688–1766).

Castiglione was a Jesuit trained in Genoa and a masterful European painter who excelled at portraiture and pictures of flowers, birds, animals, and, especially, horses. As court painter to three emperors (Kangxi, Yongzheng, and Qianlong), Castiglione achieved a marvelous synthesis of Chinese and Western painting techniques and was considerably influential on the later course of Chinese painting.[52] Castiglione's works were an enormous help to Ma in his efforts at portraiture and became his essential guides and models. Drawing from Castiglione's and traditional Chinese painting techniques, Ma learned how to use black and white contrasts and tonal variations in ink application to create the illusion that light was illuminating his subjects and to use various

52. For a brief survey of Castiglione's career at the Qing court, see Michael Sullivan, *The Meeting of Eastern and Western Art*, pp. 66–71; for more details, see Cécile and Michel Beurdeley, *Giuseppe Castiglione: A Jesuit Painter at the Court of the Chinese Emperors* and Elisabeth Kardos, "Giuseppe Castiglione," *Journal of the International Chinese Snuff Bottle Society*, March 1978, pp. 3–16.

methods of traditional Chinese shading and texturing to depict different shapes in all their structural and surface detail. He also experimented to see what kind of effects he could achieve with various brush idioms and techniques.

Ma devoted himself to inside-painted snuff bottle portraits throughout the rest of his career, roughly the first three decades of the twentieth century. Although his later works exhibit a much greater sophistication of technique, his first efforts deserve attention since they occupy a pivotal position in his artistic development.

Only a few bottle portraits survive from this first period, but, when examined in chronological sequence, they mark the speed with which Ma acquired his new skills. These include:

(1) Portrait of Xiechen,[53] undated but appears to be Ma's earliest portrait (fig. 36).[54]

(2) Portrait of an Anonymous Man, painted in the year *renyin* (1902) (fig. 37).

(3) Portrait of Zaifu,[55] painted in the year *yisi* (1905) (fig. 38).

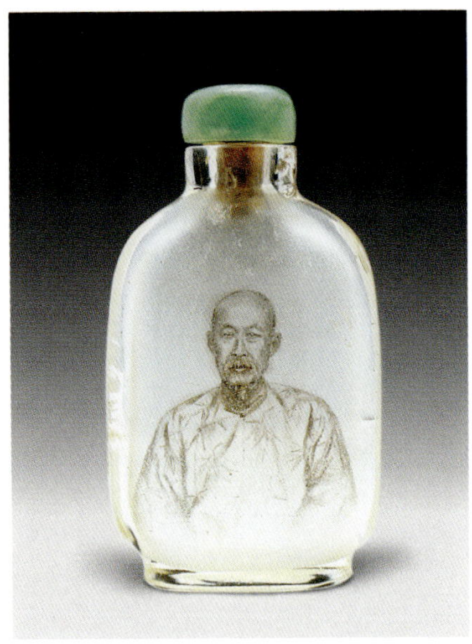

Fig. 36. Portrait of Sun Jianai, whose personal name was Xiechen, undated (The Collection of Carlos Soler)

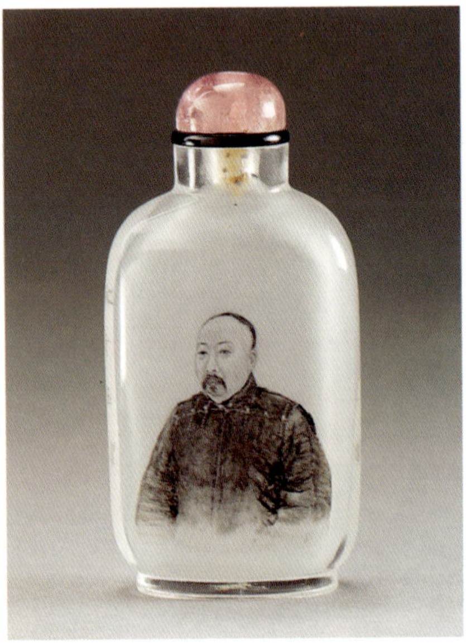

Fig. 37. Portrait of an Anonymous Man (identified by Emily Curtis as Na Tung-a), dated 1902 (The Collection of Mary and George Bloch)

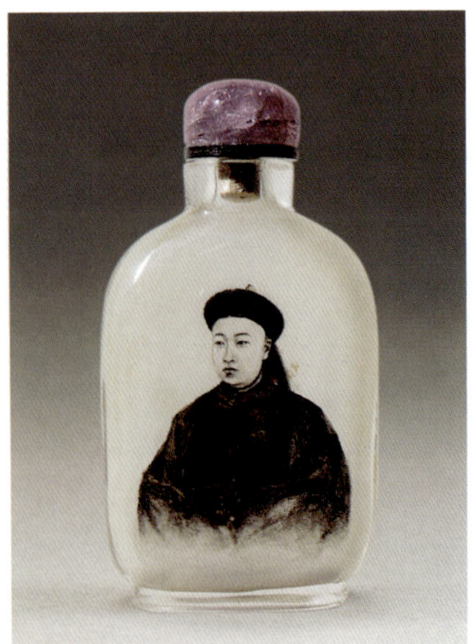

Fig. 38. Portrait of Zaifu, dated 1905 (The Collection of Ann Kreuger)

53. Xiechen was the personal name of Sun Jianai (1827–1909), tutor to the Guangxu emperor (1871–1908) from 1878 to 1887. He later served as President of the Board of Ceremonies and the Board of Civil Appointment and was an Associate Grand Secretary. He was a major figure in the reform movement of 1898. Surviving the Empress Dowager's conservative coup and the Boxer Rebellion, he was made Grand Secretary in 1902. See his biographical entry in Arthur W. Hummel, ed., *Eminent Chinese of the Ch'ing Period*, vol. 2, pp. 673-675.

54. It may have been painted in 1901 or 1902. See Curtis, *Reflected Glory*, pp. 22–23 and fig. 28.

55. Zaifu (b. 1887) was the second son of the Manchu Yikuang (1836–1918), whose title was Prince Qing and who served as Head of the Office of Foreign Affairs (*Zongli yamen*) from 1884 to 1911. He is remembered primarily as the notoriously corrupt and effete confidant and advisor of Empress Dowager Cixi. In 1908, his son Zaifu, a "military aristocrat," was given command of the New Palace Guard, which was established on the German imperial model. That same year, Zaifu was sent to the United States as part of a diplomatic mission, ostensibly as First Secretary to the Embassy. See *ibid.*, pp. 29-30 and figs. 38-41.

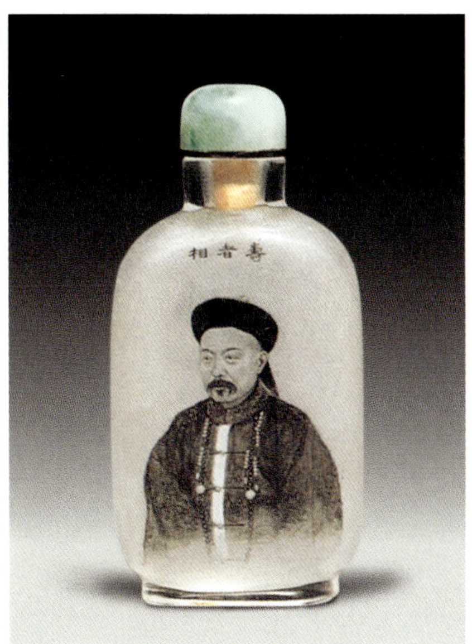

Fig. 39. Portrait of Baofen, dated 1905 (formerly in the collections of Bob Stevens and Eric Young)

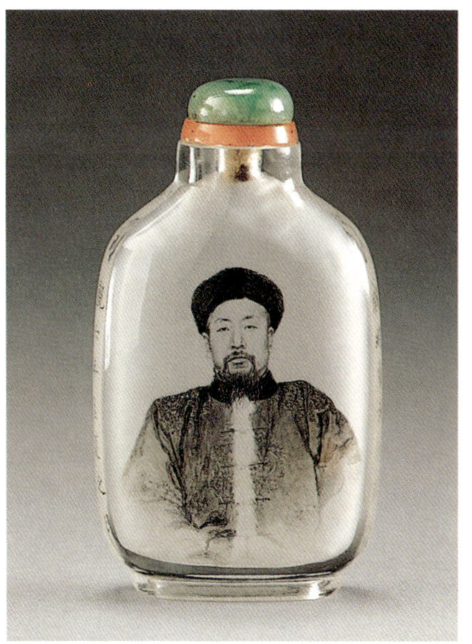

Fig. 40. Portrait of Duanfang, dated 1907 (The Collection of Mary and George Bloch)

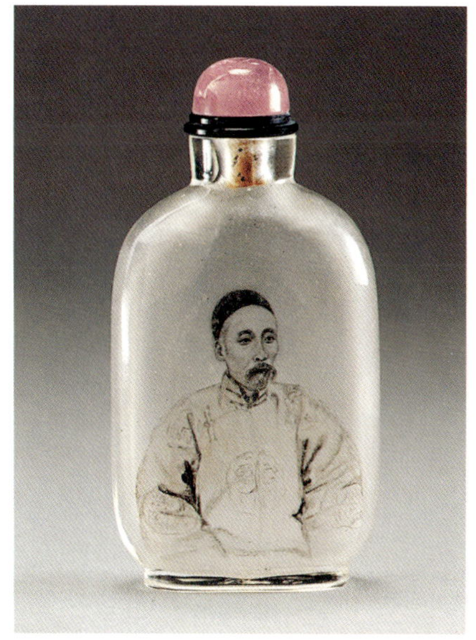

Fig. 41. Portrait of Liang Dunyan, undated (The Collection of Mary and George Bloch)

56. The Manchu Baofen (b. 1862) was Governor of Hunan at the time of the 1911 revolution. *Ibid.*, pp. 32–34 and figs. 45–47.

57. The Manchu Bannerman Duanfang (1861–1911), whose family was originally Chinese, was a progressive high-ranking official and supporter of the moderate reform policies of Zhang Zhidong (1837–1909). He was Acting Governor-General of Sichuan when he was killed during the 1911 revolution. See his biographical entry in Hummel, ed., *Eminent Chinese*, vol. 2, pp. 780–782, and Curtis, *Reflected Glory*, pp. 31–33 and figs. 42–44. The bottle in the collection of Neal Hunter is identical to the one in the Bloch Collection in every respect.

58. Liang Dunyan (1857–1924) was among the first group of students sent to the United States in 1872 as part of an educational mission designed by Li Hongzhang (1823–1901). He studied first in Hartford, Connecticut, then at Yale University. Along with other students, he was recalled to China in 1881, just before he could finish the B.A.. degree. Liang became secretary and advisor to Zhang Zhidong in 1885 and served in various high offices during the last decades of the Qing dynasty and under the early Republic. See Curtis, *Reflected Glory*, pp. 12–16 and figs. 15-21. A version of the bottle portrait listed here in informal attire is illustrated in fig. 20; one of him in formal court dress is shown in fig. 16.

(4) Portrait of Baofen,[56] painted in the year *yisi* (1905) (fig. 39).

(5) Portrait of Duanfang,[57] painted in the year *dingwei* (1907) (fig. 40).

(6) Portrait of Liang Dunyan, probably also dates from this period (fig. 41).[58]

LOVING FATHER, FILIAL SON

One of the beneficial factors contributing to the success of Ma Shaoxuan's career as an inside-painted snuff bottle artist was the fact that he had a loving father who nurtured a great passion for calligraphy and painting. Unfortunately, in 1908, when he was forty-two, his father died at the age of seventy-five.

In the spring of that year, when Ma's father became seriously ill, Ma not only hired the best doctor to look after him but also stationed himself by his bedside, comforting him and dispensing the prescribed medicine to him. In spite of all human efforts, however, his father was unable to recover. In the following days when he grieved over the loss of his father, Ma recalled the loving care his father had bestowed on him ever since he was born. From the time when he, as a toddler, learned to walk, to the time when he learned to write with a brush, his father was by his side, a mentor who opened up for him a whole new world. At eighteen, his father pointed out to him the bright future he would have if he were to learn the skill of painting inside the snuff bottle. Then, never losing sight of him, his father also always gave him timely advice, making sure that he would proceed on a level road and avoid circuitous bends. Indeed, his father was his indispensable guide in his career as well as in his life. During forty-two years, whether in good or bad times, and at crossroads when he felt indecisive, he could always count on his father's support and instructions. His father's presence inspired his confidence, making him feel that there was nothing he needed to fear. Now that this loving father, exacting mentor, and good friend had passed away, there was no way to bring him back. Ma began to realize that up till then he had not paid enough attention to his father and he felt totally devastated.

Ma was actually very close to his parents. Being an obedient son, he was always receptive to their instructions. Because he and his parents thought alike, he was quite willing to heed their suggestions and accept their arrangements. Likewise, in matters where differences of opinion arose, his parents never forced him to comply with their wishes.

During the few years when his father was ill Ma had painted a number of times inside snuff bottles the story of Wang Xiang (184–268) lying on the ice to seek a carp. Wang Xiang, whose literary name was Xiuzheng, was a native of Linyin in Shandong province. According to *Shishuo xinyu* (A New Account of Tales of the World), Wang Xiang was well known for his filial piety, manifested in his interaction with his stepmother Madam Zhu.[59] Ma Shaoxuan illustrated this theme repeatedly because he wanted to express, through this, his filial love for his parents, as well as to remind himself of nurturing this sentiment. When he illustrated this subject on one side of a snuff bottle, he would invariably paint on the reverse a grouping of narcissi, cabbages and turnips, commonly called *Qingbai tu* (A Picture of Purity) (fig. 42),[60] to express his great admiration for his parents' honorable way of conducting their lives and to reiterate his determination to follow in their footsteps. In a way it served as a kind of declaration of the honorable reputation of his family, also a manifestation of his filial sentiment for his parents.

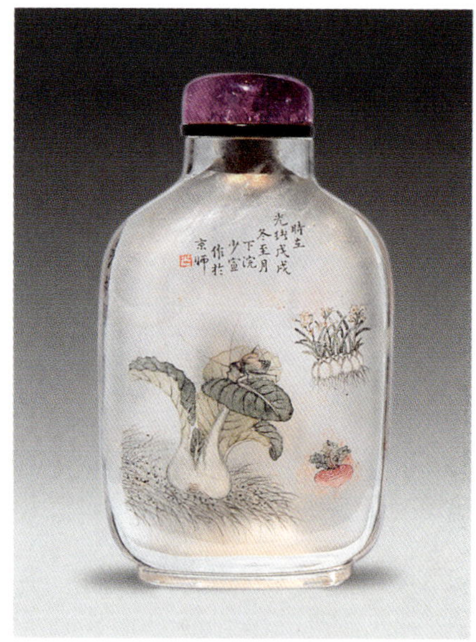

Fig. 42. "A Picture of Purity" (*Qingbai tu*), the reverse of fig. 24, dated 1898 (Private Hawaiian Collection)

59. *Shishuo xinyu* was a collection of novels written by Liu Yiqing of the Song dynasty (420–479) of the Northern and Southern Dynasties period (420–589). For the story of Wang Xiang, see Li Zhuowu, annot., *Shishuo xinyu bu, juan* 1, pp. 10a–11a.

60. The leaves of the cabbages depicted in this pictorial pun provide the green color, the character for which is pronounced "*qing.*" The turnips and the petals of the narcissi are white. The character meaning "white" is pronounced "*bai.*" Thus, these pictorial components suggest the term *qingbai* which signifies purity, in turn, the notion of an unblemished reputation.

It is commonly said that behind each achiever there must be at least one supportive family member. Ma Shaoxuan owed his success to his father who had played a crucial advisory role. Now with his passing, no similarly beneficial mentor was to be found. Henceforth, Ma would have to be entirely on his own. He would have to rely on his self-esteem and strive to continue the path his father had shown him.

PRELUDE

A snuff bottle portrait of Kaiser Wilhelm II (1859–1941) painted by Ma Shaoxuan in 1910 marks a new stage in Ma's artistic development (fig. 43). It is like a prelude to a new composition. Sometime that year, one of Ma's visitors asked him to paint a portrait of the Kaiser inside a snuff bottle, to be a present that would help improve China's international relations with Germany.[61] The bottle was to have a German inscription on the opposite side. Ma had never painted a portrait of a foreigner nor did he know any foreign language. Nevertheless, he accepted the commission.

Ma based his painting on a popular official photograph of the Kaiser then in circulation.[62] He was provided with the German inscription, which was to say: "His Majesty, the German Kaiser, Made by Ma Shaoxuan, Beijing 1910." Not knowing German or even Roman letters, Ma inscribed the letters of the text as a series of graphic shapes. The actual text, as it appears, reads, "Seiner Majestät dem Deutschen Kaiser gewidmet Ma shao hsuan Peking China 1910."[63]

Ma's bottle portrait of Kaiser Wilhem II attracted much attention in Beijing. Some members of Chinese officialdom and the Manchu aristocracy began to ask why Ma should not paint a bottle portrait of the current Qing monarch, the Xuantong Emperor.

Having painted the Kaiser's portrait, was it going to bring good or bad luck? At this point, nobody knew.

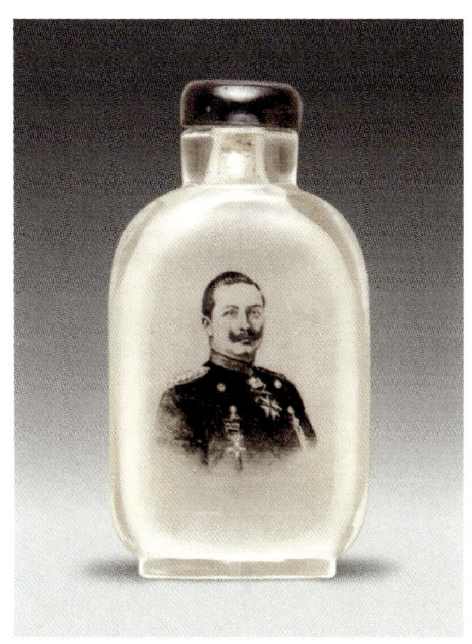

Fig. 43. Portrait of Kaiser Wilhelm II, dated 1910 (formerly in the Wolferz Collection)

61. Relations between China and Germany were strained at the time because Germany's Minister, Baron von Ketteler, had been killed by the Boxers in 1900. See Emily Byrne Curtis, "China's Republican Period History as Mirrored in Portrait Bottles," *Journal of the International Chinese Snuff Bottle Society*, December 1978, p. 6, fig. 5.

62. *Ibid.*, p. 6, fig. 6.

63. See Curtis, *Reflected Glory*, pp. 35–37 and figs. 48–49.

1911: THE HECTIC YEAR

During the cold, windy winter of 1910, an official from the Household of Prince Su, one of the Eight Great Houses,[64] arrived at Ma's residence and presented the order that he paint a bottle portrait of the Xuantong emperor. Naturally, Ma could not refuse. He accepted with some trepidation, for such a commission, while holding the promise of fame and fortune, also meant danger and worry. Soon, a messenger dispatched from the Prince's Household arrived bearing a photograph of the Xuantong emperor, with an order from His Highness that it be used as a model for the portrait. The photograph of the five-year-old Puyi was far from satisfactory (fig. 44). It showed the child-emperor as a tender infant, swaddled in a thick cotton-padded jacket with a high collar that tightly hugged his neck. His eyes were half closed, and the child seemed listless and displeased. It was impossible to paint an emperor from such a photograph. But when Ma sent a request to the Prince's Household for one or two more photographs, he was told that none existed and that he must do the portrait based on the one he had.

Ma could not refuse an order from someone of Prince Su's elevation, so he took up the photograph and tried to determine how it might be used. After studying it for a week or so, Ma had a possible solution to his problem. The photograph was undoubtedly taken when the emperor was unhappy. He was wearing ordinary clothes instead of court dress, and the thick, cotton-padded jacket made him look dumpy and clumsy. He was not facing the camera squarely, but leaned back, with his face slightly tipped up. The child seemed utterly without spirit. Ma thought it might be possible to correct these deficiencies. He should let his imagination supply an ideal setting but use the photograph as the basis for the portrait.

He devised a new composition featuring the following changes:

The portrait should not be placed too low on the bottle. It should be centrally located, or even slightly pushed to the top.

In the photograph, Puyi leans slightly to the right, which makes him seem narrow across the shoulders, so Ma would

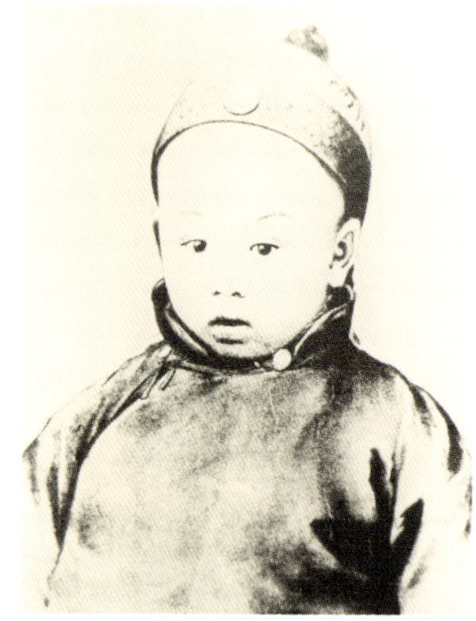

Fig. 44. Photograph of the Xuantong emperor, Puyi, 1910 (courtesy of Emily Byrne Curtis)

64. The Manchu Shanqi (1863–1921) was the last Prince Su, a hereditary rank that dated back to a seventeenth century ancestor, Haoge (1609–1648). The Su Princely Household was the fourth among the so-called "Eight Great Houses" (*Badajia*) among the Manchu nobility. See the "Haoge" biographical entry in Hummel, ed., *Eminent Chinese*, vol. 1, pp. 280–281.

position him squarely to the front, which would make his shoulders seem broader.

In the photograph, Puyi leans back and faces upward. He would seem more dignified by having him face directly forward, pulling back the lower body, and tightening the lips. This would make the forehead more prominent and dispel the impression of unhappiness, while creating a sense of energy and well-being. All this could be done without radically changing the appearance of the photograph.

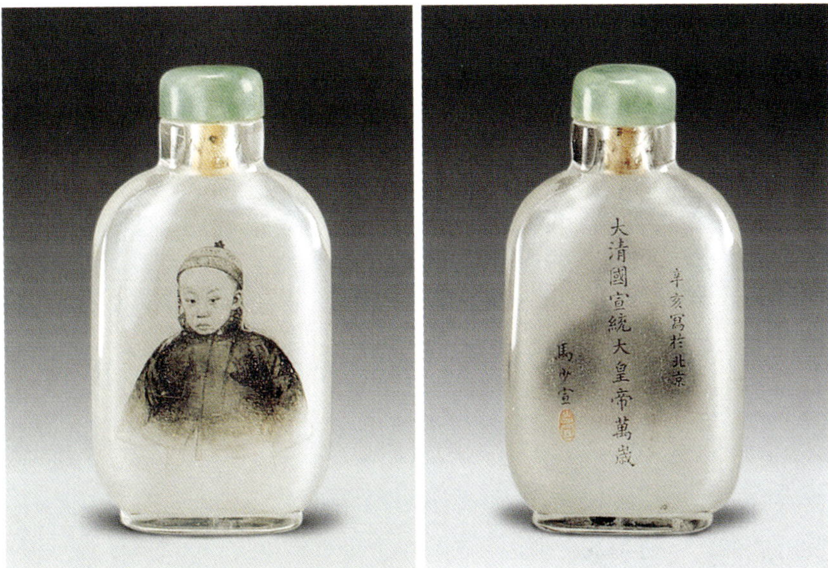

Figs. 45 and 46. Portrait of the Xuantong emperor, Puyi, with inscription on the reverse, dated 1911 (Trojan Collection)

Because the subject was a child with a rather nondescript expression lacking feeling, the face should not be emphasized. A smaller face would improve the composition.

By the beginning of the new year, Ma had the design worked out. He selected a fine, medium-size glass bottle and began to paint. Never had he taken such care with a bottle portrait. But it was soon finished, and, following instructions, he added the inscription to the opposite side, signed it, and painted his seal (figs. 45 and 46). He did not deliver it immediately but kept it at home for several days, every once in a while comparing it to the photograph. He convinced himself that he could not be blamed for failing in any significant way. After a time, he thought that he had even considerably improved on the photograph, so he got ready to send it to his patrons.[65]

65. See Curtis, *Reflected Glory*, pp. 38–40 and figs. 54–56.

However, just then, an emissary from the Household of Prince Su arrived with a second photograph of the emperor and an order to do a second portrait based on it. This was a new photograph and much more suitable. In it, the child-emperor now faced the camera squarely, and his expression was alert, dignified, but utterly natural. Ma painted a second bottle portrait (fig. 47).[66] When it had been completed, word was sent and a member of the Prince's Household came for both bottles.

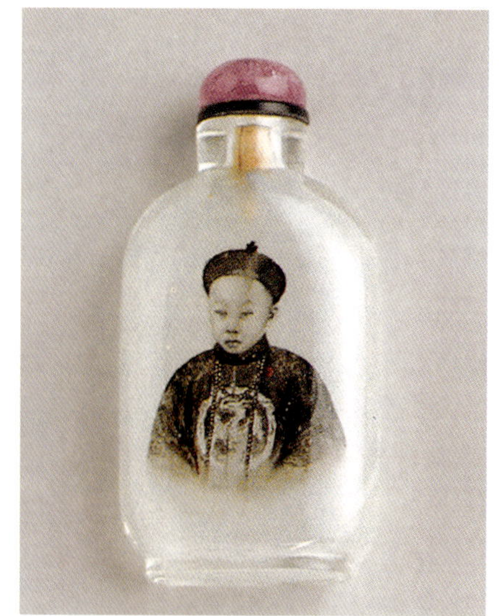

Fig. 47. Second portrait of the Xuantong emperor, Puyi, dated 1911 (formerly in the collection of Eric Young)

Up till now Ma worked at his art because he loved it. To him, depicting landscapes was a way of nurturing his inner nature. It also gave him a satisfying aesthetic experience. Yet, the execution of portraits on imperial command was a burden to him. Even when he had fulfilled the commission, he remained uneasy.

Not long afterwards, the Household of Prince Su again dispatched a messenger. He brought a photograph of the prince and commissioned Ma to use it as the model for a snuff bottle portrait. Ma was told that His Highness had been extremely pleased with the two portraits of the Xuantong emperor and kept singing their praises. When Ma heard this, the burden of worry lifted from his heart and he began to relax—only to realize that a new burden had been placed upon him, for it was equally difficult to paint a

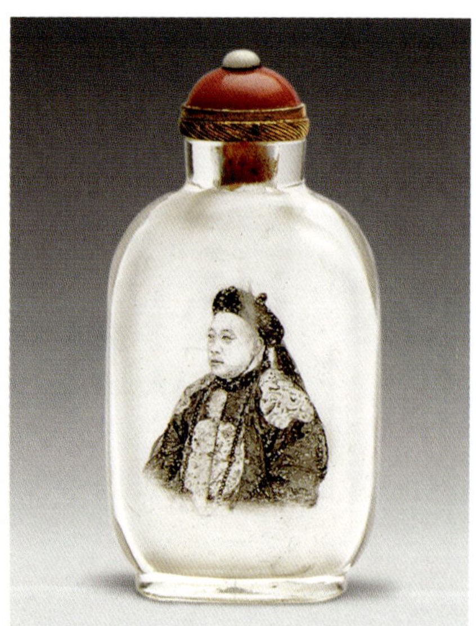

Fig. 48 Portrait of Prince Su, Shanqi, dated 1911 (The Collection of Kenneth and Marcia Hark)

66. Previously published in Curtis, "Chinese Snuff Bottle Portraits: A Supplement," *Journal of the International Chinese Snuff Bottle Society*, Autumn 1985, p. 133 and fig. 7.

67. For Prince Su's photograph and Ma's work, see Curtis, *Reflected Glory*, pp. 26–28 and figs. 34, 36 and 37.

good portrait of His Highness (fig. 48).[67] From then on, Ma received one request after another for portraits from many members of the court.

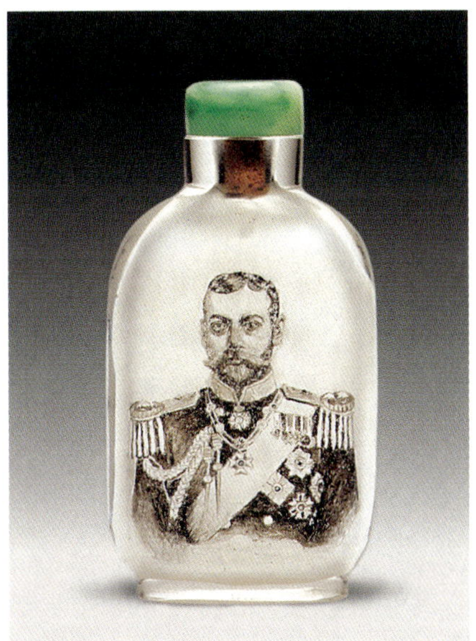

Fig. 49. Portrait of King George V, dated 1911 (Monimar Collection)

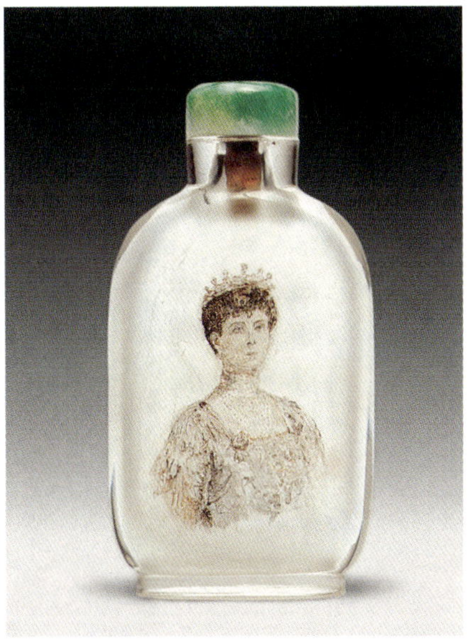

Fig. 50. Portrait of Queen Mary, dated 1911 (Monimar Collection)

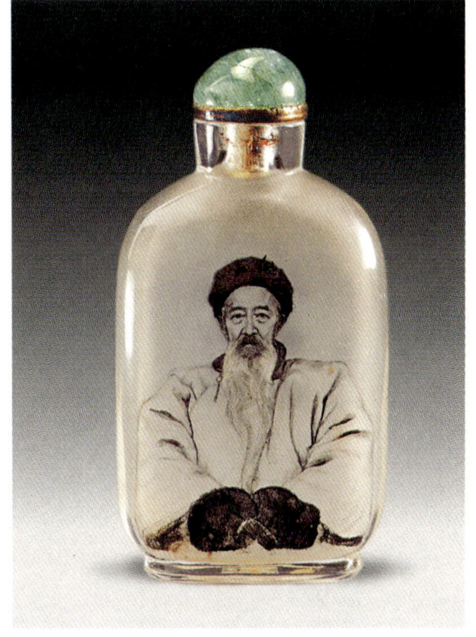

Fig. 51. Portrait of Zhang Zhidong, dated 1909 (The Collection of Mary and George Bloch)

The year 1911 saw the completion of two other major works: a pair of portraits done on separate bottles of King George V (fig. 49) and Queen Mary (fig. 50), to be presented as China's gift in celebration of their coronation,[68] and a bottle portrait of Zhang Zhidong (1837–1909), once the Grand Councilor (fig. 51).[69]

All these portraits of foreign monarchs, the Manchu emperor, Manchu aristocrats, and high-ranking officials were completed within a relatively short time, which meant that Ma lived and worked under considerable pressure. Nevertheless, his art seems to have thrived under pressure, and his splendid achievements in snuff bottle portraiture did much to raise that art form to lofty new heights and gained for it a lasting respect throughout the world.

"BUFFALO BOY'S SONG"

The year 1911 proved to be an eventful one, full of artistic and professional achievement for Ma. Nevertheless, he felt that much of his work was burdensome, for it was done to imperial order, which he could not refuse or even complete at his own

68. *Ibid.*, pp. 40–41. The coronation took place on 22nd June 1911 at Westminster Abbey. This pair of bottles was purchased from a dealer in Montreal in 1964 by Emily Byrne Curtis. There is no record in the archives of the Royal Collections at Windsor Castle that they were ever presented to King George V and Queen Mary, and it would have been impossible for them to leave the collection which does, however, include a portrait bottle of Queen Alexandra. It may have been painted by Ma Shaoxuan, but a photograph of the inscription on the reverse is not available.

69. For the biography of Zhang Zhidong, see the "Chang Chih-tung" entry in Hummel, ed., *Eminent Chinese*, vol. 1, pp. 27–32.

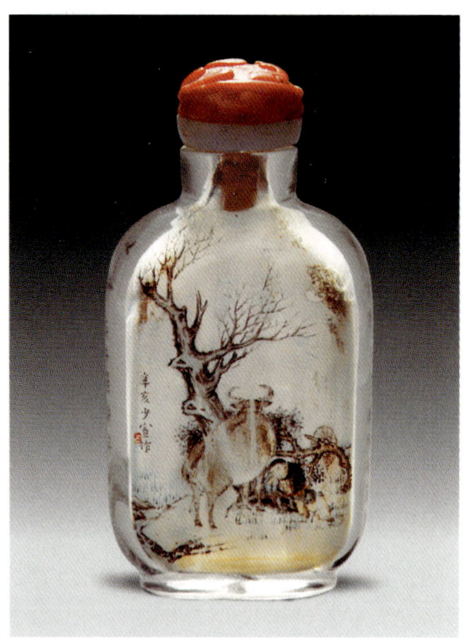

Fig. 52. "Buffalo Boy's Song" (*Muge*), dated 1911 (Ma Family Collection)

pace. He resented the hold the despotic Qing monarchy had over him, and he longed for a peaceful and serene style of life that would allow him to paint subjects of his own choice and to be more creative.

In October the forces of democracy burst free and the revolution began to rid China of Manchu rulership and to found a republic. In what state of mind was Ma Shaoxuan at this point in time? His feelings can be glimpsed from "Buffalo Boy's Song" (*Muge*), a painting he created in the winter of 1911 inside a snuff bottle (fig. 52).

On one side of a glass bottle, 6 cm high and slightly more than 3 cm wide, Ma inscribed a prose in regular script; on the other, he painted a picture of a buffalo boy at rest. The prose consists of forty-four characters arranged in four columns of eleven characters each. It reads as follows (fig. 53):

> *It's only when the moon comes up that he lets his*
> *   buffalo quit plowing,*
> *And, weary as this buffalo boy is, his weariness is*
> *   not from tending buffalo.*
> *The buffalo has a tether; there's no tether for*
> *   the human heart,*
> *But only when the buffalo rests, can the human*
> *   heart also take its ease.*
> *So, finding a place in the shallow grass for a nap,*
> *   happy, free of care, he has a rest.*

The diction is concise, simple and lively, also restrained yet richly expressive. Although couched in metaphor, the composition is an expression of Ma's feelings about his situation at the time. It is significant that it ends on such a positive and hopeful note: Ma believed that the new order would end despotism and bring

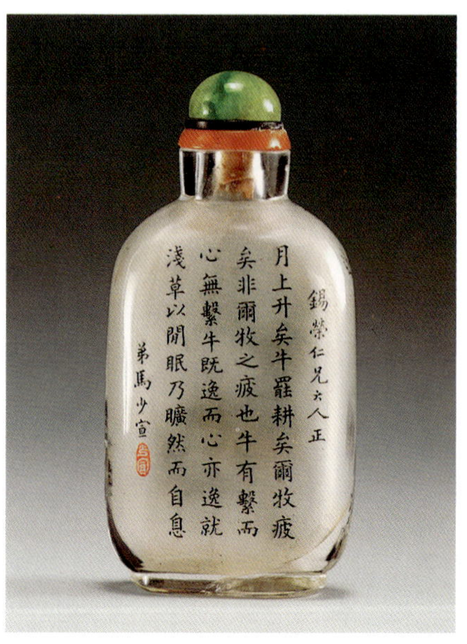

Fig. 53. Inscription written on the reverse of another bottle painted with "Buffalo Boy's Song," undated (Kleiner Collection)

about a better, more democratic society, in which he would not have to cater to the whims of the aristocracy and in which his chances to have a satisfying creative life would be improved.

On the other side of the bottle, the multi-colored picture of the buffalo boy depicts him on the short, new green grass of early spring, when the whole world again comes alive and the first plowing has been done. The buffalo, released from the plow, grazes contentedly. The boy has removed his straw hat and hung it on a tree branch. Reclining against a tree, drowsy, he falls asleep for a little nap. The moon has just risen and appears dimly beyond the spreading branches of a tall bare tree, as another smaller tree just gives off delicate new foliage, an image of vibrating life.

The work has a fresh, elegant appearance, with no thick ink or heavy colors to detract from the light green of the new grass, an obvious sign heralding the arrival of spring. The faint moon keeps company with a few thin clouds. In front of two trees, one bare and the other luxuriant, is the buffalo boy taking a nap. The composition expresses the sweetness of rest after hard labor; we envy the boy's chance to refresh himself. It is a celebration of the simple joys of pastoral life.

The writing and picture perfectly complement each other and form an integral whole, a classic masterpiece of Ma's art at its best.

The end of the nineteenth and beginning of the twentieth century were for China and Beijing momentous years, which included the Sino-Japanese War of 1894–95; the abortive Reform Movement of 1898; the Boxer Uprising, the Allied Army occupation of Beijing in 1900 and the subsequent indemnity; and the Revolution of 1911. As traumatic as all these events were, they spelled the end of Manchu despotism and the beginning of hope for the Chinese people. In addition to their value as an expression of Ma's thoughts and feelings at the end of 1911, the prose and picture of the "Buffalo Boy's Song" might also be interpreted as a statement of Ma's hopes for China. After all this toil and trouble, it was surely time for the nation to find rest and release from its enemies, rest that would allow it to forge a new future.

GOLDEN PERIOD

Ma's artistic career had two great periods of achievement: (1) when he portrayed Tan Xinpei in the role of General Huang Zhong in the later 1890s and (2) when he painted bottle portraits during 1911–15.

Bottle portraiture is a distinctive feature of Ma's art of inside-painting. Hugh Moss, the English expert on Chinese snuff bottles, made the following remarks in his book *Snuff Bottles of China* when he discussed Ma's bottle portraits: "During his lifetime Ma Shao-hsüan was the most popular and successful artist ever to paint a bottle. With his remarkable ability to paint photographic portraits on the inside of bottles. . . Ma ranks with the best of the artists in this medium. . . his portraits must rank technically as the finest interior painted bottles of all."[70]

Ma's second period fell between the years when he was forty-five and forty-nine, in the prime of life, richly experienced, and at the peak of his creative strength. Also witness to his powers at this time is Ma's full transcription of Wang Xizhi's "Lanting Preface," which consists of 325 characters all meticulously inscribed inside one tiny bottle.[71] Sixteen of Ma's bottles, all completed during 1911–15, were exhibited at the 1915 Panama-Pacific International Exposition and won an Honorable Mention award. This was indeed the golden period in the history of Ma's development as an inside-painted snuff bottle artist.

BOTTLE PORTRAITS: THE IMPORTANT WORKS

It is impossible to compile a complete inventory of Ma's bottle portraits, since such works are scattered throughout the world. All we can hope to do is draft a preliminary list of the most important works and make amendments later.

Emperors, Kings, Princes, Presidents

- The Xuantong emperor, Puyi, two portraits (figs. 45 and 47)
- Kaiser Wilhelm II, one portrait (fig. 43)
- King George V and Queen Mary, one portrait each (a matched pair) (figs. 49 and 50)[72]
- King Ibn Saʿūd of Arabia (ca. 1880–1953), one portrait

70. Hugh Moss, *Snuff Bottles of China*, pp. 57–58.

71. Ma did earlier versions of Wang Xizhi's work in 1898 and 1904. But these showed only excerpts from Wang's essay. A detailed discussion of the "Lanting Preface" is included in the next chapter.

72. See Curtis, *Reflected Glory*, pp. 40–43, figs. 58–61.

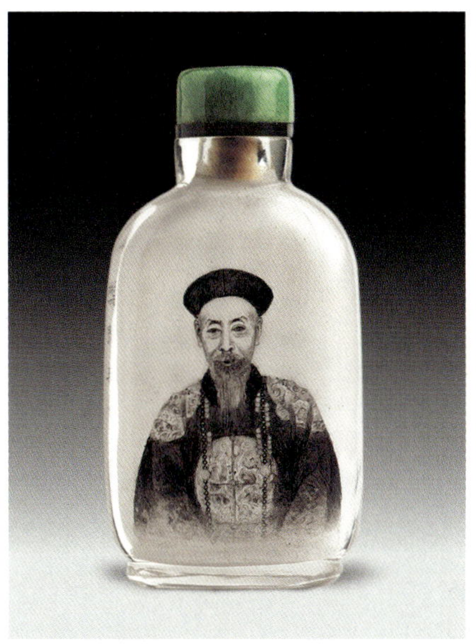

Fig. 54. Portrait of Prince Qing, Yikuang, dated 1905 (Monimar Collection)

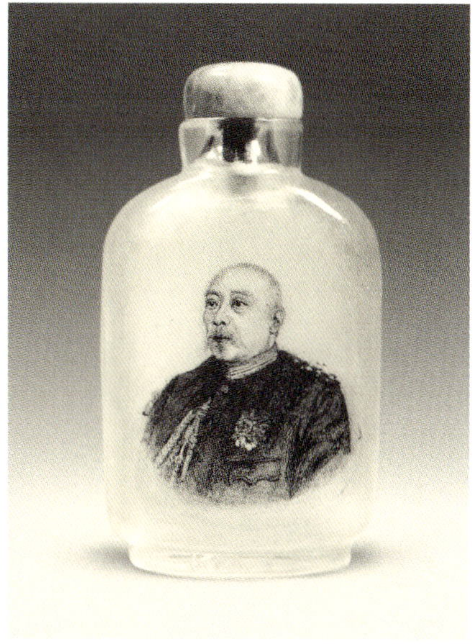

Fig. 55. Portrait of Yuan Shikai, undated (courtesy of Emily Byrne Curtis)

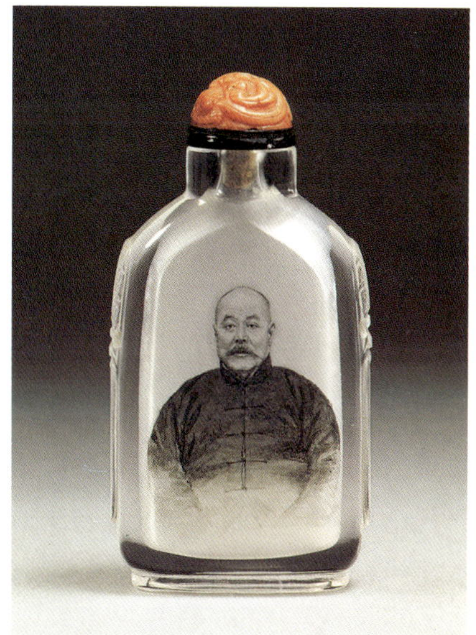

Fig. 56. Portrait of Li Yuanhong, undated (J & J Collection)

— Prince Su, Shanqi (1863–1921), one portrait (fig. 48)

— Prince Qing, Yikuang (1836–1916), one portrait (fig. 54)[73]

— President of the Republic of China, Yuan Shikai (1859–1916), three portraits (fig. 55)[74]

— President of the Republic of China, Li Yuanhong (1864–1928), two portraits (fig. 56)[75]

— President of the Republic of China, Xu Shichang (1855–1939), one portrait (fig. 57)[76]

— President of the United States, Woodrow Wilson (1856–1924) (figs. 58 and 59)[77] and Mrs. Wilson, one portrait each (a matched pair)

73. See Clare Lawrence, *Miniature Masterpieces from the Middle Kingdom: The Monimar Collection*, pp. 290–291.

74. See Curtis, *Reflected Glory*, pp. 44–49 and Geng Baochang and Zhao binghua, ed., *Zhongguo biyanhu zhenshang*, no. 367.

75. See Curtis, *Reflected Glory*, pp. 50–52, figs. 74 and 75 and Moss, Graham and Tsang, *The Art of the Chinese Snuff Bottle*, p. 701, no. 428.

76. See Curtis, *Reflected Glory*, pp. 53–55, fig. 68. The condition of this portrait bottle, formerly in the O'Dell Collection, has deteriorated somewhat. See John G. Ford, *Chinese Snuff Bottles in the Collection of Edward Choate O'Dell*, no. 187.

77. See Curtis, "Chinese Snuff Bottle Portraits: A Supplement," *Journal of the International Chinese Snuff Bottle Society*, Autumn 1985, p. 133. The bottle is seriously cracked, but this does not affect the portrait itself.

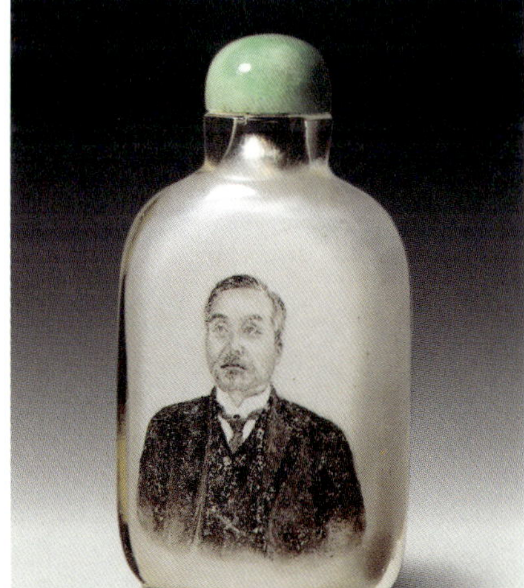

Fig. 57. Portrait of Xu Shichang, undated (O'Dell Collection)

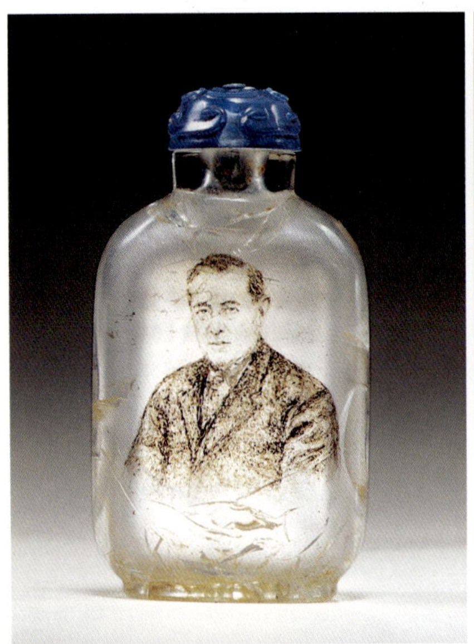
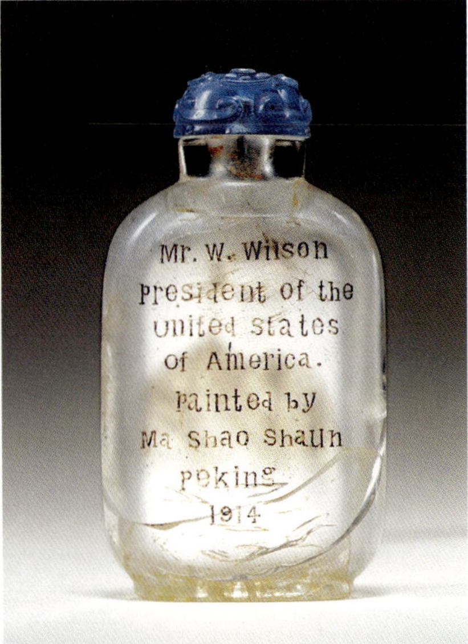

Figs. 58 and 59. Portrait of President Woodrow Wilson, with an inscription in English on the reverse, dated 1914 (The Collection of Manfred W. Arnold)

Qing Dynasty High-Ranking Officials

- Li Hongzhang (1823–1901), Commissioner of Trade for the Northern Ports and Viceroy of Zhili (fig. 60)[78]
- Zhang Zhidong (1837–1909), Grand Councilor of State (fig. 51)[79]
- Wang Wenshao (1830–1908), Grand Secretary of Military Prowess Palace (Wuying Dian)[80]

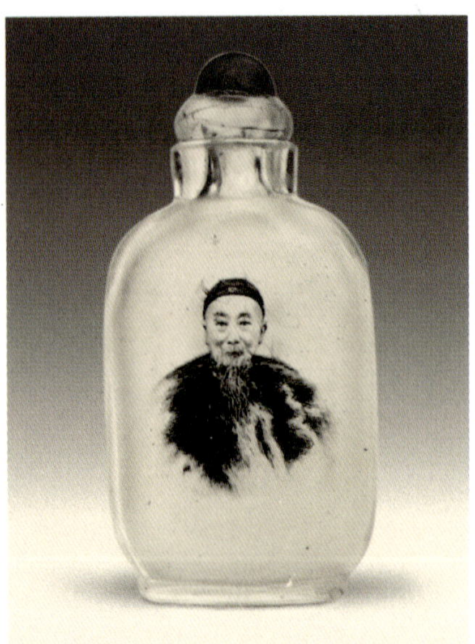

–Sun Jianai (1827–1909), a First Graduate (*zhuangyuan*) of the Xianfeng period (1851–1861) and Grand Secretary of Pavilion of Profound Literature (Wenyuan Ge) (fig. 36)[81]

Fig. 60. Portrait of Li Hongzhang, dated 1914 (Cardinal Point Collection)

78. See Curtis, *Reflected Glory*, pp. 1–7. The "Northern Ports" (Beiyang) refers to coastal regions north of Jiangsu province, such as Shandong, Hebei and Liaoning. This special term was in use during the late Qing and the early Republic period.

79. *Ibid.*, pp. 8–11.

80. Wang Wenshao held several of the highest offices during the waning years of the Qing dynasty, serving as Viceroy of Zhili and a Grand Councilor of State, concurrently a member of the Office of Foreign Affairs. Two photographs of Wang are published in *ibid.*, pp. 24-25, figs. 31 and 33, and a bottle portrait of him by Ziyizi is reproduced on p. 24, fig. 32.

81. *Ibid.*, pp. 22–23, fig. 28.

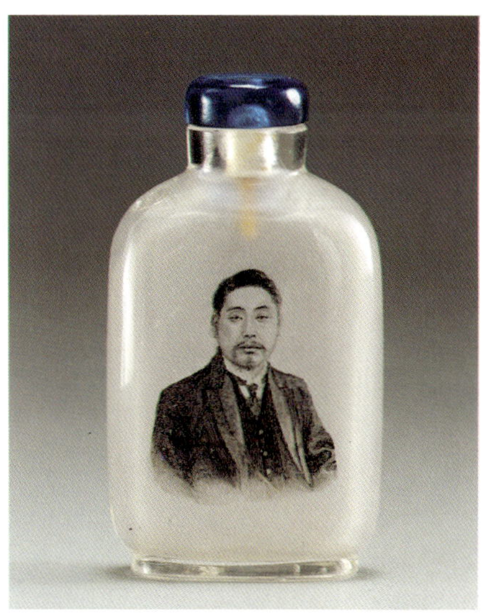

Fig. 61. Portrait of Huang Xing, c. 1912 (Kleiner Collection)

Republic of China High-Ranking Officials

- Huang Xing (1874–1916), Vice Generalissimo (fig. 61)[82]
- Cai Yuanpei (1868–1940), Minister of Education[83]
- Lu Zhengxiang (1871–1949), Minister of Foreign Affairs and Premier (fig. 62)[84]
- Zhao Bingjun (1864–1914), Minister of Internal Affairs and Premier[85]
- Zhang Jian (1853–1926), a First Graduate (*zhuangyuan*) of the Guangxu period (1875–1908) and Minister of Industries (fig. 63)[86]

82. Huang Xing was a leading anti-Manchu revolutionary and one of the founders of the Chinese Republic. See the "Huang Hsing" biographical entry in Howard L. Boorman, ed., *Biographical Dictionary of Republican China*, vol. 2, pp. 192-197, and Curtis, *Reflected Glory*, pp. 17-21 and figs. 22 and 25.

83. Cai Yuanpei was the leading liberal educator of the Republic of China. He served as Minister of Education (1912–1913), Chancellor of Beijing University (1916–1926) and was Founder and first President of the Academia Sinica. See the "Ts'ai Yüan-p'ei" biographical entry in Boorman, ed., *Biographical Dictionary*, vol. 3, pp. 295–299.

84. For more about Lu Zhengxiang, see the "Lu Cheng-hsiang" biographical entry in *ibid.*, vol. 2, pp. 441–444, and Curtis, *Reflected Glory*, pp. 66-69 and figs. 92–97.

85. See Curtis, *Reflected Glory*, pp. 56–58 and fig. 80.

86. Zhang Jian was an industrialist, social reformer, and educator. See the "Chang Chien" biographical entry in Boorman, ed., *Biographical Dictionary*, vol. 1, pp. 35–38, and Curtis, *Reflected Glory*, pp. 63–65 and fig. 91.

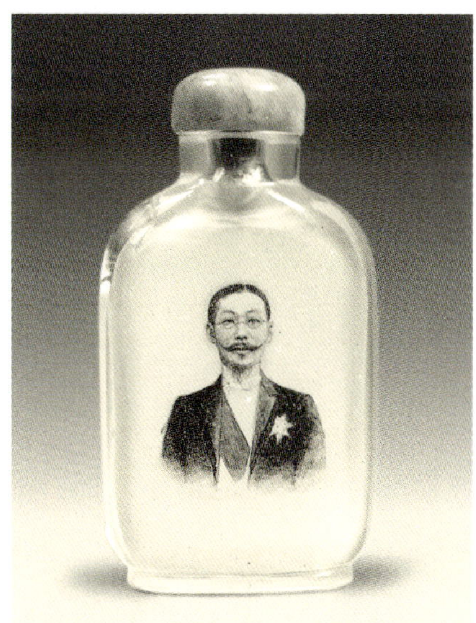

Fig. 62. Portrait of Lu Zhengxiang, undated (formerly in the Wolferz Collection)

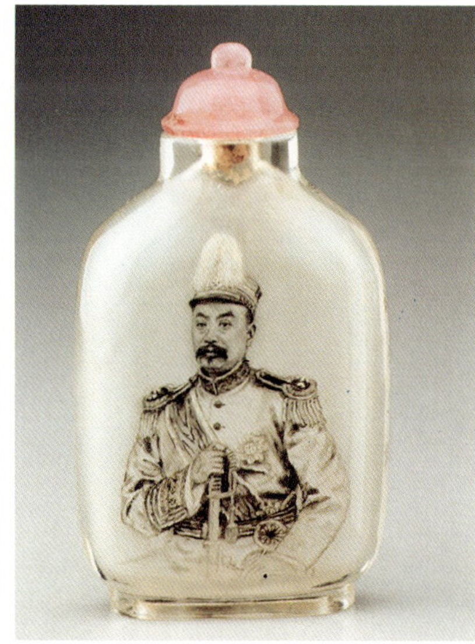

Fig. 63. Portrait of Zhang Jian, undated (The Collection of Mary Margaret Young)

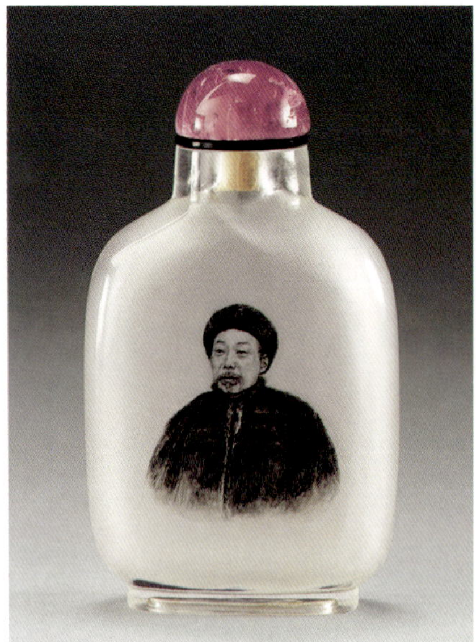
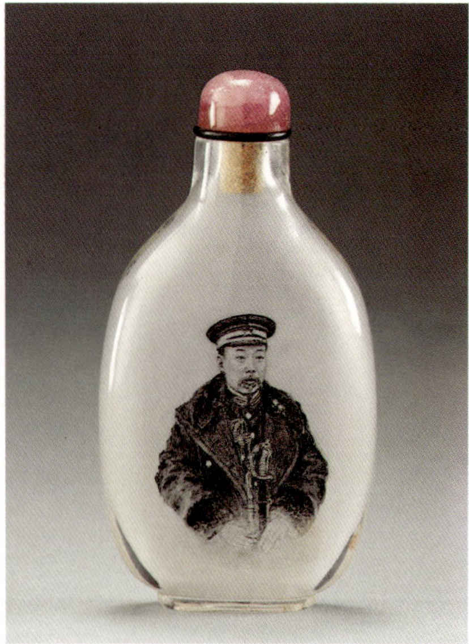

Figs. 64 and 65. Two portraits of Jiang Chaozong, one in civilian dress and the other in military attire, both with laudatory poems, unsigned and undated (The Collection of Mary and George Bloch)

– Jiang Chaozong (1858–after 1936), Commander-in-Chief of the Army (figs. 64 and 65)[87]

– Liu Guanxiong (1859–after 1923), Commander-in-Chief of the Navy (fig. 66)[88]

– Wang Zhengting (1882–1961), Minister of Foreign Affairs and Chief Councilor in the Senate (fig. 67)[89]

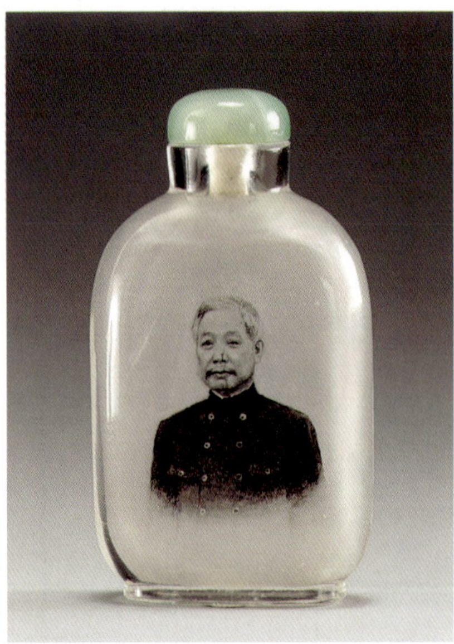

Fig. 66. Portrait of Liu Guanxiong, undated (Kleiner Collection)

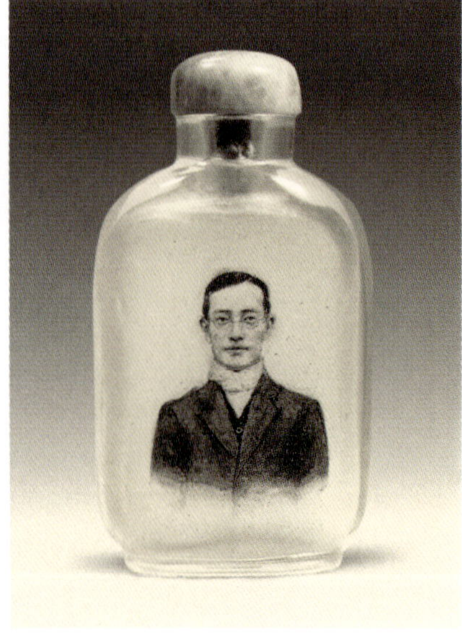

Fig. 67. Portrait of Wang Zhengting, undated (formerly in the Wolferz Collection)

87. For more information about Jiang Chaozong, see *Who's Who in China*, 3rd ed., pp. 164-165, and Curtis, "Chinese Snuff Bottle Portraits: A Supplement," *Journal of the International Chinese Snuff Bottle Society*, Autumn 1985, pp. 131–132 and figs. 3–4. These two bottles were placed together in a fitted presentation case in the style of a book.

88. For more information on Liu Guanxiong, see Curtis, *Reflected Glory*, pp. 59–60.

89. For information on Wang Zhengting, see the "Wang Cheng-t'ing" biographical entry in Boorman, ed., *Biographical Dictionary*, vol. 3, pp. 362–364, and Curtis, *Reflected Glory*, pp. 60–63.

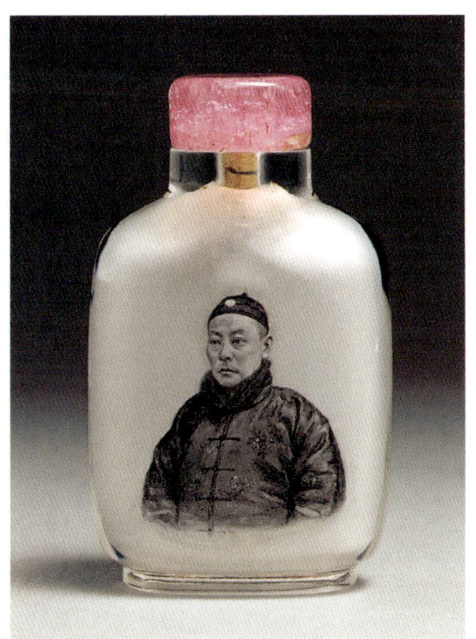

Fig. 68. Portrait of Shi Xiaofu, undated (J & J Collection)

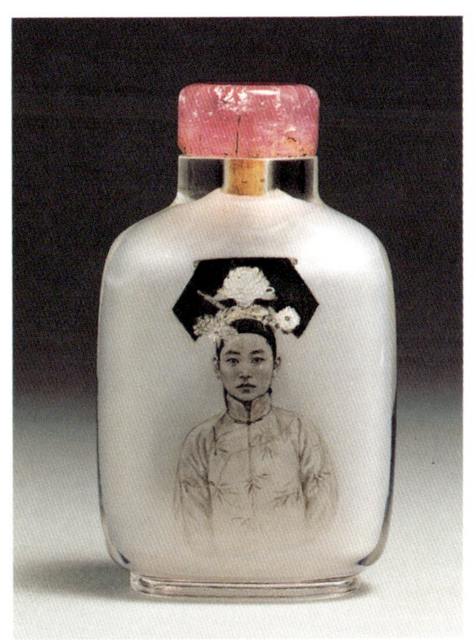

Fig. 69. Portrait of Wang Yaoqing, undated (J & J Collection)

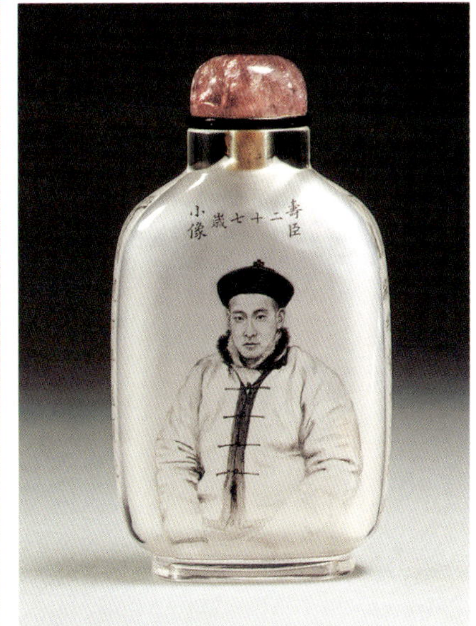

Fig. 70. Portrait of Hao Shouchen, dated 1912 (J & J Collection)

Beijing Opera Actors in Costume and in Ordinary Dress

- Tan Xinpei (1847–1917) (figs. 16, 18, 19, 20)[90]
- Shi Xiaofu (ca. 1837–ca. 1900) (fig. 68)[91]
- Wang Yaoqing (1882–1954) (fig. 69)[92]
- Gai Jiaotian (1888–1970)[93]
- Hao Shouchen (1886–1961) (fig. 70)[94]

In addition, Ma painted portraits of various other military and civil government officials of the late Qing and early Republic, including cabinet ministers, provincial governors, and army commanders, which are not listed individually here (fig. 71).[95]

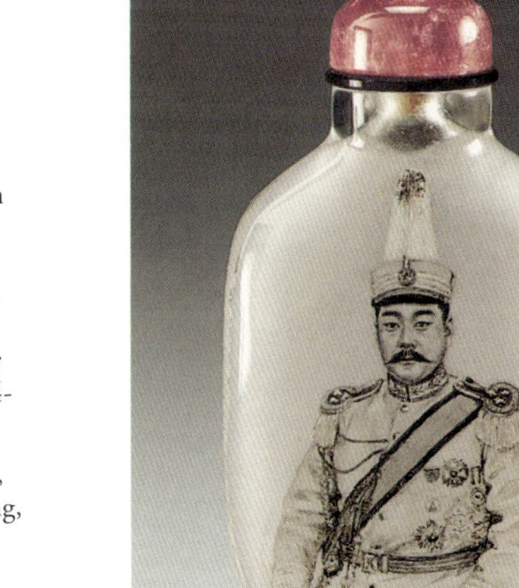

Fig. 71. Portrait of General Jiang Yanxing, undated (The Collection of Mary and George Bloch)

90. See Curtis, *Reflected Glory*, pp. 81–84.

91. *Ibid.*, p. 87, fig. 119, and Moss, Graham and Tsang, *The Art of the Chinese Snuff Bottle*, p. 700, no. 427.

92. See Curtis, *Reflected Glory*, pp. 88–90, fig. 120, and Moss, Graham and Tsang, *The Art of the Chinese Snuff Bottle*, p. 700, no. 427. Both Shi Xiaofu and Wang Yaoqing were celebrated *dan* actors playing female roles.

93. Gai Jiaotian was the stage name of Zhang Yingjie, a native of Gaoyang in Zhili province. He specialized in playing military roles. For a biographical sketch of him, see *Cihai*, vol. 3, p. 4406 and Colin Mackerras, *The Chinese Theatre in Modern Times: From 1840 to the Present Day*, pp. 114-115.

94. See Curtis, *Reflected Glory*, pp. 91–94, fig. 126, and Moss, Graham and Tsang, *The Art of the Chinese Snuff Bottle*, pp. 698–699, no. 426.

95. See Curtis, *Reflected Glory*, pp. 71–79. For Jiang Yanxing, see pp. 72–75 and fig. 100.

Ma also painted portraits of people from commercial and intellectual circles such as Min Shaoquan, Yi'an, and Yu Qing, brilliantly executed and richly expressive works from his late middle period, some of them among the best of his bottle portraits.

A PICTORIAL RECORD OF HISTORY

Ma Shaoxuan painted snuff bottle portraits from the beginning of the century until 1932. This span of thirty-odd years witnessed the surge of the high tide of the Chinese democratic revolution and the great struggle between the old and the new. Progressives, backward elements, revolutionaries, and reactionaries—people of every political stripe—all were put into Ma's bottles. Through their portraits he created chapters of past history and China's future. Since his style was genuinely realistic, the portraits capture how the subjects really looked, both in appearance and dress, and they express their personalities. Ma's portraits of political figures, government officials, military officers, common folk, and scholars—people from every walk of life and social class—constitute a priceless collection of human images that range from the prominent to the common and typical. Their value is as much historical as artistic.

PORTRAIT OF MIN SHAOQUAN

Ma's portrait of Min Shaoquan is an example of his interest in common people. Outside the Qianmen (Front Gate) is found a street called Langfangtou Tiao (Arcade Alley). Before 1949, antique and jewelry and jade shops lined both sides of this alley, where were also found silk and satin shops and the occasional banker. It was a place where the wealthy and idle liked to linger. On the south side of the alley was a jewelry and jade shop called Yubao Zhai (Plentiful Precious Things Studio), whose proprietor was Min Deren, a Muslim who lived in Ox Street, also a relative in close contact with the Ma family. Mr. Min's oldest son, Min Shaoquan, was born in 1891. In the 1920s, when he reached about thirty years of age, he already helped his father run the business, which prospered to their complete satisfaction.

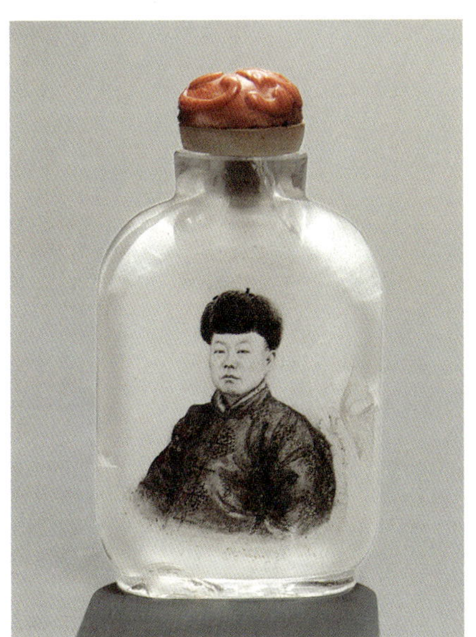

Fig. 72. Portrait of Min Shaoquan, undated (Ma Family Collection)

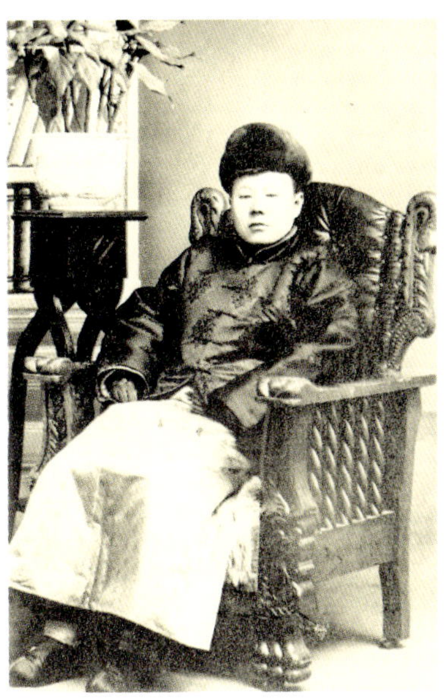

Fig. 73. Photograph of Min Shaoquan (Ma Family Collection)

Min Shaoquan greatly admired Ma's bottle painting, so he asked Ma to paint his portrait. The resulting work is inside a glass bottle 6 cm high and 4 cm wide (fig. 72). The portrait on the front is of Min wearing a sea otter fur hat on his head and a long gown, over which is a black satin mandarin jacket with lozenge-shaped patterns. The brushwork of the face exhibits superb skill, with precise and clean strokes, subtle shading, and an ink tone that is exactly right and exceptionally balanced. The composition is well organized and imparts a strong sense of a figure in the round. The satin mandarin jacket is exquisitely painted. Its gleaming blackness suggests a strong feeling of its soft texture. The furry quality of the hat also comes across successfully. In addition, clear indication of light from above and the lower sides makes the image stand out sharply.

Min Shaoquan's character is convincingly portrayed in his tender, pale, slightly plump face. He is young, blessed with good fortune, and enjoying the fruits of a successful income pleasantly acquired, so his brow is relaxed and his eyes calm and seemingly without care. However, the life of a businessman is a perpetual struggle for wealth and profits, which one cannot afford to take lightly. Thus, Ma paints Min as if he were mulling over something, with the corners of his mouth pulled in and lips pressed tightly together. Min's expression is full of self-esteem but free from arrogance.

When we compare the painting to the photograph, we see that Ma has made some changes (fig. 73). The photograph shows Min Shaoquan leaning slightly backwards, his voluminous clothing bulging at his chest, and the hat on his head is somewhat awry, with its edge drooping a bit down his forehead. The painting corrects these defects.

On the opposite side, Ma inscribed a quadrisyllabic poem in regular script (fig. 74):

> *Embodying enough talent to govern and save*
> *the world,*
> *Radiating an elegant air suited to furs and sashes,*
> *He has great breadth of mind,*
> *And an easy-going manner.*
> *His friendships conform to the Way of the*
> *noble man,*
> *He keeps careful watch over his person,*
> *Shining with pristine honesty and frankness—*
> *Who is there to equal a gentleman such as this!*

The poem complements the portrait, forming a befitting integral part. However, even if we did not know Min Shaoquan's identity and background, if we were to look carefully at his portrait and its accompanying inscription, we would still be able to tell that he was not a dignitary, but a young, rich merchant.

PORTRAITS OF UNIDENTIFIED PERSONS

An unidentified bottle portrait, lacking any inscription, has been in the possession of the Ma family for many years (fig. 75). It is of a middle-aged man with a full head of black hair neatly barbered and combed and wearing a moustache, with a broad forehead and well-formed features, the look in his eyes deep and penetrating. He has a solemn expression, yet seems calm and in a good mood, for he smiles slightly. He is dressed in a coarse woolen coat and a sparkling white shirt, clothes that are plain yet neat. His appearance is not that of a late Qing official but someone of the early Republic who, perhaps, was associated with the reform movement.

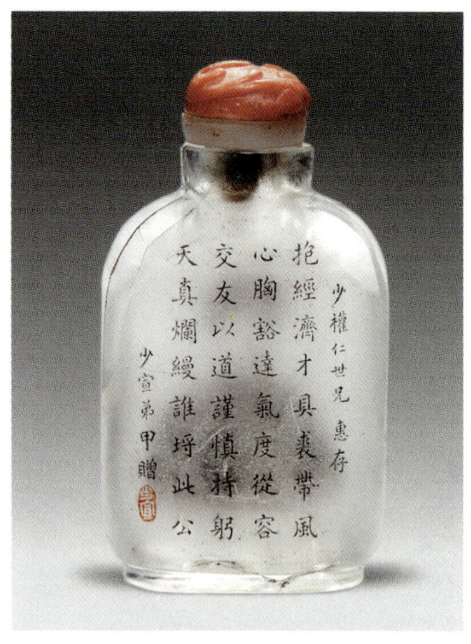

Fig. 74. Inscription on the reverse of fig. 72, portrait of Min Shaoquan (Ma Family Collection)

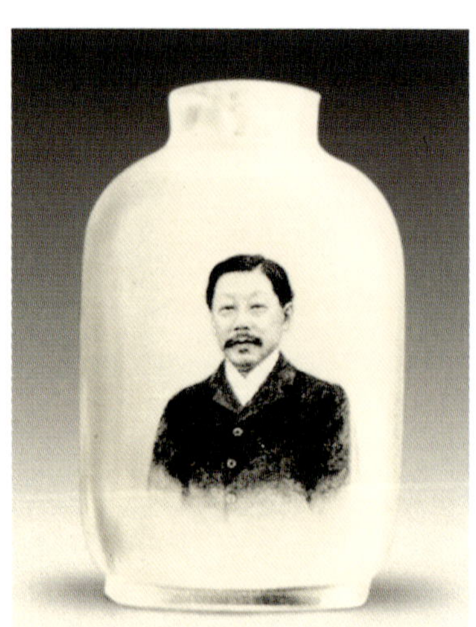

Fig. 75. Portrait of an unidentified gentleman, undated (Ma Family Collection)

Very few such unidentified bottle portraits by Ma Shaoxuan still exist. There were not more than ten up to the time of Ma's death; now, some fifty years later, no more than five seem to have survived loss or breakage.

A WORK BY AN AMERICAN FRIEND

Any study of Ma Shaoxuan's bottle portraits must mention *Reflected Glory in a Bottle: Chinese Snuff Bottle Portraits*, an important work by an American friend, Emily Byrne Curtis. This book treats mainly bottle portraits. Among the seventy-four illustrations of this type of bottles fifty-seven are devoted to works by Ma Shaoxuan, i.e., seventy-seven percent of the total number. In other words, this book can also be said to be a work focusing on the study of Ma's bottle portraits.

A valuable reference in many respects, put succinctly, however, its merits can be summed up in two points:

1. **Rich information**

    The author has collected a very significant number of photographs of bottles with inside-painted portraits by Ma that are scattered in American and European collections. These valuable and useful materials she puts together in a volume for the benefit of her readers. If it were not for this publication, it would be difficult to see at once so many bottle portraits by Ma.

2. **Inclusion of photographs of the subjects of bottle portraits**

    It is amazing how the author has succeeded in tracking down photographs from which the portraits were made. Only when the painted portraits and their original photographs are placed close to one another can readers make comparisons, and only then can they appreciate the realism Ma achieves in his portraits, and marvel at the enchanting power of inside-painting as they take note of the embellishing touches Ma puts on to make the subjects even more personable. This is a great contribution made by the author. Due respects are paid to her innovative idea and her hard work in making it a reality.

ARTISTIC CHARACTERISTICS OF
THE BOTTLE PORTRAITS

Before closing, it is pertinent to review Ma's bottle portraits and comment on his methods of execution and artistic characteristics.

1. Ma's art is based on the two principles that the artistic concept should be formed before beginning to paint and that equal emphasis should be given to form and expression. Many of Ma's portraits were of emperors, kings, princes, and high-ranking officials, people he had never seen in person for the most part. Those who commissioned him to paint the portraits merely provided him with a photograph of the subject, so Ma was forced to devise some means of extrapolating from photographs in order to create works that would achieve formal and expressive artistic excellence.

   Before beginning to paint a bottle portrait, Ma would always spend a great deal of time collecting information about the subject and studying the photograph to determine what formal and compositional features might be used to transform it into a work of art. Sometimes he asked for advice from people who were acquainted with the subject and had the opportunity for intimate observation. Sometimes he had to work solely from photographs and depend entirely on his own imagination to suggest artistic solutions. In either case, his approach was that of the great painters and calligraphers, for whom "the perfected bamboo is in the breast" (*chengzhu zaixiong*) and "the concept exists before the brushwork begins" (*yi zai bixian*).[96]

   Su Shi (1037–1101) opposed the mere attempt to capture formal likeness in painting, as he expressed himself in a poem: "If anyone discusses painting in terms of formal likeness, / His understanding is nearly that of a child."[97] A photograph captures the formal likeness, and to copy a photograph would merely reproduce that formal likeness. Such a portrait would be a lifeless image and an artistic failure. This is why Ma Shaoxuan insisted on placing equal emphasis on form and expression. A human being has both a physical appearance and a sense of life and personality—an

96. The source of "the perfected bamboo is in the breast" is "On Wen Yuke's Painting of Bamboos in the Yundang (Big Bamboo) Valley," an essay written by the renowned poet, painter and calligrapher, Su Shi (1037–1101). See Su Shi, *Su Dongpo quanji, juan* 33, p. 395. This phrase has become an idiomatic expression signifying the importance of sound planning before an endeavor is undertaken. As to "the concept exists before the brushwork begins," this idea was first recorded in Zhang Yanyuan's (ca. 847) *Lidai minghua ji, juan* 2, p. 23.

97. Translation by Susan Bush, *The Chinese Literati on Painting: Su Shih (1037–1101) to Tung Ch'i-ch'ang (1555–1636)*, p. 32.

expression of character. Gu Kaizhi (ca. 345–ca. 406), in describing how to paint human figures, said, "Describe the spirit through form" (*yi xing xie shen*),[98] and this is just what Ma succeeded so well in doing in his bottle portraits—they come alive with the spirit and personality of the subjects. When someone was accepted to have Ma paint his portrait in a bottle, he composed a brief text that Ma inscribed on the opposite side:

> *This fine painting is so filled with spirit*
> *that it makes one think General Cao painted it.*[99]
> *Thanks to you, I am embarrassed that my portrait*
> *now takes its place among those of fine*
> *gentlemen and elegant lords.*[100]

Others said that Ma's bottle portraits looked like photographs pasted inside bottles but were better than photographs, for they corrected the shortcomings of photographs and seemed more lifelike.

2. Ma placed great emphasis on the development of a sense of light in his bottle portraits, for it is this sense that creates illusions of depth, mass, and texture. Ma was a close student of the visual effects of light on flesh and clothing—light and shade, the play of light rays, and modulation of colors. He also studied the exact way that various kinds of ink application reflected light differently and how to modulate these differences. Practical experience eventually taught him how to solve the two basic problems of how to create an illusion of mass and how to suggest the sense of various kinds of surface texture. As a consequence, the bottle portraits of his middle and late periods sparkle with light; the textures of satin, silk, wool, and other fabrics look real enough to fondle and stroke, and the skin seems soft, pliant and alive to the touch.

3. In these works, the portraits are the main focus of Ma's art and the calligraphic inscriptions are secondary features. Most of the bottle portraits have inscriptions on the opposite side, the majority poems transcribed in either graceful regular script or elegant clerical script, added to enhance the portraits and to contribute to a total artistic effect. Some poems are

---

98. Gu Kaizhi, *"Lunhua"* ("Essay on Painting"), is cited in Zhang Yanyuan, *Lidai minghua ji, juan* 5, p. 118. See also Susan Bush and Hsio-yen Shih, *Early Chinese Texts on Painting*, p. 33.

99. General Cao was Cao Ba (active mid-eighth century), who was an excellent calligrapher and painter. He was particularly famous for his pictures of imperial horses and portraits of government ministers and was highly praised by the great Tang poet Du Fu, who said that he not only caught the formal likeness but also the *shen* (spirit) of his subjects. See Susan Bush and Hsio-yen Shih, *Early Chinese Texts on Painting*, p. 336.

100. Neither the subject of the portrait nor the author of the inscription is identified. However, a portrait bottle with this same inscription is published in Geng Baochang and Zhao Binghua, ed., *Zhongguo biyanhu zhenshang*, p. 299, bottle no. 366. There, the inscription is reproduced and includes the name (but not surname) of the subject and author of the inscription, a man whose personal or literary name was Shunmu, and the date, "last month of spring in the year *gengxu* [1910]."

meant to praise or address the person whose figure is portrayed, as, for example, the poem that accompanies the portrait of Min Shaoquan presented above. Another example is the poem inscribed on the opposite side of the bottle portrait of Yu Qing:

> *At the same age as Zhong and Jia,[101]*
> *You are off to seek teachers thousands of miles*
> *   away.*
> *The Unicorn Pavilion and Cloud Terrace,[102]*
> *May this be the start of your way up to them.*
> *It's easier to color a man with companions and habits*
> *Than to apply reds or blues to his portrait.*
> *So when you need help to stay on the path of virtue,*
> *Just look at this picture and inscription.*

This inscription was actually a piece of sincere advice written for a young man about to embark on a long journey to seek guidance in his personal development.[103] Other inscriptions criticize figures and even poke fun at them, as, for example, a poem that accompanies a portrait of an anonymous man (figs. 37 and 76):

> *The virtues of clear ice and pure jade*
> *Are united in equal measure in his own person,*
> *So when he enters the realm of many fragrances,[104]*
> *He can frolic in the muck and never come up black!*

Other inscriptions, of course, consist of conventional wishes for happiness and long life. In general, some poems are original compositions by Ma himself, and some were first drafted by those who sought portraits from him.

4. Ma's snuff bottle portraits, regardless of the subject, are characterized by refinement and elegance. The subjects are portrayed as if beyond the concerns of fame or wealth. Although this quality is not at all apparent upon viewing only a few bottle portraits, once one becomes familiar with Ma's oeuvre, it is obvious that all his figures are painted to appear to share in the higher virtues. They are never tainted by frivolity or meanness nor subject to worldly cares. This idealism typifies Ma's art and helps to make his work unique.

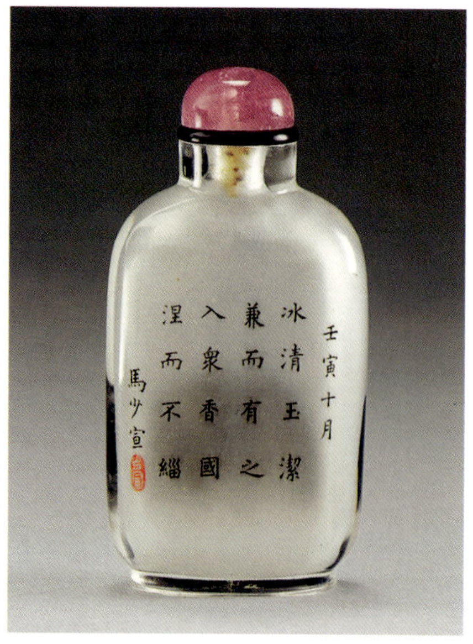

Fig. 76. Poem inscribed on the reverse of fig. 37, portrait of an anonymous man, dated 1902 (The Collection of Mary and George Bloch)

101. Zhong Jun (d. 112 B.C.) and Jia Yi (200–168 B.C.) were precocious youths of the early Han period who gained high office and imperial favor. Later they were often cited as exemplars of talented young men.

102. The Unicorn Pavilion (Qilin Ge) and Cloud Terrace (Yun Tai) were constructed respectively during the reigns of Emperor Xuandi (73–49 B.C.) and Emperor Mingdi (A.D. 58–75) of the Han period; in them were arrayed portraits of illustrious ministers.

103. This bottle is illustrated in Geng Baochang and Zhao Binghua, ed., *Zhongguo biyanhu zhenshang*, p. 281, no. 342.

104. "Realm of many fragrances" (*zhongxiangguo*) refers to taking snuff; i.e., the owner of the bottle can indulge his habit of taking snuff as much as he likes, yet will never be soiled by it.

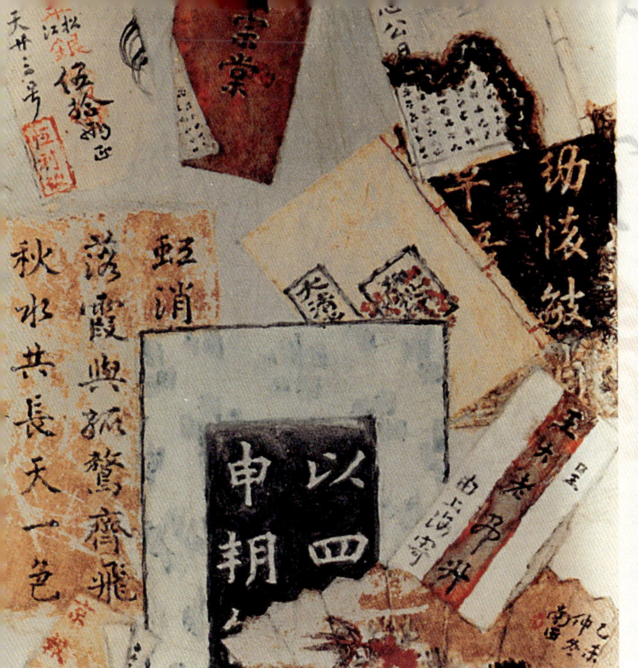

CHAPTER FOUR

Calligraphic Works

The basic format of Ma Shaoxuan's inside-painted snuff bottles consists of a painting on one side and a piece of calligraphy on the other, with equal emphasis given to both and each used to enhance the other.

TWIN-HEADED LOTUS

In China, painting and calligraphy are traditionally done on paper or silk. Although both arts originate from the same source, each has its independent form of expression, and as well, its own aesthetic value. Since the Ming dynasty (1368–1644), writing inscribed on paintings has been increased considerably. As a result, the viewer's visual experience has been much enhanced. Yet, as a rule, writing is incorporated into painting, but never the other way round. This phenomenon reflects the limitation inherent in their degree of integration. Painting inside snuff bottles, however, provides a means that breaks through this limitation.

Both paper and silk are two-dimensional. A snuff bottle, however, is three-dimensional. It provides surfaces for painting on one side and writing on the other; these can be enjoyed singly or as an integrated piece of work. An artist can add an inscription beside a painting; he can also add illustrations to a text. In letting the two arts complement each other on equal terms, he intensifies the close relationship that binds them together.

Ma Shaoxuan made full use of the advantage innate within bottles suitable for inside-painting. He painted pictures on one side and wrote inscriptions on the reverse, allowing them to be enjoyed as independent works or as unified compositions. "Rhapsody on the Sounds of Autumn," for example, is a work in which the painting is created to illustrate Ouyang Xiu's famous prose (figs. 12 and 13), while the inscription that accompanies the bottle portrait of Min Shaoquan is added to provide more information about the subject (figs. 72 and 74). This flexibility of combining text to visual images and vice versa opens up a whole new horizon for the artist. He no longer needs to worry about the restrictions imposed on him while painting on paper or silk. With regard to the two basic elements—painting and calligraphy—it is entirely up to him to plan their best means of combination. The following poem gives some idea of the magnitude of this creative freedom:

> *Between heaven and earth, a vast realm for you*
> *   to roam about.*
> *Why conform with old rules?*
> *Unfold your ambitious plans; flap your wings*
> *   to soar;*
> *Gorgeous mountains and rivers will take shape*
> *   under your brush!*

INSIDE-CALLIGRAPHY FORMATS

Ma's inside-painted bottles often have calligraphy on both sides: one side shows a text; the other side is decorated with a picture, with calligraphy incorporated in it. His methods of presentation are as follows:

1. When calligraphy is integrated into a picture, it usually takes the form of an inscription which varies in length from only a few characters to more than twenty characters. Some just indicate the subject matter, such as the one made up of only four characters, *Wuniao xulun* (The Essential Human Relationships Represented by Five Species of Birds) (fig. 9). Some include the artist's signature and date of completion, as in the bottle, "Buffalo Boy's Song," on which to the left of the painting is written in a vertical line five characters, *Xinhai Shaoxuan zuo* (Executed by Shaoxuan in the year *xinhai* [1911]) (fig. 52). There are also instances where the inscription embodies the title, signature and date of completion, as in this example made up of ten characters:

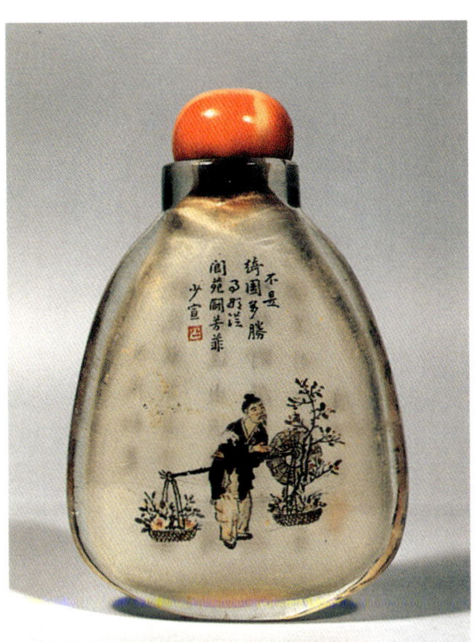

Fig. 77. "Picture of a Flower Peddler," dated 1898 (The Collection of Susan B. Hacker)

Huantian xidi, yiwei dongri, Shaoxuan ("Boundless Joy," [painted by] Shaoxuan on a winter day in the year *yiwei* [1895]) (fig. 4). Furthermore, in yet another case, the inscription may include poetic lines, such as "Picture of a Flower Peddler" made in 1898, on which no less than twenty characters are inscribed: *Bushi qiyuan duo shengshi, nacong langyuan dou fangfei, Shaoxuan zuo yu jingshi* ("If the beautiful garden were not pulsing with numerous activities, / How could [the flowers] compete in beauty and fragrance in the fairyland?" Executed by Shaoxuan at the capital) (fig. 77).

Ma always inscribed his paintings with extreme care. Whether the inscriptions were written in regular, or running, script, whether they were long or short, he was very particular about their positioning, making sure that as part of the pictorial compositions, they could stand on their own as fine pieces of calligraphic works, yet also enhance the artistic significance of the themes portrayed.

2. Ma's principal method of presenting calligraphy inside snuff bottles was to write a poem or prose in standard script on one side. The nature of their content varied from piece to piece, including the following:

Literary compositions —the majority comprised short and antithetical sentences. Sometimes these were maxims created by celebrities, while at other times they were made up of idiomatic expressions and allusions. The number of characters constituting such inscriptions varied considerably in length, ranging from as few as a handful to as many as up to a hundred. Yet, whether short or long, they were all designed to complement the illustration on the other side of the bottle, either amplifying the meaning of the pictorial composition, or expressing good wishes for the person portrayed, or conveying more fully the feelings embodied in the picture.

Poems —these appeared in different formats, such as quadrisyllabic, pentasyllabic, septasyllabic, ancient form, regulated form, and prose with rhymes. They might be famous compositions by renowned writers of the past, or Ma's own creations improvised on the spur of the moment, or productions provided by people who commissioned the bottles.

Well-known prose writings, fully quoted or excerpted—
frequently copied works include "The Lanting Preface" by
Wang Xizhi, the highly acclaimed literary writer and
calligrapher of the Jin dynasty (265–420), "Rhapsody on the
Sounds of Autumn" by Ouyang Xiu, and "Rhapsody on Red
Cliff" by Su Shi. Because such works are quite long, often the
text occupies not just one side of the bottle, but both sides;
and in certain cases, all four sides are covered with characters. As a result, these works are devoid of paintings; calligraphy becomes the sole decorative element.

Imitations of steles and calligraphic specimens —
Ma was especially fond of the calligraphic style of
Ouyang Xun. More than once he copied on one side of a bottle the first few sentences of Ouyang's "An Account of the Sweet Spring in the Palace of Nine Accomplishments" which
produced extremely satisfactory results. In addition, Ma liked
to paint "Pictures of Antiquities" (*Bogu tu*) and "Pictures of
Longevity" (*Baisui tu*). The former illustrates a collection of
antique vessels, tiles, calligraphic specimens, paintings, books,
and correspondence (figs. 78 and 79). The latter depicts a
collage of damaged objects (fig. 80). The fragmentary (*sui*)
state of these numerous (*bai*) burnt, broken, rotten, or torn
objects calls to mind a homonym meaning "year." Thus, the
image of a number of broken (*baisui*) objects actually
constitutes a rebus having the auspicious meaning of wishing
someone might enjoy a long life. Both types of composition
incorporate characters which are written out in a variety of
scripts, including the writing style used for inscriptions on
ancient bronzes, big seal, running and regular. In imitating

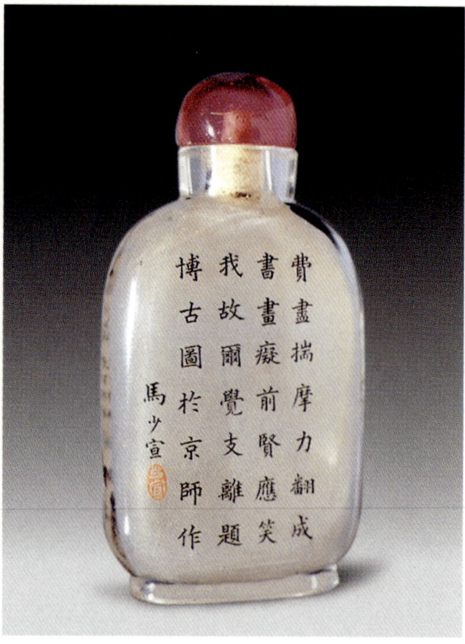

Figs. 78 and 79. "Picture of Antiquities" (*Bogu tu*), with a poem inscribed on the reverse, undated (The Collection of Ann Kreuger)

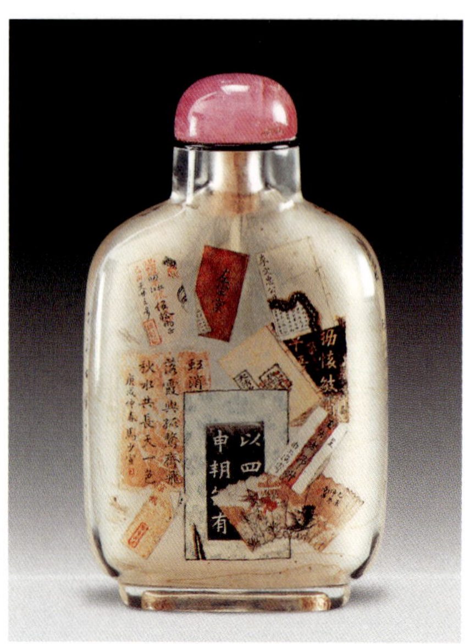

Fig. 80. "Picture of Longevity" (*Baisui tu*), undated (The Collection of Mary and George Bloch)

these scripts one must first acquire a sound training in calligraphy. Such renditions, therefore, should also be regarded as another form of Ma's calligraphic works.

CALLIGRAPHIC STYLES

The term "calligraphic styles" means different forms of writing, such as regular, cursive, clerical, and seal, scripts. It also means different schools of calligraphy, such as those originated by Yan Zhenqing (709–785), Liu Gongquan (778–865), Ouyang Xun, and Zhao Mengfu (1254–1322).[105]

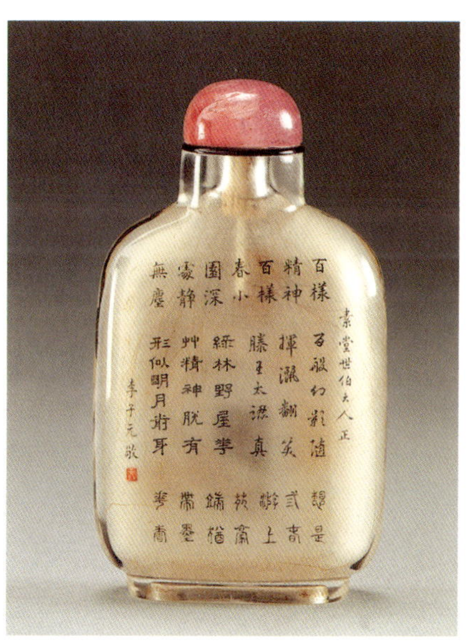

Fig. 81. Inscription on the reverse of fig. 80, undated, with two poetic lines in regular script (upper section), two poetic lines in a combination of regular and running scripts, and four poetic lines in clerical script (middle section), two poetic lines in seal script (The Collection of Mary and George Bloch)

105. Yan Zhenqing, Liu Gongquan and Ouyang Xun were all renowned calligraphers of the Tang dynasty. They also held important positions in the government. Yan's calligraphy is characterized by an air of dignity and strength. Liu's handwriting is valued for its well integrated structure imbued with vigor. Ouyang's calligraphy is noted for his propensity for unpredictable effects. Zhao Mengfu, a Yuan official, painter, and calligrapher, is respected for the fluidity and beguiling beauty inherent in his writing.

106. The composition would have been similar to that of fig. 4 although the inscriptions on the reverse of these bottles, both dated 1895, are not the same.

107. Except for the two lines written at the top about butterflies, the inscription on the reverse of fig. 80 is identical to the text quoted. The differing poetic lines shown in fig. 81 read, "A hundred aspects of spring; a hundred moods; / In the depth of a small garden— peaceful and free from the dust [of this world]."

108. The Prince of Teng was the twenty-second son of Emperor Gaozu of the Tang dynasty (r. 618–626). His name was Li Yuanying.

Among Ma's inside-written works regular script was the style he favoured, although he also wrote in running, seal, and clerical, scripts. On a work which he produced in 1895 he inscribed poems in four different scripts. One side of it depicts blossoms and butterflies, a scene exuding feelings of spring and vitality.[106] The inscriptions on the reverse, written out in regular, running, clerical, and seal, scripts, are chosen specifically to complement the subject matter of the painting (fig. 81). At the top is written in regular script, "A hundred butterflies [flit about] the bushes, [leaving behind] a hundred souls, / A hundred flowers from a hundred species also seem to be rootless."[107] In the middle, on the right, written in running script is: "[With my brush] I sketch as many illusory images as I like. / How I laugh at the Prince of Teng for being too serious."[108] On the left are written in clerical script these four lines: "[Like] a rustic cottage in a luxuriant grove, / [Or] the essence of flowers and foliage, / [If one] discards [the notion of] outward resemblance, / The bright moon [could well have been these] in its former lives." At the bottom, written in seal script is "[I] believe [he] must have visited the imperial park during the three [months of] spring, [So that his] brush-tip still exudes the fragrance of ink blossoms." Altogether, the fifty-eight characters rendered in four styles form a perfect piece of inside-written calligraphic work. In other examples two styles of writing may appear together in the inscription, such as on the bottle depicting a portrait of Li Hongzhang, the Commissioner of Trade for the Northern Ports, where the eulogy is written in seal script, while the signature is done in regular script.[109]

Regular script is definitely Ma's favourite writing style.

"THE LANTING PREFACE"

Ma Shaoxuan left for his descendants as an heirloom a snuff bottle inscribed in regular script on the inside with the full text of the great Jin-dynasty calligrapher Wang Xizhi's renowned essay, "The Lanting Preface" (figs. 82–85). This he regarded as a fruit of labor most dear to his heart.

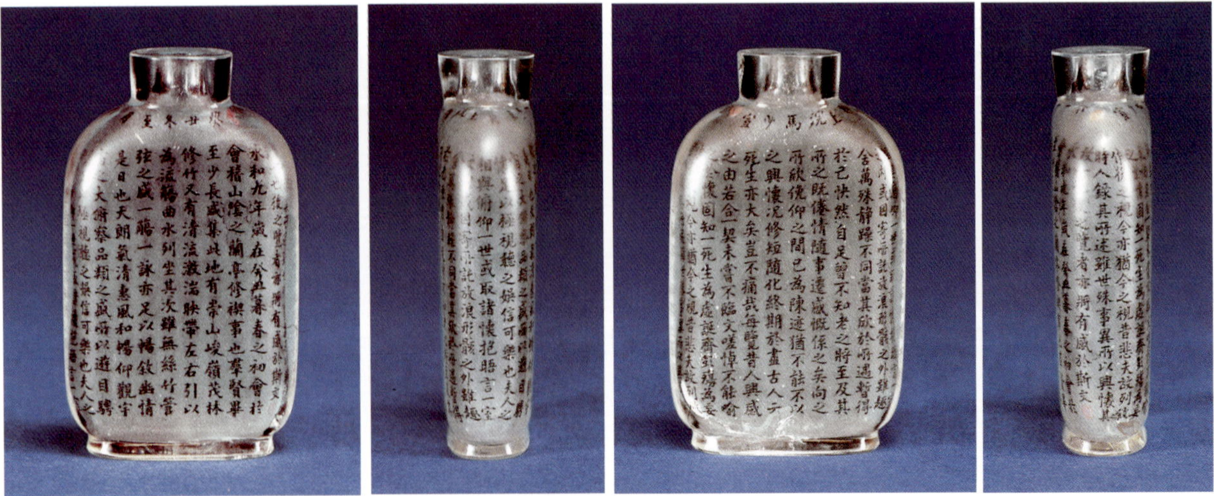

Figs. 82-85. Complete text of "The Lanting Preface" written in regular script inside a bottle, four views, dated 1913 (Ma Family Collection)

---

109. See Curtis, *Reflected Glory*, p. 2, fig. 4.

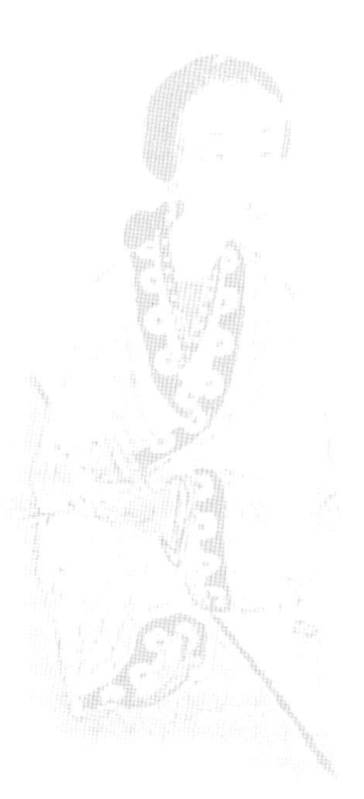

The bottle is 6 cm high and 3.6 cm wide. The full text, totalling 325 characters, is distributed on all four sides of the bottle in 22 columns that run from right to left. Each line consists of 14 to 15 characters; each character measures approximately 0.28 cm high and 0.25 cm wide. The inscription and signature, made up of ten characters, are positioned on the neck, reading, "[Executed by] Ma Shaoxuan during the first ten days of the month of the winter solstice in the year *kuichou*." Two seals are painted in. The one placed after the signature is as small as a rice grain. Its legend, *Shao*, is written in seal script in intaglio mode. The other one, the size of a green bean, is located after the inscription. It shows the single character *Xuan* in relief, also written in seal script.

The year *kuichou* is equivalent to 1913. In that year Ma was forty-seven years old. "The Lanting Preface" by Wang Xizhi was also composed in the year *kuichou*. However, as indicated in the beginning sentences of the essay, this was equivalent to the ninth year of the Yonghe period (353). According to ancient customs, people observed purification rites on the third day of the third month. On this particular day Wang Xizhi and some of his friends gathered at the Orchid Pavilion (Lanting) at Shanyin county in the region of Mount Guiji in Zhejiang province. They cleansed their bodies in a stream to rid themselves of evil influences and hoped for blessings from heaven. After this ceremony all of the participants sat along the bank and drank wine as cups filled with it floated down the stream. In high spirits they composed many poems which Wang Xizhi collected, adding a preface to record the event. More than two hundred years later, Wang's work, written in running script, was greatly admired by Emperor Taizong of the Tang dynasty (r. 627–649), who ordered that copies be made so that reproductions could be generated from stone engravings. From then on, copies of Wang Xizhi's "Lanting Preface" spread far and wide. Praised as "the preeminent exemplar of running script," this masterpiece has exerted immense influence on later calligraphers. The essay itself has also been given an important place in the historical development of literature.

Ma Shaoxuan always held in great respect Wang Xizhi's literary works and calligraphy. He learned Wang's writing style from his father. He also passed on what he had mastered to his sons and grandsons. Learning the Wang calligraphic style has thus become a family tradition. In the early stages of his career as an inside-painted snuff bottle artist, more than once Ma had already inscribed excerpts from the "Lanting Preface" on bottles. As an example, on a work completed in 1897 he wrote altogether fifty-one characters, seven of which made up the inscription and signature, while the remaining forty-four words were excerpted from the "Lanting Preface," beginning from *Yonghe jiunian* (In the ninth year of the Yonghe period) and ending with *moulin xiuzhu* (luxuriant groves and slender bamboo) (fig. 86).[110]

In 1898 Ma introduced a new format: both sides of the bottle were inscribed with a literary composition; no illustration was incorporated with it (figs. 25 and 26 and 87 and 88). The composition chosen was again the "Lanting Preface." The text ran from *Yonghe jiunian* to *yangguan yuzhou zhi da* (Looking up [we] marvel at the vastness of the universe), which consisted of 101 characters. These, together with two more characters added at the very end, *jielu* (an abridgment), amounted to a total of 103 words, which were written out in eight columns, each having thirteen characters. Following the excerpt was a painted square

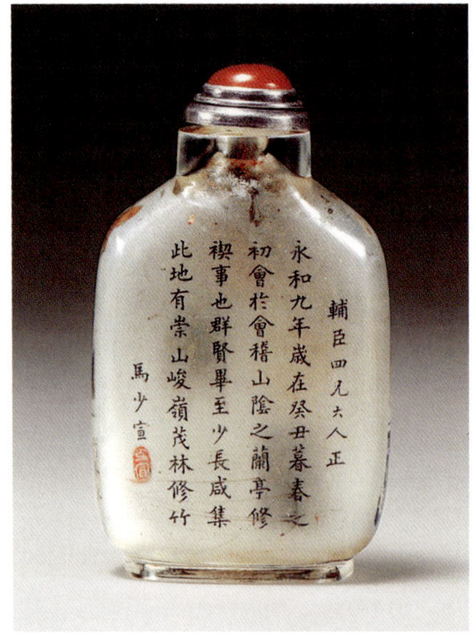

Fig. 86. "The Lanting Preface," an extract, undated (The Collection of Hilde Schonfeld)

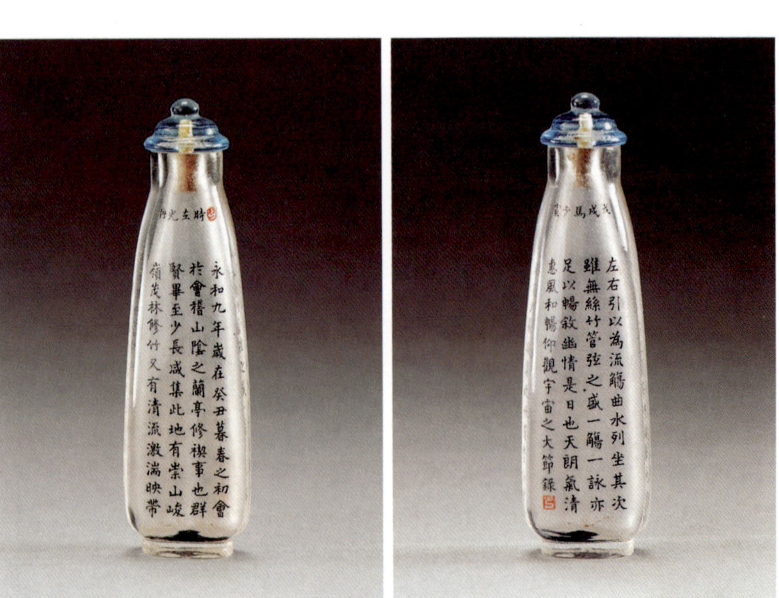

Figs. 87 and 88. "The Lanting Preface," an extract, dated 1898 (The Collection of Mary and George Bloch)

110. Although the example illustrated in fig. 86 is undated, the text quoted is identical to that inscribed on the 1897 bottle described by the author.

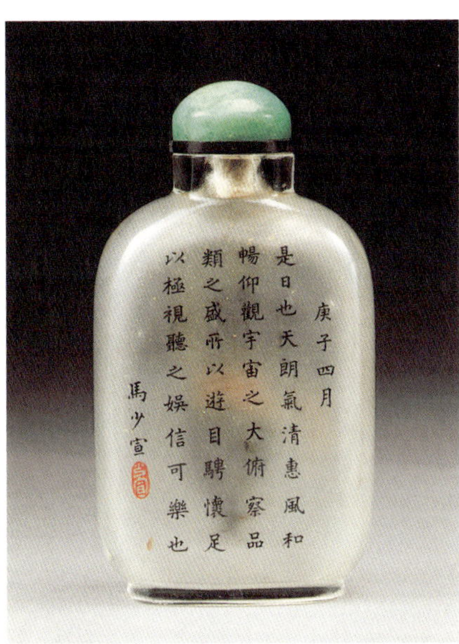

Fig. 89. "The Lanting Preface,"
an extract, inscribed on the reverse
of fig. 14, "Selling the Horse,"
dated 1900 (J & J Collection)

111. Traditionally the Chinese calculated
time by combining the Twelve Earthly
Branches with the Ten Heavenly
Stems. This produced a cycle which
would recur every sixty years.

112. According to Ma Zengshan's note,
there are differing views regarding
Wang Xizhi's chronology. Ma
Shaoxuan relied on the information
given in Lu Yitong's *Wang Youjun
nianpu* which asserted that Wang was
born in the first year of the Yongjia
period (307) during the reign of
Emperor Huaidi of the Jin dynasty.
Based on this, in 353, the year he wrote
the "Lanting Preface," he was forty-
seven by Chinese count.

seal which bore the legend of a single character, *Shao*. On the
shoulders of the bottle Ma added an inscription and his signature
which read, "[Executed] in the year *wuxu* by Ma Shaoxuan." In
addition, he painted a small round seal at the end.

Copying repeatedly the "Lanting Preface" was Ma's way to
pay tribute to Wang Xizhi (fig. 89). At the same time, repeated
copying also gave him many opportunities to practise inscribing
this composition inside bottles. Yet, up to now, all his
productions were abridgments. Would it be possible to copy the
full text inside a bottle? Decidedly this would have been a feat,
but a very meaningful one. Ma made up his mind that sooner or
later he would try to accomplish this seemingly impossible task.

By 1913 a rare coincidence happened which made Ma vow to
himself to achieve his long-cherished desire within that year.
1913 corresponded to the year *kuichou* in the Chinese lunar
calendar. Ma noted that Wang Xizhi wrote the "Lanting Preface"
in exactly the same year, only twenty-six cycles and 1560 years
earlier.[111] In addition, coincidentally, Wang was forty-seven years
old when he wrote his masterpiece.[112] Ma himself, also forty-seven
years of age in that year, therefore thought the timing was perfect
for him to attempt copying the full text of the "Lanting Preface"
inside a snuff bottle, a gesture he considered most appropriate for
commemorating Wang, the literary gathering at the Orchid
Pavilion, as well as the creation of this unsurpassed running script
model.

Recognizing the difficulty inherent in writing out more than
three hundred characters on the inside surfaces of a small bottle,
Ma knew he had to do a lot of preparation before he could
embark on this challenging project.

First of all, Ma had to tackle the problem of the style of
writing. After long periods of study, Ma already knew the
"Lanting Preface" inside out. He liked the essay's elegant wording
and succinctly expressed subject matter. However, as one had no
need to observe hard and fast rules when writing in the running
script style, Ma found that different calligraphic specimens of the
"Lanting Preface" often showed differing characters. In addition,
after a span of more than a thousand years, the usage of many
words had changed. As an example, because of the lapse of time,

it might have become unnecessary to avoid using forbidden characters identified by people of the past.[113] Yet, if Ma were to write out the text in regular script, it would mean that his work would involve not just straight copying; he would have to first transcribe the characters from running script to regular script. In the end, Ma decided to collect all available specimens. After careful research and comparison, he set down the following criteria:

1. Apocryphal words commonly used in the past would be replaced by words in current use, such as the character *ling* in the phrase *chongshan junling* (tall hills and lofty ranges); *yi* in *fuyang zhijian yiwei chenji* (In the briefest space of time it has become a trace of the past); and *you* in *yi you jin zhi shi xi* (It is as though we now look back to the past).

2. Forbidden words not used in the past in order to show deference to people in higher station would be restored, for example, Wang Xizhi's great grandfather was called Wang Lan (the character *lan* has the meaning of "to see"). Throughout the "Lanting Preface" Wang Xizhi used a homonym (the written form has a "hand" radical and the meaning of "to embrace") to replace the character *lan* (to see) in order to show respect to his forebear. This was changed back to its proper form.

3. When certain characters appeared in variant forms in different specimens, Ma would have to make a choice by relying on his own judgment. The following are some of the examples: based on the text recorded in *Pingtiwen chao* (A collection of writings composed in the euphuistically antithetical style), Ma chose the character *wu* (to see face to face) over *wu* (to become aware of) in the phrase *wuyan yishi zhi nei* (converse face to face in a room); following the practice in Wang Xizhi's biography in *Jinshu* (History of Jin), he chose *chu* (tendency) over *chu* (to take) in *chushe wanshu* ([although people] choose different ways); in the case of the phrase *kuairen zizu* (feeling happy and satisfied), some specimens, such as the famous Shenlong version and the Dingwu version,[114] used the word *yang* (dispirited) instead of *kuai* (happy), while others preferred the other way round. Ma decided to use *kuai*. Similarly, the Shenlong version and the

113. Traditionally, to show respect, the Chinese avoided using characters that made up the personal names of their elders or people in superior station. Instead, they substituted for them other similar ones.

114. The Shenlong version was considered to be the most esteemed hand-copied version of the "Lanting Preface" from the Tang dynasty. The Dingwu version was deemed the best engraved Tang copy.

Dingwu version used the character *quan* (careful and attentive) in *suozhi jijuan* ([when he got] tired of [what he] was after) instead of *juan* (to be tired of). Ma adopted the latter because to him, it made more sense in the context.

In addition, the total number of characters in the "Lanting Preface" also varied from one specimen to another: while some had 324 words, others might have 325. The difference of one single character, *ceng* (an adverb used to denote the past), occurred depending on whether or not it was added to the beginning of the phrase *buzhi lao zhi jiangzhi* (not aware of the arrival of old age). Ma was in favor of having this character in the text. Therefore, his rendition is made up of 325 characters.

If Ma had just copied the "Lanting Preface" onto the bottle without doing any textual research, the artistic and literary merits of his work would have been much less significant. Yet the studying process and decision-making were not easy tasks, for both required a good command of literature, patience, and a perceptive mind to accomplish. However, Ma, spurred by determination and a creative spirit, was adamant that the collation part of his project be done thoroughly.

After textual research had been completed, the next important thing to do was to select a good bottle. This entailed the following features: excellent material, smooth surfaces on the inside, suitable wall thickness, and well-structured corners and shoulders. In addition, before writing, other preliminary technical steps also had to be taken, such as calculating the number of characters in each column and the number of columns to be distributed around the bottle.

When all preparatory work had been completed, Ma chose the autumn season to begin writing, for he felt that this was a time when both his mind and body were at peak efficiency. He did a little bit each morning as, for him, the morning was calm, relaxing, and the time of the day when he felt most energetic and at ease. By the first decade of the eleventh month in the lunar calendar, a truly rare masterpiece emanating from a most innovative project was born.

This work was the most representative piece in Ma's oeuvre. A crystallization of many years of hard work, the bottle testified to Ma's admiration for Wang Xizhi. It was also his precious legacy left to this world, one that would always bring back memories of him. Indeed, in the study of the art of Ma's inside-painted snuff bottles, the significance of this work cannot be underestimated.

In terms of the calligraphy of Ma's work, the following are its merits:

1. **Spiritual resonance**

   Writing miniature-sized regular script inside a glass bottle with a bamboo pen is quite a challenging job. The writer has to exercise extreme caution, for no mistake is permissible. Therefore, even a skillful inside-painted bottle artist tackles this task slowly. He normally produces only a few characters a day. On good days, however, he may be able to write a few more words; but on bad days he may stop after having written a few strokes. In short, it is the kind of work that cannot be rushed. A composition like the "Lanting Preface" which consists of over three hundred characters would definitely require a long time for completion. For Ma, apart from the time devoted to preliminary preparation, the writing part actually took about two months. Is it possible to maintain the consistency of the calligraphy and the flow of spiritual resonance in a work accomplished over such a protracted period? Indeed, it is very difficult to achieve.

   Yet on close inspection, not only is the nuance of brush movement and the form of each character coherent throughout the whole piece, even the ink tonality of all the characters shows the same uniformity. There is not to be found the slightest variation in ink color or a single trace of breakage or clog in the brush strokes. Who can deny that this is truly an amazing work of art?

   Spiritual resonance is an essential quality in calligraphy. It is a common, yet very high, standard inherent in the appreciation of this special art form. Sun Guoting, a Tang theorist, in his renowned work entitled *Shupu* (Treatise on Calligraphy), pointed out that a good piece of calligraphy must be composed of coherent brushwork saturated with spiritual resonance.[115] In addition, he also theorized that with any calligraphic work, the initial stroke and the initial character already set a criterion for the remainder of the text

115. Sun Guoting was also a Tang calligrapher and calligraphy theorist. He was noted for writing the regular, running, and cursive scripts, the last of which has earned him wide respect. Only the first part of his *Shupu*, completed in the third year of the Chuigong period (687), survives today, and it treats mainly the principles of the regular and cursive scripts.

to follow. For him, stylistic consistency was part and parcel of a work of excellence. Viewed in this light, Ma's rendition of the "Lanting Preface" displays the highest degree of penmanship which runs consistently throughout the whole piece, right from the first dot in the first character, *yong*, to the downward stroke in the last character, *wen*. In between, several thousand strokes form the text. These are so coherently constructed that harmony permeates the entire work, giving it the look of one accomplished with spontaneity at one go. Indeed, this calligraphic piece exemplifies Ma's dedication, his quest for perfection, his impeccable artistic style, and his unsurpassable skills.

2. **Exquisite calligraphy and well-balanced composition**

   Chinese calligraphy calls for careful planning in the distribution of characters and spacing. Ma's presentation of the "Lanting Preface" inside a bottle is exquisitely done. Positioning more than three hundred characters, written in regular script, on the surfaces inside a tiny glass bottle would have been quite taxing. Yet, on top of this, there are also considerations for spacing between words, columns, and margins to be dealt with. In order to avoid creating a jammed look, all characters must appear in miniature size. This requirement naturally would have increased the difficulty in execution. All of the characters in Ma's "Lanting Preface" are only 0.28 cm high, the size of a green bean. In addition, many of them are composed of multiple strokes, thus making writing out each stroke neatly an even greater challenge to the writer's skills. Notwithstanding all these difficulties, Ma seemed to handle them with ease. As shown in the illustrations, the space between the columns is quite adequate; the same is true with regard to the relationship between characters. Moreover, the execution of each stroke of a character, from beginning to end, is achieved with immaculate care; the image produced is absolutely exquisite. The unsparing attention given to small details thus ensures the excellent quality of each word, column, and the entire work.

The kind of writing implement that Ma used was a bamboo pen with a hard tip, which differed from a normal brush with a soft and pliable tip made of animal hair. While the latter facilitated easy flow and the formation of strokes with variations in thickness and emphasis, the former did not have any of these advantages. In addition, Ma would have to write in an upward manner on the inner surface of the glass bottle through its small opening. Such a manner of execution was again entirely different from writing downward with the brush perpendicular to the paper. Seen in this light, it is difficult enough to master the technique of writing inside a bottle, let alone writing well, in miniature size, and even better calligraphy than that produced with a normal brush on paper. Yet Ma overcame all these difficulties. In this respect, nobody could come close to his high level of achievement.

In order to fit more than three hundred characters onto the inner surfaces of the bottle in a well-balanced schema, it was also necessary to increase the number of columns and the number of characters in each column. As a result, this meant, first of all, some columns had to be positioned at the corners. Since corner spaces inside the bottle became concave surfaces, maintaining characters written there in the same size and shape as others written on flat surfaces would be a very difficult task. Secondly, even more difficult was to write in areas that seemed to be beyond the reach of the pen, notably those inside the shoulders of the bottle. Because a stiff bamboo pen could hardly reach there through the bottle's small mouth and straight neck, artists normally would leave such areas blank. Yet, miraculously, Ma managed to defy the impossible: he wrote characters in these awkward spaces and wrote them so well that this feature provides one of the reasons why his rendition of the "Lanting Preface" was esteemed as a very rare masterpiece.

3. **A synthesis of the styles of Ouyang Xun and Wang Xizhi: a calligraphy charged with strength and vigor**

Many people think that Ma's calligraphy follows the style of Ouyang Xun. This is not entirely true. Although Ma was good at copying Ouyang's calligraphy and more than once

copied with great precision on the inside of a bottle a small section of Ouyang's "An Account of the Sweet Spring in the Palace of Nine Accomplishments," yet he was equally adept in imitating Wang Xizhi's calligraphic style. Inside snuff bottles, he also attempted with great success an excerpt from Monk Huairen's *Shengjiao xu* (Holy Religion Preface), a text written by assembling characters selected from Wang Xizhi's running script specimens.[116] Such productions testify to Ma's earnest intention to imitate the calligraphic styles of Ouyang and Wang. However, copying these two styles separately on the inside of snuff bottles was only one of Ma's ways of doing calligraphy. It was not the only way he did it. In his inside-written "Lanting Preface," the calligraphic style replicates neither that of Ouyang nor Wang. Yet somehow it seems to resemble both. In a sense, therefore, combining the styles of Wang and Ouyang may well have been another manner of practising calligraphy favoured by Ma. The end product of this synthesis is imbued with the flavor of Ouyang's style, yet Wang's characteristics are also very much in evidence. This trait is seen not only in the "Lanting Preface" but also in many of Ma's works, especially in those completed in his late period.

In brushwork and form, each character in Ma's inside-written rendition of the "Lanting Preface" calls to mind Ouyang Xun and Wang Xizhi as the stylistic models. In certain instances, however, evidence of Wang's calligraphic style is a lot more prominent, as in the characters *yong, he, kui, chou, mu, chun, zuo,* and *you.* Although underlying in them are the prim look and invincible strength particular to Ouyang's style, they are actually more endowed with the exuberance and spontaneity intrinsic in Wang's calligraphy. In brushwork, they are purged of Ouyang's penchant for austerity and angularity, displaying instead Wang's emphasis on sleekness infused with controlled energy.

In terms of format, the text of the inside-written version of the "Lanting Preface" is disposed in columns. The characters, however, are not set equidistantly. Again, this feature departs from Ouyang's style. Its sources are traceable

---

116. The "Holy Religion Preface" was written by Emperor Taizong of Tang in commemoration of Monk Xuanzhuang's (602–664) untiring effort to promote Buddhism in China. It was engraved on stone during the reign of Emperor Gaozong (r. 650–683). Four versions of the preface exist today. Three are written in regular script. The fourth one, composed by using characters collected from Wang Xizhi's works written in running script, was created by Monk Huairen of Hongfu Si (Vast Blessings Monastery), and engraved on stone in the third year of the Xianheng period (672).

to the regular-script models of Zhong You and Wang Xizhi, whose more flexible format is devoid of the regularity akin to that of the counters strung on an abacus. Yet, in execution, because each character is made up of a different number of strokes, the space each occupies would vary in size. Characters with complex forms must not be squeezed to become tiny lumps. Similarly, those comprised of a few strokes must not be stretched in order to make their images look larger. How to ensure a pleasing and harmonious appearance in the layout is not an easy task. If the characters are incorrectly spaced, there might be left only half a space at the end of a column, which is not enough for a character to fit into, and it would look awkward if left blank, as all characters at the end of the columns would not be aligned and the layout's overall unity would be destroyed. Yet, this kind of defect is not to be found in Ma's rendition: all twenty-two columns of the text are perfectly aligned, with no trace of congestion or unusable empty space.

The three points enumerated above show that Ma was extremely proficient in tapping nourishment from past traditions. They also demonstrate that he had at his command excellent skill in practising calligraphy inside snuff bottles. Both aspects played important parts in the formation of his personal calligraphic style.

In addition, in terms of creative motivation, underlying Ma's unremitting endeavor to copy Wang Xizhi's "Lanting Preface" inside a bottle was his sincere desire to commemorate the divine calligrapher through emulation. In order to be thoroughly versed in Wang's style, he devoted endless hours and spared no effort in copying Wang's calligraphic specimens. His rendition of the "Lanting Preface," therefore, was achieved not simply with a bamboo pen but also with his soul.

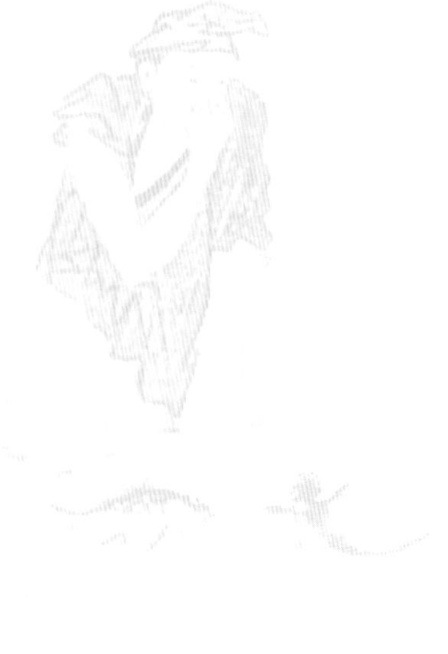

This snuff bottle, filled inside on all sides with the full text of a celebrated literary composition written out with great feeling in fine calligraphy, is not just a fruit of labor, but also a testimony of Ma's innovative venture. It signifies not just Ma's success as an artist of inside-written calligraphy, but also, even more importantly, the establishment of a firm footing for inside-written calligraphy as an independent decorative element.

Before the completion of this work, inside-painted snuff bottles were known for their paintings. As painting was the chief, or even sole, means of decoration, it was quite obvious that painting was valued more than calligraphy. Yet, since ancient times, painting and calligraphy had been regarded as two major art forms of equal standing. Calligraphy could always be appreciated on its own for its inherent merits. Seen in this light, this tradition should be carried on in the decoration of snuff bottles. The completion of the "Lanting Preface" inside a bottle proves that it was feasible to make use of calligraphy as the only decorative means, presenting famous literary works in a new light. This accomplishment also filled a big gap in the art of inside-painted bottles. Its significance cannot be overestimated.

To be able to take inside-written calligraphy one step further calls for three prerequisites. These are: (1) a mastery of the art of calligraphy; (2) excellent technical skill in writing inside a snuff bottle; and (3) a passion for executing art inside a snuff bottle. Ma possessed all three requirements. Thus he was able to expand the horizon of inside-written calligraphy. His influences encompassed two aspects. First of all, he opened up a new area for calligraphy to take form. In the past, calligraphy was written on the surfaces of paper, silk, and other objects. Now it could be fully enjoyed through glass, as a performer taking a lead role rather than a subordinate one. Secondly, he created a new subject category for inside-painted snuff bottles. From now on, painting and calligraphy were on a par.

Today, people carry on the traditions of painting and calligraphy. However, while inside-painting is highly esteemed, inside-calligraphy should be similarly regarded. Both art forms are just like the two legs of a person. Only a person with strong legs can move forward in big strides and climb up to a summit. A new attitude and a new plan of action are in order: both would be conducive to the cultivation of new blood and furthering the development of decoration inside snuff bottles.

According to Zong Baihua, a contemporary aesthetician, "Every artist must strive to create his own style. An art work that can move people relies not just on new subject matter but also on a fresh way of presentation." Seen in this light, Ma Shaoxuan was truly an innovative inside-painted snuff bottle artist.

Finally, it should be pointed out that the "Lanting Preface" was only one of several famous literary compositions of the past which Ma Shaoxuan presented in full inside a snuff bottle. Among his renditions, this, together with Zhuge Liang's *Chushi biao* (A Memorial [Submitted to the Shu Emperor before] the Embarkation of a Campaign) and Su Shi's "Rhapsody on Red Cliff" are his most representative masterpieces.[117] Unfortunately the whereabouts of these two treasures is unknown. Have they suffered damage? If not, it is hoped that they would be made known to the public.

A FEW POINTS ABOUT LEARNING INSIDE-CALLIGRAPHY

In researching inside-painted snuff bottles, it is important to include a study of Ma Shaoxuan's technique of inside-calligraphy and learn from his experience.

The renowned snuff bottle collector and writer, Bob C. Stevens, in his work entitled *The Collector's Book of Snuff Bottles*, had this to say about Ma Shaoxuan's calligraphy: "His style of calligraphy. . . was and still is imitated and appreciated by calligraphers. These elegant bottles were held in high esteem and often were presented as gifts marking anniversaries or other special occasions. In the bottles of no other artist can we find calligraphy that excels that of Ma Shao-hsüan."[118]

Calligraphy is part of traditional Chinese culture. Many books on this subject, written in Chinese and other languages, have been published. Although developed from this art form, inside-calligraphy has never received any in-depth treatment. Books on this subject, therefore, still remain to be written.

To learn to write inside a snuff bottle and to excel in it so as to surpass past masters, these are topics that preoccupy not only people involved with inside-painting but also people interested in this particular aspect of the snuff bottle, whether Chinese or occidental. Everyone looks forward to a generation of new blood to outshine the forerunners.

117. Zhuge Liang (181–234) was a politician and strategist living in the Three Kingdoms period. He was instrumental in helping Liu Bei (161–223) establish the state of Shu. *Chushi biao* was written in the fifth year of the Jianxing period (227), just before Zhuge led a combined army to reclaim the Han territory in central China. Later on, because of the emergence of another memorial supposedly written by Zhuge in the eleventh month of the following year (228) which explained why the Shu should send an expedition against the state of Wei, the first memorial became known as *Qian chushi biao*, i.e., the first *Chushi biao*, and the later one, *Hou chushi biao*, i.e., the second *Chushi biao*.

118. Bob C. Stevens, *The Collector's Book of Snuff Bottles*, p.250.

In thinking over the question of writing good calligraphy on the interior surfaces of bottles, the Song poet Lu You's (1125–1210) advice on learning to write good poems is worth noting. In a poem he instructed his son thus, "If you really want to learn to write poems, / You should work hard at things outside the realm of poetry."[119] Viewed in the same vein, if one really wants to learn to write good calligraphy inside snuff bottles, one should also work hard at things outside the realm of snuff bottles. Lu You had no intention of showing disrespect for fundamental training in composing poetry. On the contrary, he was quite aware of the importance of developing a knack in basic skills such as wording, sentence structure, rhyming, and the use of antitheses. But to him, acquiring such technical skills was not enough for writing good poems. Learn from society and the proper way to conduct one's life. Then, with the expansion of knowledge, one's vision would be broadened. It was only then that one could hope to be able to produce good poems. In the same manner, a person interested in learning to practise inside-calligraphy well must take fundamental training seriously. He should first of all grasp the rhythm of the pen as it moves on the interior surface of a bottle while forming characters and then strive to become completely at ease handling the pen. Yet, again this is not sufficient for him to be able to execute excellent calligraphy inside snuff bottles. In order to reach this high level of competence, he would need to enhance his knowledge of literature and other aspects of his own culture. In addition, a thorough understanding of calligraphy and good penmanship are also essential. Only when he combines knowledge with skill can he hope to be able to achieve first-rate performance. Anything less would be no better than "seeking a fish by climbing a tree."[120] As the whole undertaking entails dedication and hard work, anybody who cherishes the least bit of luck will not likely accomplish his goal.

There are two known examples of calligraphic works done on paper with a brush by Ma Shaoxuan and they illustrate how deeply rooted Ma's calligraphy is in traditional styles and what extraordinary ability Ma had in evolving a style of his own from his models.

119. These are two closing lines in Lu You's poem "Instructions for My Son, Yu." See Lu You, *Lu Fangweng quanji*, vol. 2, p. 1076.

120. This proverb, *yuanmu qiuyu*, signifies an inevitable futile result if one tries to achieve something using a wrong method.

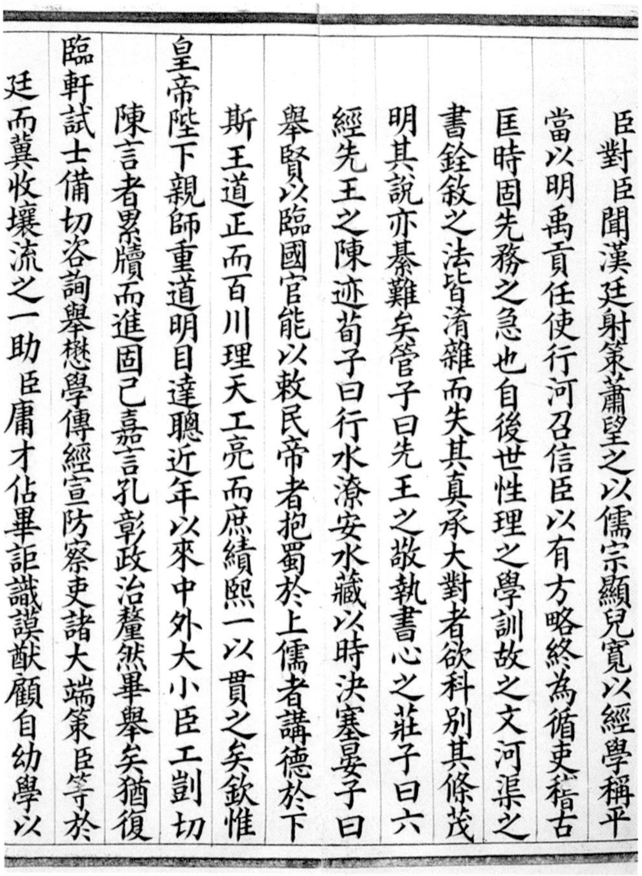

Fig. 90. A memorial to the throne, written in small regular script by Ma Shaoxuan (Ma Family Collection)

The first one is a memorial to the throne, written in small regular script (fig. 90). Measuring 30 cm high and 12 cm wide, each folio accommodates six columns made up of twenty-two to twenty-four characters. The full text takes up sixteen folios which consist of a total of eighty-eight columns and about two thousand characters.

The second example, also written in small regular script but probably completed sometime after the first one, is a transcription of the Tang literary writer Wang Bo's (650–675) famous essay entitled *Tengwangge xu* (Preface to [Poems Dedicated to] Prince Teng's Tower).[121] Measuring 30 cm high and 12 cm wide, this specimen has six folios (fig. 91). Each consists of six columns composed of twenty characters. Altogether the text is comprised of more than seven hundred characters. It starts with the beginning sentences *Nanchang gujun, Hongdu xinfu* (The old

121. When Li Yuanying, twenty-second son of the first emperor, Gaozu of Tang (r. 618–626), was governor of Hongzhou (present-day Nanchang in Jiangxi province) during the Xianqing period (656–660), he built a tower. Just when construction was completed he was given a new title, the Prince of Teng. The tower was therefore named after him. Later on, Yan Boyu became the governor. On the day of a certain Double-nine Festival, he gave a banquet in order to create an opportunity to show off the literary talent of his son-in-law, Wu Zizhang. However, Wu was completely overshadowed by Wang Bo, a precocious genius, who composed this brilliant essay in no time.

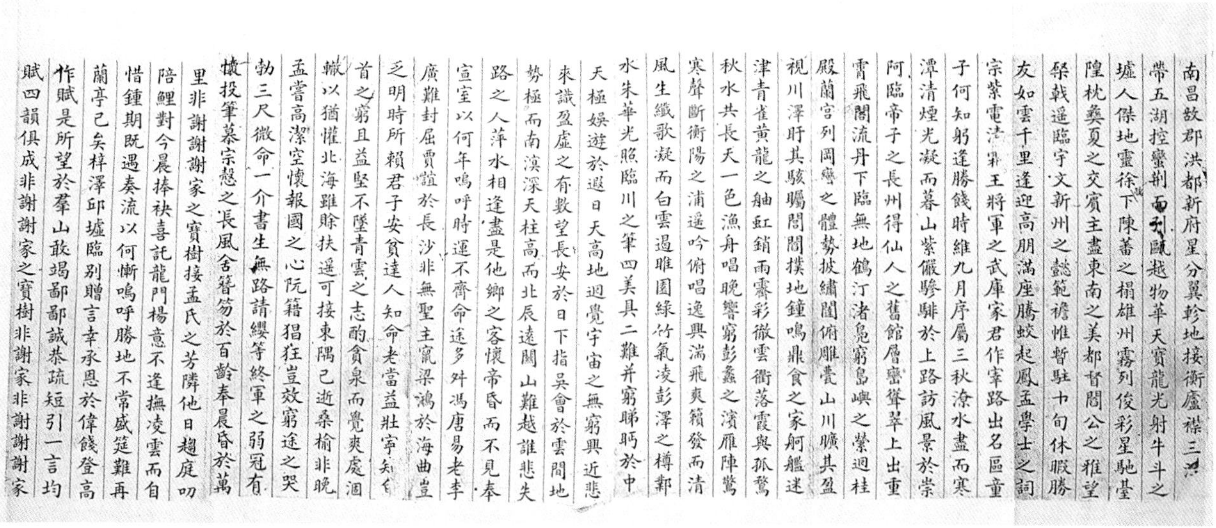

Fig. 91. A transcription of Wang Bo's "Preface to [Poems Dedicated to] Prince Teng's Tower," written in small regular script by Ma Shaoxuan (Ma Family Collection)

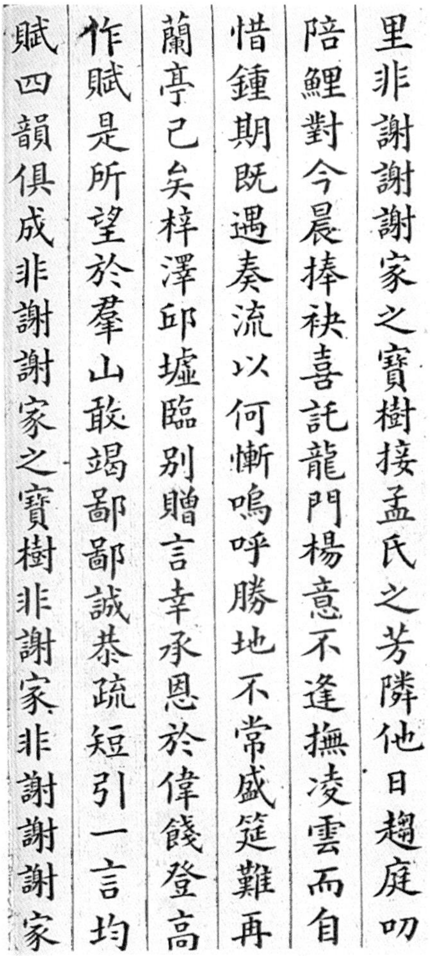

Fig. 92. Detail of fig. 91 showing superfluous characters in first and last lines (Ma Family Collection)

prefectural district Nanchang, now called Hongdu) and ends with these two sentences: *Yiyan junfu, siyun juchang* ([Let's all use] the same rhyme, and compose eight poetic lines). Most likely it is a specimen executed in his daily practice as it is marred by superfluous characters. Often several versions of the same character appear one after the other, indicating that when Ma was dissatisfied with the form of one character, he kept on practising until he was pleased with the result (fig. 92). This work, therefore, bears testimony to Ma's persistence in writing the small regular script even when he was advanced in age. As well, it also bears witness to his spirit of strong commitment.

Extremely precious, these two works form part of the Ma family heirlooms. Neither of them have been seen or described outside the family. They exemplify how well grounded Ma's calligraphy is in traditional styles and how diligent he was in his pursuit of perfection. Even though he had won wide recognition, he continued to practise writing every day, a habit he kept right into his old age. Study these two pieces of calligraphy carefully and one will surely learn a lot from them.

In learning calligraphy there is no insurmountable barrier. Three points are worth remembering: 1. Have a clear vision and determination; 2. Persevere and never stop learning; and 3. Use the correct method. If one holds fast to these guidelines, one will undoubtedly be able to develop a good hand. In addition, it would be ideal if one could start training at a tender age.

Just like waves in the Yangzi River, one succeeding another, let's hope that more skillful artists of inside-painting will appear on the scene, their performance surpassing that of their predecessors and bringing this special form of art to a new height.

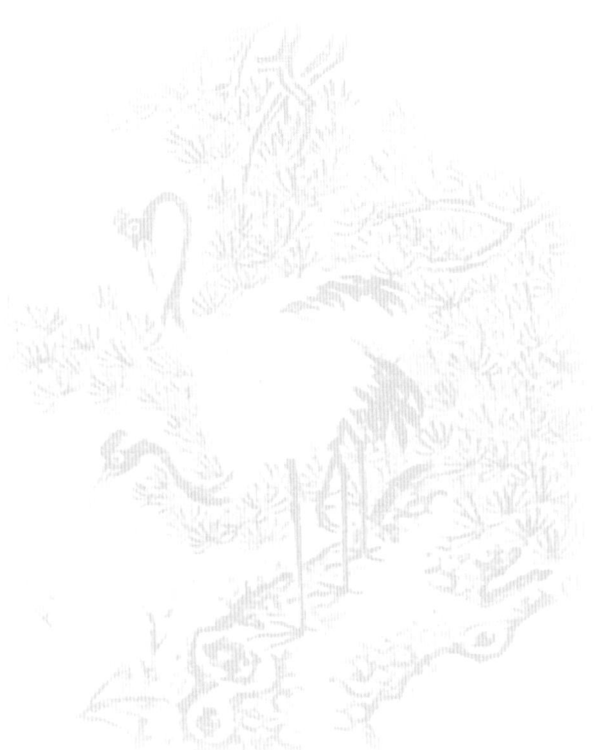

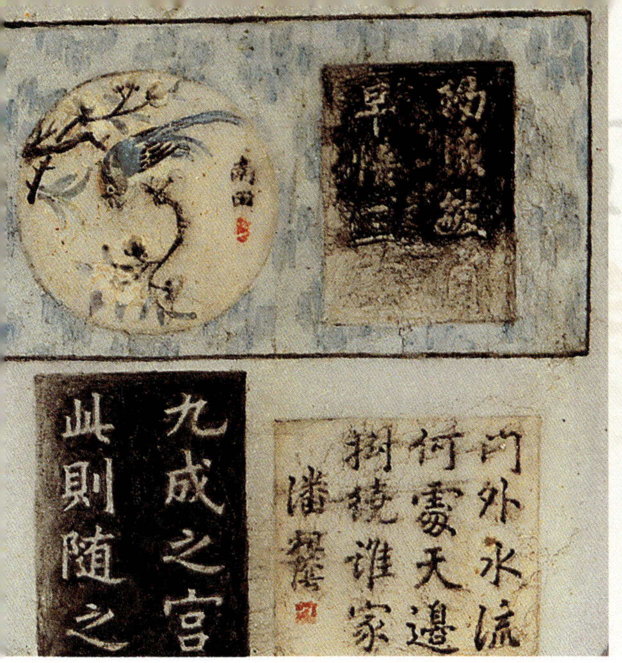

CHAPTER FIVE

Creative Literary Compositions and Seals

Ma Shaoxuan was not only one of a few great inside-painted snuff bottle artists, he was also a poet. Some of his fine compositions can be appreciated on inside-painted snuff bottles. They provide an important source for a more in-depth understanding of the history of his art of inside-painting, his personality, and the way he conducted himself in life. All these aspects have escaped attention before, and as a result, have never been discussed.

AN ASSEMBLAGE OF FOUR REFINEMENTS

Chinese painting is characterized by a fine tradition: many painters are endowed with versatile artistic skills; they are also steeped in culture. They excel in painting, calligraphy, and poetry. Some are even well versed in seal-engraving. Often their works are composed of painting, poems, calligraphy, and seal impressions—an assemblage of four refinements which impart an air of elegance while at the same time providing enjoyment in various aspects of Chinese art. Embodied in literati painting are elements of versatility, erudition, and fine brushwork. They represent ideals pursued by Chinese painters. They are also criteria used in the appreciation of Chinese painting.

Ma Shaoxuan's art of inside-painting perpetuates this fine tradition. He also set these ideals as his goals. During his whole life he never lapsed in his attempt to fulfill them. He demonstrated consummate skills in his painting and calligraphy, for which he has won wide recognition both at home and abroad.

This aspect has already been treated in previous chapters. In poetry and seal designs, he was also quite proficient. Some of his inside-painted bottles bear his own poetic creations. His painted seal designs are original, their forms always pleasing to look at. The combination of poetry, painting, calligraphy and seal design as harmoniously integrated elements, all serving the expression of a particular subject, is a major characteristic of Ma's art of inside-painting.

AUTOBIOGRAPHICAL POEMS

In the collection of the Royal Ontario Museum in Toronto, Canada is a snuff bottle decorated by Ma with a poem accompanied by an illustration (figs. 93 and 94). Measuring 6 cm high and 3 cm wide, it has a pentasyllabic quatrain on one side and a complementary illustration on the other side. It bears witness to the first time Ma used the inside-painted snuff bottle as a means of recording his learning experience, his goals, and his principles. The poem is as follows:

> *I exhausted all my powers of concentration,*
> *Turned into a madman for painting and*
> *   calligraphy.*
> *But worthies of the past would surely laugh at me,*
> *For I know my results are but trivial and*
> *   incomplete.*

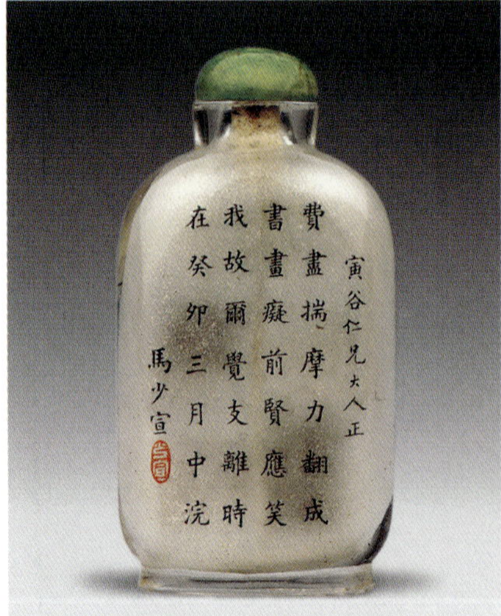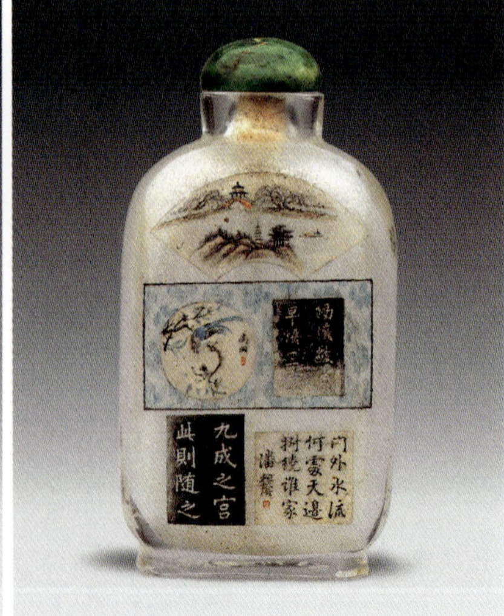

Figs. 93 and 94. Snuff bottle with an autobiographical poem on one side and miniature paintings and calligraphy on the other side, dated 1903 (Royal Ontario Museum Collection)

Right after the poem is inscribed "[Executed] in the second ten-day period of the third month of the year *kuimao*." *Kuimao* corresponds to the twenty-ninth year of the Guangxu period, 1903 in the Western calendar. At that time Ma was thirty-seven years old.

In the summer of the same year Ma produced a similar work. In order to understand this poem, it is necessary to view the illustration on the other side of the bottle as its footnote and study both together.

The illustration consists of five independent paintings and calligraphic specimens. These are, specifically, two fan paintings, two ink rubbings, and one incomplete calligraphic work. The ink rubbing positioned at mid-right is oblong in shape. The calligraphy, appearing in reserve against a black background, is arranged in two columns, each consisting of four characters. On the right are *youhuai minzhen* (clever and trustworthy at a young age); on the left, *zaowu sankong* (long ago [had nurtured a mind for the] understanding of the "Three Voids").[122] They are rendered in imitation of Wang Xizhi's calligraphic style, based on Monk Huairen's "Holy Religion Preface," a text written by assembling characters selected from Wang Xizhi's running script specimens.

During his reign in the seventh century Emperor Taizong of Tang wrote a preface for Monk Xuanzhuang's (602–664) translation of *Tripitaka*. This he entitled "Holy Religion Preface." Knowing that the emperor admired Wang Xizhi's calligraphy, Monk Huairen of Hongfu Si (Vast Blessings Monastery) searched out all extant calligraphic specimens by Wang and copied from them the relevant characters used in the emperor's text to recreate a version written in Wang's hand. This ambitious project, beginning from the twenty-second year of the Zhenguan period (648) and concluding in the third year of the Xianheng period (672), took him twenty-four years to accomplish. His rendition was later engraved on a stone stele. Today, people still learn to write in Wang's style by modelling their calligraphy after ink rubbings taken from this stele.[123]

In the preface are the following sentences: "There was a monk by the name of Xuanzhuang. A leader of the Buddhist faith, he was clever and trustworthy at a young age, and long ago had

---

122. In Buddhism there are three sets of "Three Voids." The first set relates to one form of meditation, the principles of which are 1. to empty the mind of the ideas of "me" and "mine" and suffering, which are unreal; 2. to get rid of the idea of form, or externals; 3. to be free from all wishes or desires. The second set regards the self, things, and all phenomena as "empty" or immaterial. The third set is related to charity which sees the giver, the receiver, and the gift as "empty." See William Edward Soothill and Lewis Hodous, comp., *A Dictionary of Chinese Buddhist Terms*, p. 73.

123. The stele is in the collection of Beilin (Forest of Steles), a repository of inscribed stone steles produced over the centuries located in Xi'an, Shaanxi province.

nurtured a mind for the understanding of the 'Three Voids.' Always embracing an all-encompassing spirit, he practised the 'Four Forms of Endurance'. . ."[124] On Ma's bottle, the eight characters that he imitated from this passage in the calligraphic model look exactly like a fragment of an ink rubbing. Certain areas show characters with sharp outlines, while other areas show white blots and ill-defined strokes, making the script almost illegible and yet at the same time creating a most interesting visual impact.

The other image of an ink rubbing, located in the lower left-hand corner of the bottle, has these eight characters: *Jiucheng zhi gong, ci ze Sui zhi* (The Palace of Nine Accomplishments [was built on the site of the Palace of Benevolence and Longevity] belonging to the Sui [dynasty]). When Emperor Taizong of Tang ordered the construction of the Palace of Nine Accomplishments on the former site of the Sui (589–618) Palace of Benevolence and Longevity, a spring having sweet-tasting water was discovered. Hence it was called Liquan (Sweet Spring). Wei Zheng (580–643), a high official, wrote an essay in commemoration of this event. This, *Jiucheng gong Liquan ming*, was transcribed by the renowned calligrapher of the time, Ouyang Xun. A stone stele engraved with the text was erected in the sixth year of the Zhenguan period (632). Ink rubbings obtained from this stele have since served as exemplars for people who wished to be versed in Ouyang's calligraphic style.

Wei Zheng began his essay thus: "In the sixth year of the Zhenguan period, during the first month of summer, the emperor retreated to the Palace of Nine Accomplishments to avoid the heat. The structure was [erected on the former site of] the Palace of Benevolence and Longevity of the Sui dynasty." Ma Shaoxuan extracted eight characters from two of these sentences and copied them on the bottle as a detail of an ink rubbing, their calligraphic style strongly reminiscent of Ouyang Xun's handwriting.

As to the two fan paintings, the one positioned at the top is designed in the shape of a folding fan. It depicts a landscape with an expansive vista, delightfully worked out in light ink and colors and elegant brushwork. An inscription, however, has not been

124. According to William Edward Soothill and Lewis Hodous, comp., *A Dictionary of Chinese Buddhist Terms*, the term, *ren* (patience, endurance), in Sanskrit, *kṣānti*, in the religious state appears in groups of two, three, four, five, six, ten, and fourteen, indicating various forms of patience, equanimity, repression, forbearance, endurance, constancy, or "perseverance of the saints," both in mundane and spiritual things. See p. 237.

included. The other fan painting is in the shape of a round fan bearing the name Nantian. It is placed side by side with the image simulating a fragment of Wang Xizhi's calligraphic specimen. Both are enclosed in a rectangle which separates them from the images that appear at the top and bottom.

To the left of the lowest register is the rendition of a fragment of Ouyang Xun's calligraphic specimen. To the right is an imitation of a calligraphic work from the hand of Pan Zuyin (1830–1890), a contemporary official. In square format, it is presented as characters written in black ink against a white background. The poetic text, arranged in three columns of four characters each, reads, *Menwai shuiliu, hechu tianbian, shurao shuijia* (Water flows outside the door. / Where is the horizon? / Whose house is surrounded by trees?) Since it is incomplete, it is again another fragment. A fourth column shows the signature of Pan Zuyin, the last two characters joined together as a result of a crease developed in the simulated paper. This is followed by a small square seal impression.

These five paintings and calligraphic works are all executed on one side of the bottle. Alternating in black and white and designed in a variety of shapes, they form one large composition when viewed together. They can also be enjoyed as individual works. Their delicately rendered sharp and realistic details are most interesting to look at.

This composition is not a "Picture of Antiquities" (*Bogu tu*), for Pan Zuyin was not a man of the distant past. Neither is it a "Picture of Longevity" (*Baisui tu*), as the two fan paintings are represented in good condition, not showing any trace of damage. In this case, how should the significance of this work be interpreted? What did Ma Shaoxuan have in mind when he painted this assemblage of images? What messages did he want to convey?

Taking the poem as a clue to find a way out of this maze, and analyzing both poem and illustration together, a few points are offered here for consideration. The beginning two lines of the poem are: "I exhausted all my powers of concentration, / Turned into a madman for painting and calligraphy." In other words, Ma is saying explicitly that he has striven to understand the styles of various past painters and calligraphers in order to emulate them. Now, the next question is: Who were his model calligraphers? The answer is to be found in the illustration on the other side of the bottle: one was Wang Xizhi, the "Divine Calligrapher," and the other was Ouyang Xun. The correctness of this answer is borne out by Ma's large output of inside-written snuff bottles. He was such an enthusiast of the calligraphic styles of Wang and Ouyang that he had untiringly devoted himself to studying and copying ink rubbing models of their works, even to the point of turning himself into "a mad man." His revelation is not just a self-deprecatory remark but also a self-mocking one. The two poetic lines and the two calligraphic renditions combine to reveal that Ma wanted to state the concentrated efforts he had put into attaining mastery in calligraphy and the models he had chosen to follow.

In painting, who did Ma Shaoxuan admire and emulate? The answer is also to be found in the illustration: Nantian, alias Yun Shouping (1633–1690). Yun was a well-known poet/painter who flourished in the seventeenth century. The anthologies that he left for posterity are entitled *Nantian shichao* (An Anthology of Nantian) in 5 *juan* and *Ouxiangguan ji* (A Collection of Poems from the Fragrant Cup Studio) in 10 *juan*. In painting, he belonged to the tradition of Xu Chongsi, the Song painter who established the "boneless" (*mogu*) style.[125] Of considerable importance in the history of Chinese painting, this artistic school favored the sole use of color washes in the representation of images. All practitioners of this style eschewed ink outlines in defining forms.

A devoted follower of Yun Shouping, Ma learned chiefly two things from him. These are: 1. the "boneless" style; and 2. the incorporation of calligraphy in painting. The first observation is borne out by Ma's inside-painted bottles. The birds and flowers he depicted are given form by washes of color characteristic of them. No ink outlines have been used to define the contours. To some people, this method of painting is not lacking bone structure, it is only devoid of outlines. Therefore, the term "lineless" (*moxian*) style would seem to be a more appropriate appelation.

125. Xu Chongsi was a Northern Song painter. A grandson of the renowned ink monochrome painter, Xu Xi, he later abandoned his grandfather's rustic style. Turning to the more decorative style of Huang Quan and Huang Jucai for inspiration, he developed the "boneless" style.

As to the second observation, Yun Shouping often incorporated inscriptions in his paintings. Ma's inside-painted bottles also frequently bear paintings on one side and inscriptions on the other side. Many of these inscriptions are poems he composed himself. The meanings embodied in his wonderful verses augment the ideas expressed in the paintings. As in learning calligraphy, in painting Ma did not take Yun Shouping as his only model. He also emulated Bada Shanren (1626–1705), Xia Gui (act. ca. 1180–1224) and Ma Yuan (act. before 1189–after 1225).[126] However, in painting in the "boneless" style and in incorporating calligraphy in painting, it is obvious that he was following in the steps of Yun Shouping.

The first two lines in Ma's poem disclose how totally engrossed he was in his quest for painting and calligraphic skills. What did he achieve as a result of all the hard work that he had put in? The answer is to be found in the two concluding lines which read, "But worthies of the past would surely laugh at me, / For I know my results are but trivial and incomplete." Here, Ma cleverly used an allusion. After the fall of the Ming dynasty a renowned painter and calligrapher by the name of Fu Shan (1605–1690) decided to stay out of office and make a living by practising medicine.[127] An advocate of upright conduct, in calligraphy he disliked slavish imitation to conform with popular taste. He once said, "In learning calligraphy, one should aim for the effect of clumsiness rather than artfulness, ugliness rather than prettiness, incompleteness rather than showiness, and spontaneity rather than careful planning."[128] Ma liked Fu Shan's works. In addition, he admired Fu's personality. This is why he used Fu's terminology in making a statement about his own character and the ideals he pursued in calligraphy and painting. In a self-disparaging tone, he admitted that he had not fully grasped the finer points in these two art forms, but at the same time, neither had he strayed from the right path. Although his works may be criticized for lack of "incompleteness," the same certainly do not suffer from "showiness" and "prettiness." By saying "Worthies of the past would surely laugh at me," what Ma meant was that they would have laughed at his inadequacies and

126. Bada Shanren was an individualistic painter who flourished during the transitional period of the Ming and Qing dynasties. For more information about him, see Wang Fangyu and Richard M. Barnhart, *Master of the Lotus Garden: The Life and Art of Bada Shanren (1626–1705)*. Xia Gui was a Southern Song landscape painter who specialized in using economic brushwork and ink washes to recreate impressionistic scenery. Ma Yuan was also a Southern Song painter well known for his sensitive renditions of nature.

127. For a biographical sketch of Fu Shan, see Yu Jianhua, ed., *Zhongguo meishujia renming cidian*, p. 1054. Yu notes that Fu's chronology has several versions, for example, in Guo Weiqu, ed., *Song Yuan Ming Qing shuhuajia nianbiao* it is 1607–1684 (pp. 191, 287), while in Ye Ming, *Guang yinren zhuan* it is 1609–1690 (*juan* 13, p. 5).

128. Yu Jianhua, ed., *Zhongguo meishujia renming cidian*, p. 1054.

his decision to abide by the correct way. Their laughter was made out of satisfaction, not out of ridicule. Underlying these two poetic lines, therefore, is a mixed sentiment of self-disparagement, modesty, self-respect, and self-confidence. Furthermore, these two lines not only complete the meaning of the poem, they also serve well its autobiographical objective.

When a painter/calligrapher is never satisfied with his achievements and openly admits his inadequacies in his work, this spirit is his key to success.

The last thing to be discussed is the calligraphic work ascribed to Pan Zuyin, located in the lowest register on the bottle. Pan, after attaining the *jinshi* degree in the second year of the Xianfeng period (1852), filled various posts in the capital, including Director of the Court of Imperial Entertainments, Director of the Grand Court of Revision,[129] Vice-President of the Board of War, Vice-President of the Board of Works, and Governor Adjoint of the region enclosing the imperial capital.[130] In his biography in *Qingshi gao* (Draft of Qing History), it is said that he "was fond of learning, erudite in the classics and history, and enthusiastic in amassing antiquities. His collection of bronzes and stone steles is quite rich. . ."[131] As to his character, he was particularly known for his diligence: he got up at the *yin* hour (3 to 5 a.m.) everyday and invariably arrived at his office ahead of his colleagues. For his dedication to work, the name of Wenqin (literary and diligent) was appropriately bestowed on him after his death.

Ma Shaoxuan admired the hard-working spirit of this extremely influential figure in the literary circles at the capital and looked up to him as an exemplar. For this reason, he imitated Pan's calligraphy inside the bottle, using it as a footnote to his own poem. His first line, "I exhausted all my powers of concentration," describes how assiduously he had used his brain and hands. His second line, "Turned into a madman for painting and calligraphy," draws a clear picture of him working away frantically. He spent his whole life improving his artistic skills. Diligence was an indispensable element—a cornerstone—in his success as an important inside-painted snuff bottle artist. In subtly referring to Pan's exemplary image, Ma was not only

129. This department supervised the administration of the criminal law.

130. For more information on Pan Zuyin, see Hummel, ed., *Eminent Chinese*, vol. 2, pp. 608-609.

131. See Zhao Ersun *et al.*, *Qingshi gao*, *juan* 441, p. 12416.

expressing his ideal, he was also passing on an injunction to people who followed in his footsteps.

The five components of the illustration and the poem discussed above blend into one another to form a unified entity endowed with rich significance. Together, they make clear Ma's attitude in his artistic pursuit, his personality, and his visions. These renditions, coming from his own hand, are first-hand materials he left for posterity. In his own artistic language he recounted the first half of his career. This important work makes it possible for us to understand Ma Shaoxuan himself and to study the art of his inside-painting. As with a door, those who do not know how to open it remain locked on the inside. Those who are able to open it will find a broad view outside. It is only after solving all sorts of problems that we can make progress.

This autobiographical poem is one of Ma's major works. Viewed together with his calligraphy and paintings, they testify to a very high artistic level in Ma's production. Without the poem, it would be difficult to understand the illustration on the other side of the bottle. Similarly, without the illustration, the poem would sound dry and vague. The integration of the poem and the illustration creates the feeling that Ma is actually having a heart-to-heart dialogue with the viewer of this bottle. In as few as twenty words he tells of his learning experience and his goal in the first half of his life, in this way giving later followers guidelines and encouragement. The integration of the poem and the illustration also allows us to see the beauty inherent in Ma's calligraphy, painting and poetry, in other words, the beauty of his mind.

This inside-painted snuff bottle is indeed a treasure. May it always be held in high esteem.

TWO POETIC INSCRIPTIONS

Ma Shaoxuan was extremely fond of poetry. He was thoroughly versed in famous compositions, from the poems in *The Book of Songs* to regulated verses. His own creations included quadrisyllabic, pentasyllabic, and septasyllabic poems, which are all characterized by these merits: meticulous metres, harmonious rhymes, excellent wording, long-lasting poetic feelings, succinctly expressed ideas, and simple flowing diction. The autobiographical poem and the poem inscribed on the bottle bearing Min Shaoquan's portrait discussed previously are good examples (fig. 74). Two more works will be analyzed here.

Among several poems inscribed with Huang Zhong's portraits is this septasyllabic rendition (fig. 95):

> *[Although] his eyebrows were shaggy and his head had become hoary, no one could have matched his bravery.*
>
> *[Also,] as an official of long service, he had won great distinction under the Zhaolie emperor.[132]*
>
> *[Yet,] if it had not been for the [members of the] Pear Garden who were skillful musical performers,[133]*
>
> *Nowadays who would still know [anything] about this general?*

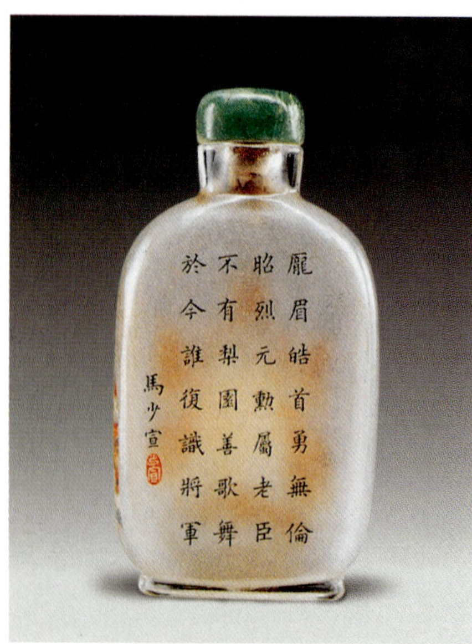

Fig. 95. Inscription on the reverse of fig. 18, paying tribute to actors recreating history on the stage (formerly in the collection of Bernice Straus Hasterlik)

Ma Shaoxuan was an aficionado of Beijing opera. After watching Tan Xinpei's expert performance in the opera "Mount Dingjun," he was so excited that he painted a portrait of Huang Zhong inside a bottle.

132. Zhaolie was the style of the monarch of the Shu kingdom, Liu Bei's reign.

133. The Pear Garden was first established in the Forbidden City in Chang'an by the Tang emperor Xuanzong (r. 712–755) for the training of singing and dancing performers. It has become a common name for opera troupes.

According to Huang Zhong's biography in Chen Shou's *Sanguo zhi*, Huang "attacked Xiahou Yuan on Mount Dingjun in the Hanzhong area. Although his opponent's troops were very well trained, Huang's strategy was precise and effective. He led his soldiers as they marched forward, beating the drums so vigorously that their rumbling noise seemed to reach the sky. His troops roared with joy, their merriment resounded in the valleys. Xiahou Yuan was killed in this battle; his troops also disintegrated."[134] The opera "Mount Dingjun" was based on this historical fact. In the role of Huang Zhong, Tan Xinpei's portrayal of the aged general's courage and valor was both moving and invigorating. Inspired by Tan's performance, Ma not only painted him in the guise of Huang but also composed this accompanying poem. The first line describes Huang's appearance. In spite of his thick eyebrows and silvery white hair, this old man demonstrated peerless bravery. The second line alludes to his outstanding performance in combat. Liu Bei, as the Zhaolie emperor, awarded him the title of General in Charge of Western Expeditions (*Zhengxi jiangjun*) after he had won the victory at Mount Dingjun. The third and fourth lines point out that more than one thousand and seven hundred years later Tan Xinpei and other troupe members gave an impressive operatic performance which recreated Huang's valiant act. If it was not for them, who in this day and age would have any idea about Huang's image? In the poem, the first two lines praise Huang Zhong. The following two lines extoll Tan Xinpei. Read together, they applaud Tan's masterly portrayal of Huang. The same composition also expresses perfectly Ma's feeling. It is a wonderful work, both lyrical and narrative, created to complement a painting.

The poem begins with a character with an even tone. The last character in the first line also ends with an even tone. In addition, it introduces a rhyme pattern (*lun*, *chen*, and *jun*) belonging to the *zhen* category. The four lines conform with the standard metric scheme. The pairing and antithetical arrangement of imagery are adroitly handled. Viewed in the context of the rules of poetic composition, this poem is in compliance with all set requirements.

134. See Chen Shou, *Sanguo zhi*, *juan* 36, p. 948.

Another pentasyllabic poem that Ma wrote is one inscribed with a portrait of Queen Mary of England (1867–1953). It was composed in 1911 (fig. 96). The poem reads:

> *Her graceful mien skilfully painted,*
> *As though she is seen in light make-up.*
> *This face is like one from the fairy kingdom;*
> *Its beauty stands alone in the Western world.*

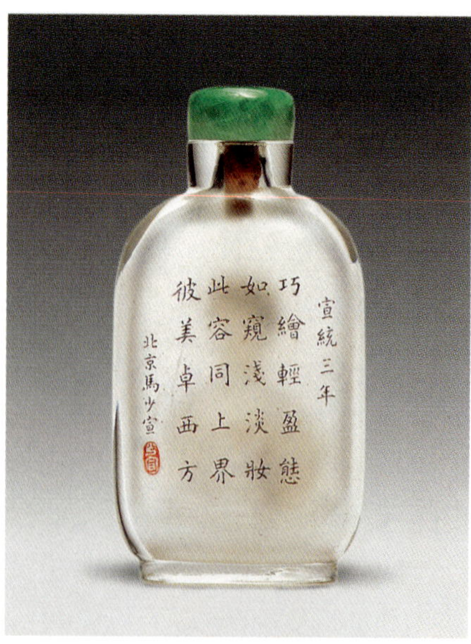

Fig. 96. Poem inscribed on the reverse of fig. 50, with the portrait of Queen Mary, dated 1911 (Monimar Collection)

The bottle portrait that Ma was commissioned to paint is a bust portrait in light colors (fig. 50). The queen is shown wearing a short-sleeved white lace dress. She also wears a tiara on her head, her chestnut-colored hair pulled back to reveal her ears. She has red lips, blue eyes, and on her neck and chest is a multi-strand pearl necklace.

Ma was indebted to Li Bai (701–762), the celebrated Tang poet, for his comparison of the beauty of the queen to that of a celestial in the fairy kingdom. In the first year of the Tianbao period (742) during the reign of Emperor Xuanzong, Li Bai was in Chang'an, serving as *Hanlin gongfeng* (Compiler-in-Attendance at the Hanlin Academy). One day, when the emperor and his beloved court lady Yang *guifei* were enjoying peonies in Chenxiang Ting (Heavy Fragrance Pavilion), Li Bai was summoned to compose poems. Li wrote three compositions to the tune of *Qingping diao* (Peaceful Time). The following is one of them:

> *Her garments remind me of clouds; her face, a flower.*
> *The spring breeze, blowing past the balustrade, sways the dew-laden peonies.*
> *If I did not see her before among the peaks of the Jade Mountain,*
> *I must have met her in moonlight on the Jasper Terrace.*[135]

In mythology Jade Mountain (Qunyu Shan) is the place where the patroness of all fairies, Xiwangmu (Queen Mother of the West) resides. Here, Li Bai pays tribute to the beguiling beauty of Yang *guifei*. He likens her to these immortal beings, and ponders that if he has not set eyes on her before on the peaks of Jade Mountain where Xiwangmu usually receives the immortals, then he must have met her under the moon in Xiwangmu's palace.

Ma Shaoxuan's poem follows the tradition of romantic poetry. In it he lets his imagination take rein. Also likening Queen Mary to a heavenly being, he asserts that she must be the prettiest in the West.

Although this quatrain consists of only twenty words, its concise diction and imaginative thinking fully express the subject. As a presentation item for the purpose of promoting international relationship, this work which has amalgamated poetry, calligraphy and painting is both a handsome gift and a perfect choice. In the light of technical skills, the poem conforms with the standard tonal pattern. However, its phonetic effect is varied and its rhymes harmonious. It is also easy to recite as repeated reading brings out its musical quality.

SEALS

Seal-engraving is a unique Chinese art form. Ma Shaoxuan's art of inside-painting encompasses many kinds of artistic skills. Seal-designing also counts among them. On examining his oeuvre, it is clear that throughout all periods of development he

135. See Wang Qi, annot., *Li Taibai quanji, juan* 5, p. 304.

regarded seal design as an important element. He never simply painted a single character, *yin* (seal), to stand for the seal. Instead, he followed exactly the traditional regulations governing the application of seals on paintings and calligraphic specimens. To him, it was essential to first decide on a suitable location before painting in a tiny image of a seal which might bear his personal name or his literary name or his studio name. This exquisitely rendered detail would then become an integral part of the whole composition. Whether the bottle painting is in ink monochrome or in color, the addition of one or two vermilion seal designs will enliven its overall visual impact. As the seal design, together with calligraphy, painting, and poetry, forms an indispensable component of Ma's art, it is an aspect that cannot be ignored.

Ma used seal script for most of his seals, their legends delineated in intaglio. Designed in a variety of formats, they are most interesting to look at. In terms of the number of characters that make up the legend, there are one-, two-, and four-character examples. *Shao* (fig. 4), *Xuan* (fig. 26), and *Guang* are words that appear most often in single-character seal designs. *Shaoxuan* is to be found in a two-character example (fig. 6); and in a four-character one, *Ma Guangjia yin* (fig. 5). In terms of shapes, some seal designs are round, while others may be square, oval, or free-formed. Also, the number of seals that accompany a bottle painting may vary from one, two, to three. Some examples, however, have no seal designs at all.

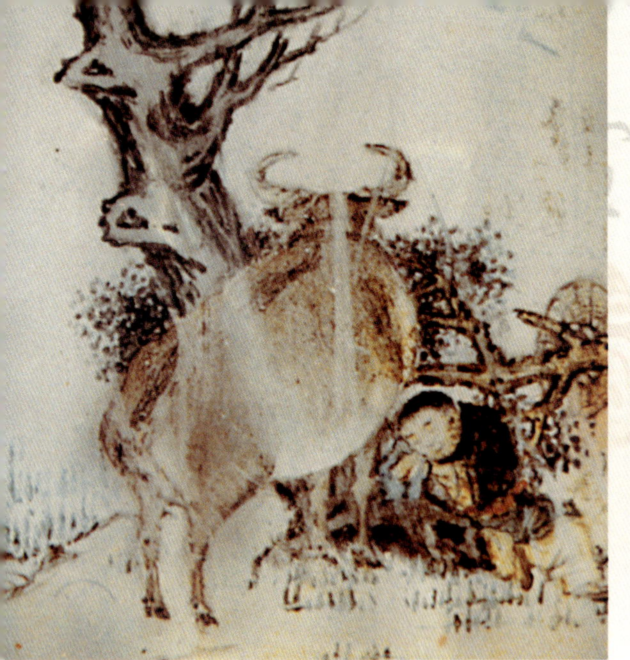

CHAPTER SIX

Winning a Gold Award at Fifty

In 1915 a large-scale international exposition was held in San Francisco in the United States. Ma Shaoxuan won an award that was even more distinguished than the gold medal. This was the first time that inside-painted snuff bottles won a highly esteemed international honor. From then on, the art of the Chinese inside-painted snuff bottle began to shine on the stage of international arts and crafts.

ENTRY ITEMS

The United States started to organize an international exposition in 1904. In February 1915 the twelfth exposition was held in San Francisco in the state of California. In celebration of the completion of the Panama Canal in 1914, which made possible direct access between the Pacific Ocean and the Atlantic Ocean, the exposition was called "An International Exposition in Commemoration of the Inauguration of the Panama Canal." It was also referred to as "The Panama-Pacific International Exposition."

As early as 1911 the American government had already formally invited China to participate in the international exposition. This happened at the time when the revolutionaries had just succeeded in overthrowing the Manchu-ruled Qing dynasty and established a republic. Everyone thought highly of the exposition and it was decided that China should participate in this important event. Subsequently an Exposition Commission was set up to oversee the operation. In October 1912 the Commission sent personnel over to the United States to start building a pavilion. In the following year, every province in China had set up an Exposition Commission Office which undertook the responsibility of assembling and selecting entry items. The province of Zhili established its office in October 1913. Yan Zhiyi, at the time Head of the Department of Industry and Commerce in the Ministry of Industries and later a Minister of the same ministry, was appointed its commissioner. Following suit, fourteen provinces, among which Guangdong, Fujian, Jiangsu, Zhejiang and Sichuan, also set up similar commissions one after the other.

In the process of selecting entry items the staff of the Exposition Commission of Zhili held Ma Shaoxuan's inside-painted snuff bottles in high esteem because they had already heard of Ma's great reputation and were sure that his works would stand out among Chinese and Western paintings. They sent a representative to visit Ma, who explained to him the objectives of the Panama-Pacific International Exposition, the establishment of the Zhili Exposition Commission, and the imminent plan of selecting entry items. He also expressed the wish that Ma would agree to participate in this event and submit the best of his works. Ma fully supported the idea; he was more than willing to introduce China's art of inside-painted snuff bottles to the rest of the world. He submitted for selection about a dozen or so extremely fine bottles, works he had painted within the last few years and kept for his own enjoyment. Members of the Exposition Commission were very pleased with his submission. However, they suggested that Ma should increase the number of bottles to be submitted, so as to ensure that they be displayed prominently as a larger group and catch people's attention; for otherwise they might not be noticed in a big exhibition hall because of their small size. Also, in consideration of the fact that the exposition would be taking place in the United States, they strongly encouraged Ma to do bottle portraits of Woodrow Wilson (fig. 58), then President of the United States, and his wife, which should be augmented by bottle portraits of the most important political figures of the time in China, such as the

President, Yuan Shikai (fig. 55), and the Vice President, Li Yuanhong (fig. 56). Ma accepted these suggestions. He requested assistance in securing photographs of these illustrious people, and immediately committed himself to creating his additional entry items.

During the half year that spanned the winter of 1913 and the spring of 1914 Ma gave up all activities in order to concentrate on the production of several works of the highest quality for competition in the international exposition. In the end, together with the more than a dozen bottles completed in recent years, he put together about twenty works, out of which he selected sixteen, and these he offered as a set to the Exposition Commission of Zhili. It was comprised of mainly bottle portraits, which were complemented with portraits of operatic actors assuming different roles, landscapes and bird-and-flower themes.[136]

In consideration of the long journey across the ocean, the susceptibility to damage in transit, and also a visually appealing packaging, Ma commissioned a large brocade-covered box inside which were sixteen slots arranged in a four-in-a-row manner. Each slot was fitted with a small brocade-bound box, inside of which was inserted a white satin pouch containing a snuff bottle. In this way, the sixteen works could be enjoyed independently; they could also be viewed as a group. In addition, each bottle would be protected by the pouch. When all sixteen of them were put in the large box, they made a handsome set that was easy and safe to carry. Also, during transportation the risk of breakage would be reduced to a minimum. When everything was in order, Ma handed the set over to the Exposition Commission.

Officials of the Exposition Commission were exceedingly pleased with Ma's submission. They extolled it as the best among all entry items.

WINNING AN AWARD IN TIANJIN

The Exposition Commission was very successful in soliciting entry items for the Panama-Pacific International Exposition. Many people, both Chinese and foreigners, submitted creative works for consideration. In arts and crafts, in addition to Ma

136. Ma's sixteen snuff bottles are listed under the name of Ma Hsao-shien in the official catalogue of the Panama-Pacific International Exposition. Their descriptions are as follows: "no. 222 Belle; no. 223 Rabbits in the Field; no. 224 Antiques; no. 225 Hill Scene in Winter; no. 226 Lotus, Swallows and Fish; no. 227 Cowboy; no. 228 Portrait of President Wilson; no. 229 Portrait of President Yuen; no. 230 Looking for Prunus Blossoms; no. 231 Looking at Lotus Flowers; no. 232 Crickets Playing; no. 233 Portrait of Vice-President Li; no. 234 Studying in Autumn Night; no. 235 Portrait of Late Statesman Li; no. 236 Portraits of President and Mrs. Wilson; no. 237 Portrait of Ma Hsao-shien." See *Panama-Pacific International Exposition Official Catalogue: Department of Fine Arts*, p. 84.

Shaoxuan, participants in this event included Jiang Yun (1847–1919),[137] Lin Shu (1852–1924),[138] Wang Luonian (1870–1925),[139] Xing Yunqin, Xiao Xun (1883–1944),[140] and Shi Chenglian, who submitted paintings; and Yu Xiaoxuan who submitted an ivory carving. In all, the entry items, which reached a total of several tens of thousands, were categorized under these nine headings: jewelry and gold and silver ware, cloisonné, embroidery, musical instruments, opera costumes, four treasures of calligraphy stationery (paper, brush, ink and inkstone), carved lacquerware, ceramics, and medicine. Among such masterpieces were magnificent cloisonné lion figures, a giant censer and a huge flower basket manufactured by the shop called Dechang Hao in Beijing. Also from Beijing, another shop, Baohua Lou, specially made a pair of three-feet tall gold-plated silver flower baskets. Inlaid with semi-precious stones, these opulent works truly dazzled the eye.

At the end of eight months of hard work the Exposition Commission of Zhili had collected many splendid entry items. Officials decided to first exhibit them in the city of Tianjin, so that people could have a chance to see them. As the items were diverse in nature, exquisite in workmanship, and novel to look at, the exhibition proved to be a big attraction. In the span of a month, from 14th June to 16th July 1914, a total of a hundred thousand people visited this preview.

Before the preview closed, the Exposition Commission invited well-known experts and scholars to form a judging committee. Members of this committee were charged with the mandate of selecting suitable items from the exhibit for entry into the Panama-Pacific International Exposition, and at the same time, grading the three best works of art, the creators of which would be awarded either a gold, silver, or bronze, medal. Ma Shaoxuan's inside-painted bottles were judged to merit the gold medal. They were also recommended to be included in the overseas display.

Selections from all provinces were shipped from Shanghai to San Francisco in December 1914 after they had been assembled there.

137. Jiang Yun's chronology is also recorded as 1847–1918. A native of Huaining in Anhui province, he was also known under his sobriquet, Yingsheng. An official, a poet, and a painter of landscape and flower subjects, he also practised calligraphy and seal engraving. For his biographical sketch, see Yu Jianhua, ed., *Zhongguo meishujia renming cidain*, p. 581.

138. Lin Shu was a native of Min district. A celebrated pioneer in the translation of European novels into Chinese, he was also much admired as a painter of landscape and bird-and-flower themes. For his biographical sketch, see *ibid.*, p. 530.

139. Wang Luonian was a native of Hangzhou. In painting he followed the orthodox styles of the Four Wangs of the early Qing. He was also known for his proficiency in calligraphy and seal engraving. For his biographical sketch, see *ibid.*, pp. 452–453.

140. Xiao Xun was a native of Huaining in Anhui province. He was a student of Jiang Yun and often did paintings for his teacher. However, later in life he developed his own style after he had seen works by Monk Daoji (1642–1707) and Gong Xian (1619–1689). For his biographical sketch, see *ibid.*, p. 1415.

WINNING AN AWARD IN SAN FRANCISCO

On 20th February 1915 the Panama-Pacific International Exposition opened on its new seashore site in San Francisco. It was a big show and a big competition featuring the very best of the economy and culture of the participating countries. The Exposition occupied an area of 635 acres. The exhibition halls, which covered eleven departments, sprawled over 250 acres. They were: fine arts, education, literature, manufacture, crafts, engineering, mining, communication, agriculture, food, and gardening. In addition, each of the forty-one participating countries was represented by a pavilion built by its own government. This showcased national architectural features on the outside and typical products inside.

According to *Banama saihui Zhili guanhui congbian* (A Collection of Notes Made by Delegates of Zhili at the Panama Exposition) by Yan Zhiyi, the main objective of the Exposition was to "provide an opportunity for all civilizations to directly compare the results of their cultures." In carrying out this motto, the Exposition set up displays, facilitated viewing, encouraged criticism, promoted sales, and stimulated exchange of technology—activities which assisted extensive economic, cultural and technological exchanges on an international scale. It not only caused a great sensation within the United States and other parts of the world but it also inspired governments of different countries to send delegations to San Francisco. From the Republic of China came a large delegation which, in addition to taking charge of China's exhibit, visited other displays and exchanged dialogues with representatives from other countries.

Within China's exhibition galleries it was the fine arts and crafts sections that had attracted the biggest crowd and the highest praise. During their sojourn in the United States Yan Zhiyi sent the delegates in small groups to various parts of the host country to see and to learn. They all benefitted from this experience. Later, Yan made this comment with a sigh: "Most people are afflicted with a lack of self-knowledge. They prefer to live behind closed doors and think the world is too mean for their notice. It is only when they emerge from their cocoons and make contact with other people that they will realize that what they have entertained in their minds in the past were crazy and ridiculous ideas. . . If, knowing that we lag behind other countries, we still feel content as if this were our fate, this frame of mind would be quite abnormal. It is also one that my countrymen definitely should not nurture."

The Exposition closed on 4th December of the same year after staying open for a period of ten months. It was the longest duration since its inception.

The Exposition appointed a judging panel, its members selected from representatives recommended by the visiting delegations. After reviewing the entry items the panel set down these five categories of award: grand prize, honorable mention, gold medal, silver medal, and bronze medal. Among China's entries it was the fine arts section that won the most awards. Ma Shaoxuan's inside-painted snuff bottles won an honorable mention.[141] In this year he was forty-nine years old.

Also in the fine arts section, other winners included Jiang Yun, who won an honorable mention for his landscape painting, Shi Chenglian and Xing Yunqin, who each won gold medals for their paintings, Yu Xiaoxuan, who also won a gold medal for his ivory carving, and the shop named Dechang Hao, which was awarded a grand prize for its cloisonné works of art.

The sixteen bottles that earned Ma Shaoxuan an award were all masterpieces. They are important evidence for researching Ma's art of inside-painting and for understanding the cultural exchange that took place between China and overseas countries. After the Exposition was over, the Exposition Commission purchased some of the bottles. The rest were donated either to museums and various institutions in the United States for display or to the Commodities Display Center in Tianjin.

CELEBRATION

As soon as members of the delegation from Zhili returned to Tianjin, a messenger was dispatched to Beijing to announce the good news to Ma Shaoxuan. Ma's family was overjoyed and excited. Word spread quickly among relatives, friends and neighbors: "Sixth uncle won an award in the United States!" "Sixth master won an honor award in the International

141. In the official catalogue of the Panama Pacific International Exposition, however, no award is indicated under Ma's name. See *Panama-Pacific International Exposition Official Catalogue: Department of Fine Arts*, p. 84.

Exposition!"[142] Friends and relatives came one after the other to congratulate Ma. Neighbors rejoiced: they were proud of Ma because the distinction meant not only that the Ma family had produced a talent in the field of snuff bottles but also that the Hui minority had produced a talent. They exclaimed, "Sixth master of the Ma family has won honor for us Muslims! He has made the inhabitants of Ox Street stand taller!"

M'as fiftieth birthday fell in the month of April, 1916. His wife, children, friends and relatives busied themselves to prepare a big celebration. They had men put up an awning in the courtyard; they slaughtered sheep; they hired chefs; and they even rented space in a guildhall and commissioned a Beijing opera troupe to put on performances. Friends and relatives sent Ma gifts of magnificently mounted scrolls in celebration of his double happiness—his birthday and his award. In high spirits, Ma and his well-wishers enjoyed a hearty banquet. For Ma, it was the happiest day of his life. On this day he had received the most impressive birthday presents.

A TRIP TO TIANJIN

In the following year Ma Shaoxuan received a letter from the Exposition Commission, which requested his presence at a ceremony, to be held on 27th December 1917, in which a full report of China's participation in the Panama-Pacific International Exposition would be given and awards won in this event would be handed over to the winners.

For a long time Ma had wanted to visit Tianjin. However, because he had decided to devote his time wholeheartedly to pursuing the art of inside-painting, he never took time off to travel anywhere outside Beijing. On this occasion he felt he could not decline the Exposition Commission's invitation to go to Tianjin. At that time Beijing and Tianjin were already connected by railway. From the perspective of someone living in the present age, it is no big deal to take a trip to Tianjin. Yet, in the early part of this century, a man of some age who had never ventured outside Beijing would consider going to Tianjin as taking a long-distance trip. The whole family worried a lot about the clothes Ma should wear, the food he should bring, the accommodation

142. Ma Shaoxuan was referred to as "sixth uncle" or "sixth master" because he was sixth in line among boys of his generation in the Ma clan.

he would need, and the means of transportation available to him. They even searched out friends who knew Tianjin well to ask about the way to the Exposition Commission's office. After all arrangements had been made, Mrs. Ma somehow still felt uneasy. She repeated one instruction after another to her husband. She also prayed to Allah for his safe return. On the day of Ma's departure she led all family members to the railway station to see him off.

After Ma had arrived at Tianjin he went straight to attend the ceremony. Officials of the Exposition Commission had put on display some of the award-winning items so invited guests could enjoy them. During the ceremony the Commissioner, Yan Zhiyi, made a speech in which he gave a detailed account of the Exposition and the results of the contest held in conjunction with this event. To Ma he handed over the certificate of honor won in the Panama-Pacific International Exposition and the gold medal won in the Tianjin preview.

Winning an award in the Tianjin preview reflected the Chinese government's appreciation of Ma's art of inside-painting. Winning an award in the Panama-Pacific International Exposition—an important international contest judged by a panel of experts from different countries—however, meant worldwide recognition. The significance was remarkable. It acknowledged the distinctively national character and the high artistic quality inherent in Ma's art, as well as his inheritance of China's long tradition in painting and calligraphy and his contribution to further development. For Ma, the award was akin to a large fruit transformed from a flower, this blossom he had spent scores of years to nurture. It was the greatest encouragement he received in his whole life. Ma's award also signified an effective worldwide promotion of China's inside-painted snuff bottles. Since then, his works have become known all over the world. Museums in the United States and in other parts of the world have collected them. Although before this event took place Ma's bottles had been in circulation outside China, the award was like, for the first time, the international community officially firing a salute in honor of China's art of inside-painted snuff bottles making its premiere on the world stage.

After the ceremony, in high spirits Ma visited the Commodities Display Center, enjoyed Tianjin's operatic performances, and toured the market. He then returned home safely. When friends and relatives heard about his homecoming, a stream of jubilant well-wishers came to see him and to congratulate him.

A TRAIN OF THOUGHT

From the time Ma received news of his winning a major award to the time he claimed it, more than a year had elapsed. During this long period this major event must have caused quite a ripple in his mind. There were times highlighted by visitations of congratulatory friends. There were also times when he ruminated in the stillness of the night all by himself. Among these friends and relatives some paid tribute to his achievements; others made suggestions as to what direction he should follow in the future. Ma found himself caught between two kinds of mood: exhilaration on the one hand and complete composure on the other. In reminiscing over the past he seemed to taste one more time the bitterness, the spiciness, the sourness, and the sweetness he had experienced before, with all kinds of feelings welling up in his heart. When he pondered on the future, he was fully aware that there was no end to the pursuit of perfection in the realms of calligraphy, painting, poetry and literature. He knew that his interest was in these refined pursuits, not in fame and profit. Winning an international award no doubt made him feel excited, but basically he was an artist practising inside-painting. His passion for this branch of art was so intense that all other things seemed to become unimportant. What other people deemed extremely significant would be, in his eyes, secondary when compared with the art of inside-painting. It was this reasoning that helped Ma keep his composure.

When all the fanfare was over, Ma resumed his normal life: with the bamboo pen his companion, he continued to enjoy painting different scenes inside the snuff bottle and while his life away dappling ink.

THE GOLD MEDAL AND THE CERTIFICATE OF HONORABLE MENTION

The Certificate of Honorable Mention that Ma Shaoxuan received from the Panama-Pacific International Exposition was printed on dowling paper in quarto size. The left- and right-hand borders were decorated with standing nudes and along the lower border, seated ones. Written in English in the space in the center were the reason for the award and its category. After Ma had returned home, he had it nicely framed and hung on a wall in his studio.

By the late 1930s, the gold medal that Ma had won in the Tianjin preview was already kept in his grandsons' quarters. At that time his two eldest grandsons were teenagers. They lived in the inner room of the eastern chamber. In the middle room a side table was placed against the gable wall. On it was a table-clock. The gold medal was put inside its glass cover. Unfortunately one day the gable wall collapsed. The clock, the medal, and everything placed along the wall were smashed. Oblivious of the danger, old Mrs. Ma rushed to the inner room to get her grandsons out. Although no one was hurt, everybody in the house was stunned. Later, workmen were called in to remove the rubble and rebuild the wall. After all the clean-up was done and people began to feel a little easier, they thought of the gold medal. However, by that time there was no trace of it at all.

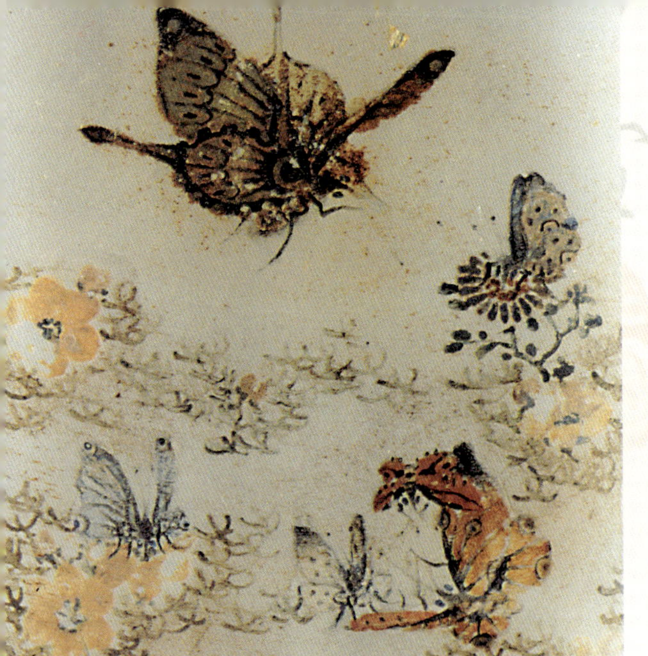

CHAPTER SEVEN

Life and Works at the Age of Sixty and Afterwards

The time-frame discussed in this chapter is rather extensive, spanning sixteen years from about 1915 to 1932, when Ma Shaoxuan was fifty to sixty-six years old. During this period significant changes occurred in China's political situation and Ma's personal life. The art of his inside-painting entered a new phase of development.

GREAT CHANGES

From the time when Ma won his award at the Panama-Pacific International Exposition to the early part of the 1930s, many things happened in Ma's surroundings and in his personal life. These can be summed up in three main points:

1. From 1914 to 1918 many countries became embroiled, either directly or indirectly, in the First World War. Communication broke down as a result of incessant exchanges of gunfire. Normal intercourse that had been carried on during peacetime was destroyed. Also, people lost interest in buying art. This was not the case just during wartime, for even years after the conclusion of the War there was hardly any transaction on the international art market. Under the circumstances demands for Ma's inside-painted snuff bottles were drastically reduced.

2. The situation in China was not much better. The warlords never stopped fighting against each other. Beijing's political arena was topsy-turvy. Military factions flexed muscles, vying for power and control. One person might be in command

one day, only to be toppled by another person the next day. During the eleven years between 1916 and 1927 no less than seven people were instated as the President in the so-called Beiyang Military Clique, not to mention the restoration of a monarchy staged by Zhang Xun.[143] As to the position of Premier, the turnover rate was even faster. In a matter of eleven years, no less than twenty-seven Premiers were appointed and discharged. If Acting Premiers were taken into consideration as well, a total of forty-eight incumbents came and went. On average, each term of service would have lasted less than three months. In actual fact, some officially appointed Premiers were ousted only a couple of weeks after they had been sworn into office. The longest period of service on record was no more than a year and four months. When the administrators of the state were so affected by instability, who would have the time to think of art? Fewer distinguished patrons commissioned Ma to paint bottle portraits or bought inside-painted snuff bottles from him.

3. In sharp contrast to the above-mentioned grim prospects was Ma's spirit of making further progress which he developed after receiving an award from the Panama-Pacific International Exposition. No doubt this prestigious international award had produced a positive effect on Ma: it fired his desire to create.

 When a passionate heart is suddenly placed in a chilly surrounding, what will become of it? As the idiomatic expression says, "When a vehicle is blocked by a hill, there must be a path for it to get through."

CHARACTERISTICS OF MA'S LATER WORKS

Taken together, the three major changes enumerated above contribute to five characteristics in Ma Shaoxuan's later works. These are:

1. From filling out orders back to creating art at his own will

 In his early works Ma chose the subject matter as he pleased. During the latter half of his middle period a majority of his bottle-portrait production was made to fulfill requests. In the final period, although the number of wealthy and

143. Zhang Xun was a warlord who seized control of Beijing on July 1, 1917 and restored the Manchu emperor to the throne.

illustrious patrons who commissioned bottle portraits from him dropped drastically, it hardly produced any adverse effect on his art of inside-painting. As a matter of fact, the reduction of commissioned work gave Ma an opportunity to work on subjects that he liked, to create with greater freedom and more leisure, to express himself more fully, and to put forward works with brand new themes. As a result, in comparing his later works with those completed during his middle period, it is obvious that there were fewer portraits, but more depictions of landscapes and themes related to daily life. As far as subject matter was concerned, there was more variety in his later production.

2. Reduced output

With diminished high-society clients and fewer commissions, Ma could work on subjects of his own choice and create of his own free will. He began to slow down his speed of production and, as a result, his output was reduced.

Time is merciless. When Ma was in his early fifties, he painted away passionately, each day working at it for the same number of hours. After he had turned fifty-five years old, the time he spent each day on painting was not as long as before. When he reached sixty and beyond, he spent less and less time painting; there were even days when he stopped altogether. Therefore, during these sixteen years the volume of his annual production varied: sometimes greater, while other times smaller. But generally speaking, in graphic terms his output would have appeared as a descending wavy line on a chart.

3. Works characterized by more refined and sensitive brushwork, exhibiting a well-rounded quality typifying full maturity

Ma's faculties were still quite sound when he was sixty. Having accumulated more than forty years of experience in painting inside snuff bottles, his technical skills were consummate, his compositions well designed, and the calligraphic and painting elements in his works full of feelings of serenity and purity. He had overcome his shortcomings and reinforced his strengths. Therefore, not only had the quality of his works not suffered any setback, in certain respects his productions even showed signs of further development and individuality. These observations are supported by examples such as the bottle portrait of Min Shaoquan (fig. 72) and "Boundless Joy" (fig. 100).

4. Painting more often for the general public

   Before 1915, under great pressure Ma was fully occupied with producing commissioned works. His productions were beyond the reach of the middle- and lower-class people. After the 1920s things began to change. Increasingly he painted for the general populace, either as gifts or for a fee. Many of his works were acquired by the middle and lower classes.

5. Because of the stalemate in international communications, fewer of Ma's works were circulated on overseas markets and more became accessible to the ordinary people in China.

GATHERING IDEAS

Ever since his youthful days Ma Shaoxuan had been fond of painting fresh, lively and interesting subjects, as can be witnessed by examples such as "Boundless Joy" (fig. 4), "Lotuses and a Dragonfly" (fig. 32), and "Boy Catching a Butterfly." Later, he had to stop doing this type of subject matter because he was too busy painting formal portraits and actors in operatic roles. After he had turned fifty years old, he had more time on his hands, more freedom to choose his subjects, and more latitude to create. It was only then that he could feel once more the happiness of painting with the heart of a child. However, resuming painting with a child's heart does not mean repeating old themes and old compositions. On the contrary, Ma wanted to create new moods and new designs. He knew very well that splendid scenery and feelings were part and parcel of a good life; and it was also in life that catalysts existed which sparked inspiration. Therefore, driven by a passionate desire to create, and fired by an energetic mind, Ma delved into a good life to earnestly look for painting themes. Here are two incidents which illustrate how he would seek out new subjects.

On a warm spring day, when the foliage of the willows was green and fresh, Ma left home to visit one of his cousins. While several people sat down comfortably to sip tea and have a chat,

Ma caught sight of the blooming flowers in the courtyard. He got up and sauntered off to admire the flowers, leaving his companions behind to continue their conversation. After a while the cousin looked for Ma and found him standing transfixed by a flowering shrub, watching a mottled kitten attracted by several butterflies which fluttered about among the blossoms. The kitten wanted to catch one of them. He struck with a fore-paw but failed to reach his target. The butterfly did not fly away. It lingered, however, now and then moving from one bloom to another. The kitten was in no hurry: it hit out the moment the butterfly interrupted its flight. Ma was mesmerized by this hit-and-chase game. As he watched he was busy thinking about the best angle he should take to capture the scene. As soon as he hit upon an idea, he seized a piece of toilet paper and quickly made a sketch. At this point Ma's companions were quite moved by seeing him search for ideas in real life. They commended him thus, "You are over fifty, but you still have the heart of a child." In other words, to them, he was not an old man yet, for his art always stayed youthful.

A few days later, an inside-painted snuff bottle with a new theme appeared. It was decorated with a mottled kitten stretching out a fore-paw to catch a butterfly by a flowering shrub. Both the kitten and the butterfly were represented in the liveliest manner imaginable.

Then, there was another story about a painting of a fish and a fish-hawk.

One day Ma went to see an elderly friend who was a doctor. While chatting Ma noticed a scroll depicting a fish and a fish-hawk hanging on a wall in the reception hall. In a very realistic manner it showed a small fish swimming leisurely in a lotus pond full of gorgeous flowers and luxuriant leaves. Yet, danger lurked right beside the fish: a fish-hawk was gazing intently at the fish; with neck outstretched, it was poised to attack momentarily. The fish, however, seemed totally oblivious of its plight. With his brush the painter had brought to life both the fish and the fish-hawk. Like a magnet, the painting held Ma's attention. He stopped talking abruptly. The host took note of his dazed look, and, following his eyes, realized that he was absorbed in the painting. Holding his tongue too, the host let Ma enjoy it with undivided attention. Ma studied it for a long time, now standing back to view it from afar; now moving closer to inspect it detail by detail. He was pondering a compositional design that would allow him to transfer perfectly this subject onto a tiny snuff bottle. He did not take his leave until he had found a solution. Some time later, a bottle painted on the inside with a fish and a fish-hawk was produced: it depicted the life and death of a small fish in a tranquil lotus pond.

These stories make clear that Ma was kind-hearted by nature; he also enjoyed life with gusto. Such stories also testify to Ma manifesting his passion for the art of inside-painting in all aspects of his life. This passion was all pervasive. Even though after he had turned fifty, Ma still nurtured a strong desire to give the whole of himself—body and mind—to practising painting and calligraphy. This is why in the realm of art he could continue to explore and create.

FRIENDSHIP

Painting on the interior walls of snuff bottles is a meticulous form of artistic work that taxes one's eyesight. It entails slow progress. In addition, in the case of Ma Shaoxuan, after he had turned fifty years old, he further slowed down his work pace. Therefore, his output during this period became smaller than before. Nevertheless, his reputation was still very high and many of his friends knew all too well how difficult it was and what an honor it would be to be able to own a bottle painted by him. In the past he had painted portraits for monarchs and presidents. Now, people tried every means to acquire at least one bottle from him, if it was at all possible. Ma himself, however, was a man who regarded friendship a lot more highly than money. Whenever friends requested bottles from him, he would try to satisfy them.

The following anecdote has been in circulation:

Ma's wife became ill when she was in her fifties. On a relative's recommendation Ma wanted to secure the service of Zhi Ti'an, one of the most reputable doctors in the capital, to look after her. Mr. Zhi originally was on the medical staff in the imperial palace. After the establishment of the Republic he left the imperial medical board and set up his own practice. It was not easy to have him pay a house call. However, when he learned that it was Ma Shaoxuan who had requested his service for Mrs. Ma, he immediately went. He lived in the east side of the city. Twice every week he went to Ma's home in a hired vehicle. There, he took the patient's pulse and wrote the prescription. Thanks to his care and infinite patience, not long after, Mrs. Ma fully recovered. The Ma family was very grateful. Members of the family talked about recompensing Mr. Zhi with a gift to show their appreciation. Through a friend Mr. Zhi expressed the wish that in place of a monetary reward he would like to have an inside-painted snuff bottle from Ma. When this wish was conveyed to Ma, Ma complied with gladness, for he wanted to thank Mr. Zhi for his friendship and, at the same time, express his admiration for Mr. Zhi's medical skills and ethical conduct. Needless to say, Mr. Zhi was overjoyed when he received the bottle. For him, it was indeed a great treasure.

PHOTO-TAKING

For Ma Shaoxuan 1925 was a happy year. In the third lunar month of this year his eldest son, Ma Zhenduo, who worked in the Bank of China in Shanghai, returned to Beijing with his wife and children to see his parents. It was a reunion that all looked forward to.

Ma Zhenduo started working in the Bank of China when he was seventeen. For a long time he lived in Shanghai. Busy work schedules at the bank prevented him from visiting his parents from time to time. In 1925 he was twenty-eight years old. He decided to pay his parents a visit, bringing along with him his wife, née Hei, their four-year-old son, Zengxiang, and two-year-old daughter, Lifang. It was a very rare occasion.

Ma Shaoxuan lived with his second son, Zhensheng. In this year Zhensheng was twenty-five years old. He had a two-year-old son named Zengrui.

Ma Shaoxuan was exceedingly happy to be surrounded by his children and grandchildren. In order to keep a record of this

joyful reunion for future remembrance, he took his grandchildren
to a studio to have some pictures taken. The one illustrated here
shows him holding Zengrui with one hand and Lifang with the
other hand (fig. 97). For a long time many people who like Ma's
inside-painted snuff bottles and collect them had no idea what he
looked like. Although unsure whether Ma had ever been
photographed, they expressed the wish to see a picture of him.
This photograph is published in response to such a request. With
its publication, we, the descendants of Ma Shaoxuan, have also
fulfilled our desire to publicize Ma, one of the main objectives of
the present biography.

Now, all three of them in the picture have passed away.
Looking at the picture is just like seeing them in the flesh.
However, we can only reminisce about them and pay our respects
to them.

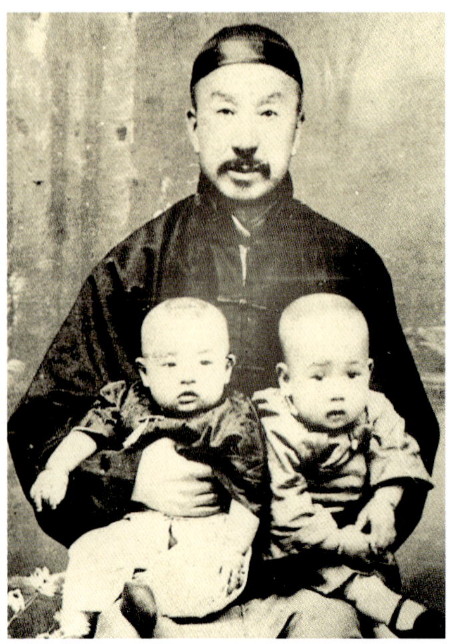

Fig. 97. Photograph showing Ma Shaoxuan
holding his grandchildren, Zengrui (left)
and Lifang (right), 1925 (Ma Family
Collection)

The present writer remembers clearly what Ma Shaoxuan was
like. He was an elderly man with a kind heart and an easy-going
temperament. He had always enjoyed good health. Even when he
reached seventy his mind was still very alert. A typical member of

the Hui minority, he was tall; his back was always straight; he had a broad forehead, shiny black eyes, high nose-bridge and thick-set moustache. He led a simple and plain lifestyle. At home he always wore old but clean clothes. Only when he went out did he change into better garments. He neither smoked nor drank. He took three meals a day. What he partook of was just simple fare. He shunned delicacies but craved for noodles. Noodle soup and noodles with diced meat and spicy sauce were favorites that he had all the time. A kind and doting father and grandfather, whether at home or outside, he was never seen in argument with anyone or losing control of himself.

Although a bottle painted in 1932 seems to have been Ma's last work, Ma still occasionally seated himself at his work station to paint a little bit of this or to write a little bit of that. These exercises, however, were done only to kill time. When painting bottles Ma required himself to assume a proper posture. He would seat himself on the west side of an eight-immortals table placed against a window in the southern chamber.[144] He never hunched foreward, instead he kept his back erect. In addition, he would never allow himself to squint. On the table was always placed a blue cloth-bound box that had once stored ink containers. No longer serving this purpose, this empty box was now used as a stand that provided elevation for the bottle to be worked on. As Ma inserted the bamboo pen into the bottle to paint, his elbows would be positioned on the table, his wrists would be raised and the heels of his hands would rest on the box. At this time, he would be so focused on his work that everything else would seem to be non-existent.

In 1992 the present writer wrote a pentasyllabic poem in memory of Ma. It reads,

> *I raise my head to look at the rosy clouds,*
> *I saw an elderly painter standing there*
> *   majestically.*
> *His poems and paintings will be transmitted far*
> *   and wide;*
> *His love will be all-embracing like the spring*
> *   breeze.*

---

144. The eight-immortals table is a square
    table that can seat eight people.

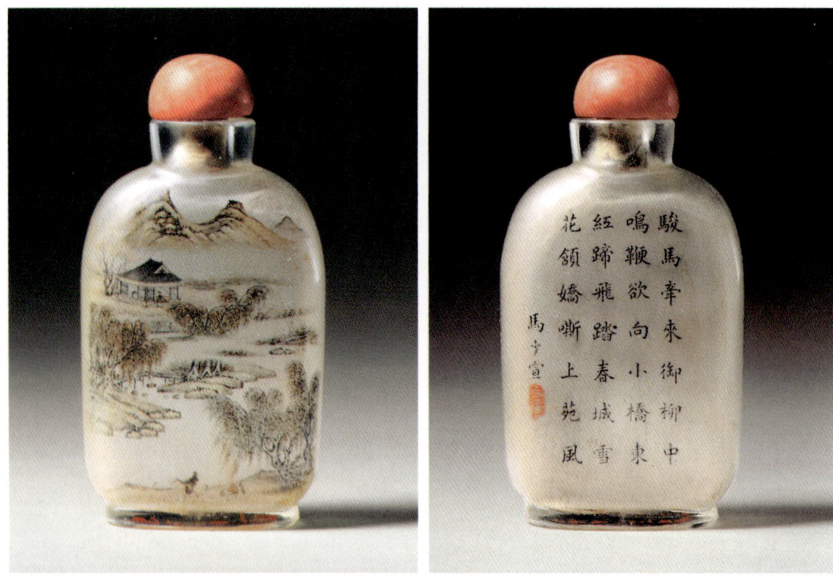

Figs. 98 and 99. Landscape, with a poem inscribed on the reverse, undated (Ma Family Collection)

ART HAS NO LIMIT

In addition to his usual artistic qualities, Ma Shaoxuan's inside-painted snuff bottles produced during his last years were also imbued with a carefree spirit typical of a man of some age. At this time, having become a veteran artist, he not only had an excellent command of painting techniques but also a receptive mind. Better still, he no longer had to work under stress to fill orders as he had done before. His works produced during these years, therefore, exuded feelings of broad-mindedness, purity and tranquility. Three examples of his output belonging to this period are discussed here:

1. Among Ma's representative inside-painted portraits can be counted the portrait of Min Shaoquan (see Chapter 3 for its description).

2. With bird-and-flower themes, "Boundless Joy" completed in 1925 was a representative work. It will be introduced below, using another example of identical subject matter, made in 1895, for comparison.

3. For landscape, see the bottle illustrated in figs. 98 and 99. Although undated, its painting and calligraphy demonstrate features characteristic of Ma's last period.

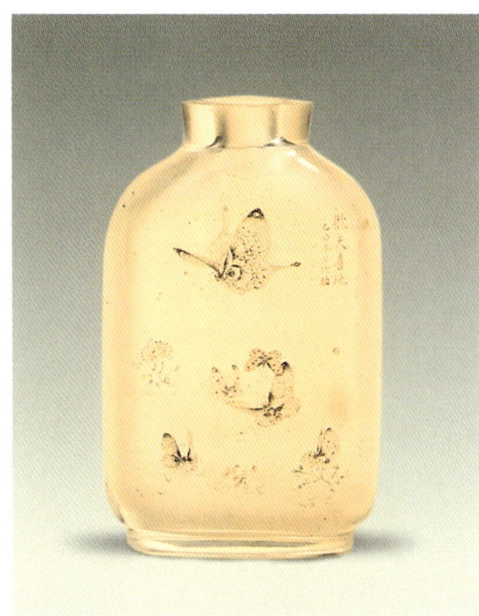

Fig. 100. *"Boundless Joy"* (*Huantian xidi*), dated 1925 (Ma Family Collection)

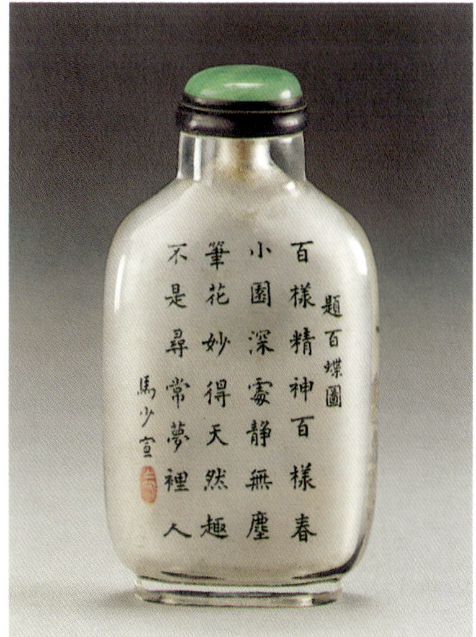

Fig. 101. Poem inscribed on the reverse of fig. 4, dated 1895 (The Collection of Mary and George Bloch)

---

145. Li Bai, the renowned Tang poet, is said to have had a dream when he was young. In this dream he saw flowers coming out of the tip of his brush. Because his literary talents were widely recognized later in his life, people started to use this allusion to denote exceptional skills and talents.

"Boundless Joy" depicts flowers on the interior wall of a snuff bottle. According to the inscription, "Painted on a winter day in the year *yichou*," it was painted in 1925 when Ma was fifty-nine years old (fig. 100).

"Boundless Joy" was a theme that Ma had already used in his early period (fig. 4). In 1895 alone several examples were made. Why did Ma paint this theme again after thirty years? Did the later version show significant differences? What connotation did it embody? In order to clarify these questions, let us first review the 1895 example, then compare the two versions, and hopefully come to understand its meaning.

In the upper centre of the painted side of the 1895 bottle is the four-character title, *Huantian xidi*. Adjacent to it are three lines of small characters, which read, "[Painted by] Shaoxuan on a winter day in the year *yiwei*." This short inscription is followed by a small seal with a single-character legend, *Shao*. Underneath are depicted in color a few clumps of flowers and several hovering butterflies. The scene is suggestive of spring, a time when all living things, soothed by the warm breezes, begin to come alive and thrive, imparting in turn a sense of happiness. The vibrant colors and animated images indeed conjure up feelings of youthful vigor and boundless joy. It should be noted that Ma was twenty-nine years old in 1895. The youthful air that pervaded the painting reflected the artist's exuberant years and his fervor to better himself.

On the reverse, written in regular script is this septasyllabic quatrain entitled, "On a Picture of One Hundred Butterflies" (fig. 101):

A hundred aspects of spring; a hundred moods;
In the depth of a small garden -- peaceful and free
  from the dust [of this world].
Like flowers blossoming from the tip of the
  brush, [145]
[I] skilfully captured the wonders of Nature.
[Yet, I] am not the dreamer [that people] always
  talk about.

The "dreamer" in the last line is an allusion to the story of Zhuang Zhou (369 B.C.–A.D. 286) dreaming of the butterfly.

Zhuang was a philosopher who lived in the Warring States period (476–221 B.C.). In the chapter "Discussion on Making All Things Equal" (*Qiwu lun*) in *Zhuangzi* is this passage: "Once Chuang Chou dreamt he was a butterfly, a butterfly flitting and fluttering around, happy with himself and doing as he pleased. He didn't know he was Chuang Chou. Suddenly he woke up and there he was, solid and unmistakably Chuang Chou. But he didn't know if he was Chuang Chou who had dreamt he was a butterfly, or a butterfly dreaming he was Chuang Chou. Between Chuang Chou and a butterfly there must be *some* distinction! This is called the Transformation of Things."[146]

When poets compose poems, this phenomenon often occurs: when they deny being something or someone, they are actually making a statement that they are akin to that something or someone. This has been a common practice in ancient poems. The same is true with Ma's poem. Although the text says "[Yet, I] am not the dreamer [that people] always talk about," what Ma actually had in mind was Zhuang Zhou and he identified himself with Zhuang Zhou. Zhuang dreamed of a butterfly and he felt he was the butterfly. He was even unsure whether he had dreamt of becoming a butterfly or the butterfly had dreamt of becoming him. To Ma, as he was painting along, he felt he had become one of the butterflies which hovered over the blossoms, drunk with the alluring fragrances that pervaded the warm air and feeling exceedingly elated. It is only when a person immerses himself like this in painting, becoming one with the subject he engages himself in and arriving at such an imaginative feeling, that he can produce an absorbing work with moving power such as this painting and this poem.

In the history of Ma's inside-painting this 1895 work holds an important place.

Thirty years later Ma was almost sixty years old. Often people who are getting on in years like to reminisce about the past and savor bygone times. Happy events would replay in their minds one after the other. Similarly, when Ma looked back on works that he had made as a young man, his memory would bring back scene after scene before his mind's eye, such as his motives of creation, the ideas he wanted to communicate, and the process of

146. Chuang Tzu is the Wade-Giles form of romanization of Zhuangzi. The same is true with Chuang Chou and Zhuang Zhou. The translation is by Burton Watson. See *Chuang Tzu: Basic Writings*, p. 45.

production. Inevitably successes and failures would have also been reassessed.

When he looked at his old work "Boundless Joy," he would have thought that it was after all not so satisfactory. The main setback would have been the centrally positioned inscription on the upper part of the bottle, which occupied approximately one third of the painted space, leaving the flowers and butterflies in the lower half appearing to be compressed together. The whole composition, as a result, looked too spacious at the top and too crowded at the bottom. In short, the positioning of various elements was less than ideal. However, if the inscription were to be moved to the side and written vertically, the upper centre would be left empty, and the flowers and butterflies would be surrounded by more space. Wouldn't rendering the composition more spacious be a more logical solution to overcome the setback inherent in the old design? On thinking things over, Ma hit upon a new design. A strong desire to repaint "Boundless Joy" was revived. He therefore picked up his bamboo pen and redid this old theme, and in doing so, gave it new life. That was how "Boundless Joy" was reborn in 1925.

The poem inscribed on the reverse of the bottle remained the same. No changes were made (fig. 102).

The change in the compositional structure of this particular work was like an enlightenment following an explosion of inspirations. It was also the result of an intense meditation. This change testified to his continued effort in emphasizing the importance of a design after having spent several decades pursuing the art of inside-painting. It also represented a concrete summing-up of his invaluable experience in this respect. In addition, it embodied countless words and important reflections. The comparison between Ma's old and new works certainly provokes us to think further.

MOVING TO A NEW HOUSE

In the latter part of the 1920s the Ma family moved from number 3, Menlou Hutong to number 53, Xizhuan Hutong (West Brick Alley). It was a bigger compound with high steps leading to a wide main entrance. Directly opposite was a huge

百樣精神百樣春
小園深夜靜無塵
筆花妙得天然趣
不是尋常夢裡人
馬少宣

Fig. 102. Poem inscribed on the reverse of fig. 100, "Boundless Joy," dated 1925 (Ma Family Collection)

stone screen. As one entered the main gate, one would be greeted
by a gigantic and lofty garden rock resembling a sword with the
tip of its blade pointing upward to the sky. To the east of the gate
was a hall with four north-facing chambers. Richly decorated, it
was used as a reception hall. On entering the second gate, three
side-chambers were disposed to the east and west sides of the
courtyard. Further ahead, facing the front were five south-facing
chambers. The one to the extreme right and the one to the
extreme left were dark rooms. Ma Shaoxuan used the one on the
left as his bedroom; his second son, Zhensheng, and his spouse
lived in the one on the right. The three middle ones served as
Ma's studio. They were furnished with hardwood furniture.
Calligraphic specimens and paintings by celebrated artists
adorned the walls. The building complexes in the mansion had
high ceilings and were connected by covered corridors. It
afforded warmth in the winter and coolness in the summer. On
the west side of the studio a hardwood eight-immortals table was
placed beneath the window. That constituted Ma's workplace.

A smaller courtyard was connected to each side of this
courtyard. The rooms in the smaller eastern courtyard were well-
built. They were used as guest-rooms. Ma's eldest son and family
stayed there when they returned from Shanghai for a visit. The
kitchen and storerooms were located in the smaller western
courtyard.

The first thing that Ma did after moving into the new house
was to display his hall name. This meant hanging on both sides
of the main gate a vertical wooden tablet: the one on the right
inscribed with three characters, *Xinglin Tang* (Hall of the Apricot
Grove); the one on the left bearing only two characters, *Mayu*
(Residence of the Ma [family]).

People might ask, "Ma Shaoxuan was an inside-painted snuff
bottle artist. Why did he choose "Apricot Grove" as his hall
name?"

Inherent in this name was Ma's love and respect for his
parents. He once communicated to his family the answer to this
question. He said: "Now that we have moved into a new house,
we should be grateful to our forebears. It was thanks to my
parents' upbringing and every single bit of advice of my father

that I can do inside-painting on the snuff bottle. Unfortunately they had worked hard all their lives, but were never able to live in a decent house. Now that we have a new house, we should not forget them, just as a person who drinks water from a well does not forget those who made the well." As to the reason for calling the hall "Apricot Grove" in memory of his parents, Ma also recounted a story to his family. During the Three Kingdoms period there was in the state of Wu a medical practitioner by the name of Dong Feng who did not charge his patients any fees. All he asked for was that if his patients recovered from their illnesses they would plant a few apricot saplings in front of his house. Over the years the saplings grew to become a grove. Later, people used the term "apricot grove" to allude to a doctor with compassion and dedication to save lives. This story makes clear why Ma wanted to adopt this term as his hall name: it was his way to remember his father. In doing so, he was also not only passing on the good family tradition he had inherited from his father to later generations but also, by setting himself as an example, reminding them not to forget their forebears.

Ma had a passion for gardening. He was all for making the surroundings of his living quarters beautiful. His courtyards were adorned with fresh flowers all year round. Sometimes potted flowers would also be placed in the residential areas. Each year, during the New Year's observances there were narcissi, which would be followed by peach blossoms in early spring, pomegranates, oleanders and lotuses in summer, chrysanthemums in autumn, and prunuses in winter. The flowers were all supplied by a nursery on a regular basis when they were about to bloom and would be taken away by the supplier when the blossoms were over.

Among a variety of flowers Ma liked best the lotus. In summertime high scaffoldings would be installed in the courtyard. These would be covered with rush mats on top so that the whole courtyard would be shaded. The four sides were further screened off with blinds that could be opened or rolled up to regulate the light level and temperature. A dozen or so potted lotuses would be placed in the center. When they bloomed, the flowers, as large as a bowl and in hues of red and white, vied with one another against a background of lush green leaves, some of which were big and round, while others—unfurled shoots— looked like needles. The subtle fragrance released by the blossoms pervaded the whole courtyard. As whiffs of light breeze passed by, the scent would even drift through the bamboo blinds and enter the living quarters.

A charming surrounding is usually created by a man with refined tastes. Man, in addition, often creates not only his surrounding but also a peaceful and harmonious atmosphere in daily life. Ma had an orderly family life. Whenever he was at work the whole courtyard would become especially quiet. Grown-ups would walk lightly and talk softly; children would also stop making noises. The silence would only be broken occasionally by cheery birdsongs. The tranquillity was conducive to Ma's immersion in artistic pursuits: he could paint and compose poems with a peaceful mind. As soon as he finished working, the whole family joined in a variety of amusements. They chatted and laughed together, listened to radio broadcasts, and sang Beijing operas. They epitomized a harmonious and happy family life charged with zest.

LAST WORK

The inside-painted bottle portrait of King Ibn Sa'ūd of the Kingdom of Saudi Arabia, made in 1932, was Ma Shaoxuan's last work.

Ordinarily calligraphers and painters continue to wield their brushes right up to old age. However, it is a different thing with inside-painted snuff bottles. As they involve painting and writing on the interior of the bottle, it is a miniature art that does not permit shaky hands and weakened vision. It is therefore extremely rare for an artist to be able to continue to do this kind of work right up to the time when he is in his fifties or sixties.

The last work that Ma did in response to a request was painted when he was sixty-six years old. In that year, Ma Songting, the very distinguished imam in the Muslim community in China, had planned to make a pilgrimage to the Kingdom of Saudi Arabia. In addition, he would be presented to King Sa'ūd at a ceremony celebrating the second anniversary of the incorporation of Mecca into the Kingdom of Saudi Arabia.[147] The imam was a great admirer of Ma Shaoxuan's art of painting inside snuff bottles. He requested from Ma a painted bottle to be used as a gift to the king. Pilgrimages to the Sacred Mosque in Mecca were undertaken only by Muslims of a certain standing to pay homage to the almighty Allah. In order to show support to imam Ma Songting's religious duty and, through the snuff bottle as a gift, to contribute his share in bolstering the friendship between the Muslim communities in China and Saudi Arabia, Ma Shaoxuan gladly accepted the imam's request. He completed the portrait with great care, handed it over to the imam and asked to be remembered in the worship of Allah.

At the end of February 1933 imam Ma Songting attended the celebratory ceremony. When he was presented to King Ibn Sa'ūd, he represented the Chinese Muslims to extend their regards to him. He also presented the king with a number of gifts. These the king accepted happily. In his conversation with the imam he expressed his gratitude and also concern over the condition of the Muslims in China.

On 25th May 1933 the imam returned to Beijing. Later he recounted to Ma Shaoxuan all that had transpired during his pilgrimage and the celebratory ceremony. He also gave Ma religious memorabilia which he had brought back from Mecca, among which was a very fine miniature volume of the Koran. The size of half a matchbox, it was even equipped with a tiny magnifying glass. In addition, there were also a bottle of spring water taken from the mosque and some preserved dates. All these were given to Ma in appreciation of his contribution. As well, they were given in the spirit of sharing gifts brought back from the pilgrimage.

More than fifty years later, in 1987 and the spring of 1990, the present writer twice talked to Ma Songting about this event. Though already in his nineties, Ma Songting still had a vivid recollection of it. He praised Ma Shaoxuan highly for his contribution toward strengthening the friendship between the Chinese and Saudi Arabian Muslims. He was also most impressed by Ma's miraculous art of inside-painting.

147. According to *Encyclopaedia Britannica*, King Ibn Sa'ūd entered the city of Mecca in 1925, at which time it was proclaimed part of the Kingdom of Saudi Arabia, and the capital of Makkah province. See vol. 11, p. 753. Instead of the second anniversary, as the author asserts, it should have been the eighth anniversary.

Perhaps it was more than just a coincidence. When Ma was eighteen years old, he saw a snuff bottle for the first time from a Hui minority relative and from then on crossed the threshold of the art of inside-painted snuff bottles. Since then, he had received moral support and real help from his family as well as from the brotherhood and sisterhood of the Muslim religion. Moreover, his last work was done in service of the Muslim, the pilgrimage, and the fortification of the friendship between the Muslims in China and Saudi Arabia. It was indeed meaningful for him to have chosen this work to conclude his career.

We look forward eagerly to seeing this snuff bottle.

In the summer of 1990 the present writer went to Saudi Arabia in the capacity of assistant-leader of a Chinese Muslim pilgrimage group. Although I tried every way to locate this precious work, it was to no avail. To this day, these questions are still very much on my mind: Does it still exist? Will I ever be able to see it?

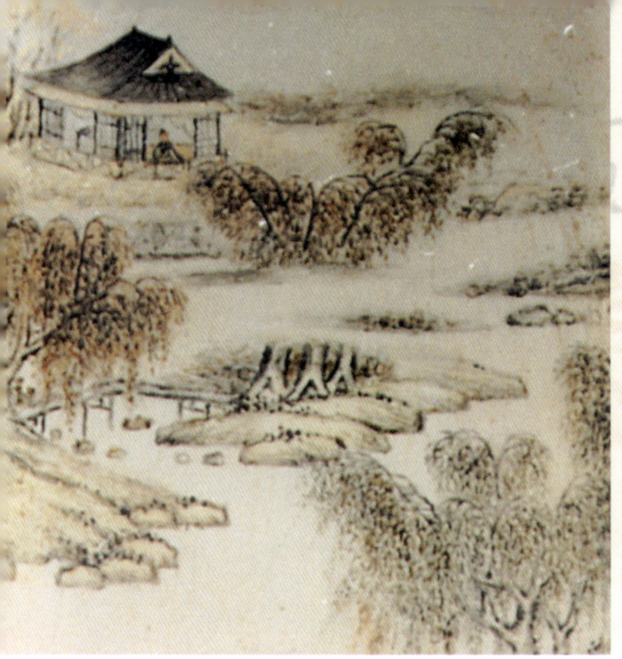

CHAPTER EIGHT

Life During Ma's Last Years

Ma Shaoxuan stopped painting snuff bottles after he had completed the bottle portrait of the king of Saudi Arabia in 1932. After more than forty years his spectacular artistic career came to an end.

This chapter discusses Ma's life during the six or seven years between 1932 and 1939. The time span can be divided into two periods: before the incident that happened at the Lugou Bridge in July 1937,[148] at which time he was still leading a rather comfortable life; and after the incident when Beijing came under Japanese occupation, at which time his life was beset with misery and worries and he soon died.

REUNION IN SHANGHAI

When Ma was in the process of painting the portrait of King Ibn Saʻūd, he already felt that there was something wrong with his eyes. Later, as the condition worsened, he went for a check-up. It was diagnosed that he had glaucoma. He received treatment and his condition improved somewhat. The oculist advised him not to strain his eyes any further, or else he would suffer serious consequences. Everyone in the family urged him to take a rest and so from then on he put aside his bamboo pens.

After he had stopped painting Ma's mind was full of contradictory feelings. On the one hand he was leading a leisurely life and feeling enormously light-hearted with the disappearance of the stress that accompanied a huge workload; yet on the other hand, he felt sad secretly. Indeed his whole life-long career has come to a full stop. He wondered, "Is old age analogous to the

148. The Lugou Bridge incident signified the beginning of a large-scale Japanese invasion in China. On 7th July 1937 a Japanese regiment practising in the vicinity of Wanping, located to the southwest of Beijing, demanded entry into Wanping in order to search for a missing soldier. On being refused entry, the Japanese fired cannon balls at the city of Wanping and the Lugou Bridge. This incident eventually led to the Chinese government making a formal declaration of war on Japan.

setting sun?" Moreover, he was not used to not doing anything the whole day long. He seated himself before his work-table, picked up a bamboo pen, and painted a few strokes. But his vision was not as good as before. His eyes became strained after a little while and he had to stop.

Mrs. Ma, seeing that he was bored, became very worried. She came up with an idea: let's take a trip to Shanghai.

Ma's eldest son worked in Shanghai. Many times he wrote to his parents inviting them to spend some time in Shanghai with him so he could have a chance to fulfill his duty as a son. In the past, Ma was busy painting and therefore unable to make the trip. Now would be the time to go. As soon as Mrs. Ma put this idea forward, Ma's spirits rose. He discussed the matter with his younger son, and it was decided that the whole family would go to Shanghai. In addition, Hangzhou would be included in their travel plan so that they could all see the scenic West Lake. Everyone was quite excited about this idea and preparations got underway.

On a splendid day in April 1933 eight members of the Ma family—Ma Shaoxuan and his wife, his younger son and daughter-in-law, three grandsons and one granddaughter—departed for Shanghai.

It was not easy for this group of people to make this extended trip because among them four were small children: the youngest, Zengqi, was only one hundred days old, while the other three were four (Zengshan), seven (Lihua), and nine (Zengrui) years old respectively. Although four adults looked after these four children, in actual fact, Ma Shaoxuan and his wife were both already in their late sixties. The situation was such that the old were too old and the young were too young. Only Ma's second son and daughter-in-law were in the prime of life. Yet, the daughter-in-law had to carry the baby all the time. So it was up to Ma's second son to run back and forth to look after the whole group. How true it was that people used to say, "Stay put at home a thousand days and everything will be fine; venture outside just once and you will be confronted with all sorts of difficulties." Whether getting on and off vehicles or having their meals here and there, they were forever worried about losing someone, or somebody getting hurt. Seeing one chaotic scene after another nerve-wrecking one, Ma Shaoxuan offered to help. He lifted his four-year-old second grandson on and off vehicles and boats. As he was getting on in years, it was quite tiring for him in spite of his good health. The most scary thing happened when they were about to cross the Huangpu River on a ferry. It was drizzling at the time. The road was slippery and there was a big crowd of people. Ma Shaoxuan had his grandson in his arms and, as he alighted from the pier to get on the ferry, he slipped. Letting out a cry, his body bent backward and he almost fell into the river. In this split second he still held fast to the child. Fortunately he was surrounded by people. A strong man beside him immediately grabbed him around the waist. More people lent a hand and both Ma and the child were steadied, their lives saved. Everyone in the family was so shocked that they all turned pale. With indescribable gratitude they thanked the surrounding people. Afterwards, whenever this incident was mentioned, everyone felt unnerved. All agreed that both Ma and his second grandson were extremely lucky.

In Shanghai they stayed in the home of Ma's eldest son on Avenue Joffre. Ma was happy to see this son well established and living a good life. With the whole family congregated in Shanghai, there were twelve members in three generations. Happily reunited, they were all very excited. In this way the boredom that troubled Ma after he had stopped painting was lifted.

A few days after their arrival, life began to return to a normal pace. Ma Shaoxuan sometimes went to the Bund to take a stroll. At other times his son might take his parents to watch Beijing opera or acrobatic shows. There were also times when the whole family would just sit down to chat and enjoy a cup of tea together. From time to time Ma's son would bring home delicious dishes and pastries to treat his aged parents. Occasionally Ma and his two sons would spend time together singing Beijing opera at home. The younger son was good at playing the *erhu* and he would sing the part of a lady to his own accompaniment. Ma would sing the part of a "painted face,"[149] while his eldest son would sing the part of a man. They had lots of fun engaging themselves in this pastime. In order to leave something for future memory, the eldest son suggested recording a Beijing opera sung

149. "Painted face," or *hualian*, is a male role that portrays a character with unusual personality traits or facial peculiarities. The actor wears heavy and dramatic make-up, sings with an exaggerated pitch, and acts with great flourish in order to emphasize the unusual characteristics of his role.

by them. After discussion they decided to select an act from "Twice Entering the Palace."[150] The elderly Ma would sing the part of Xu Yanzhao, his eldest son that of Yang Bo, and his younger son that of Imperial Concubine Li.[151] They then hired several musicians to play the melodies and practised a few times at home until they were happy with the result. The next thing they did was to book a time with a recording company. Both their performance and recording were very successful. The record became an invaluable souvenir of Ma's family reunion in Shanghai. After returning to Beijing, Ma played the record from time to time. While listening over and over to the beautiful operatic singing of this father-sons trio, Ma reminisced about the Shanghai trip. He felt happy as he let his thoughts take flight.

BOATING ON THE WEST LAKE

After spending some time in Shanghai, the eldest son accompanied his parents and younger brother on a trip to the West Lake in Hangzhou. Years ago Ma Shaoxuan had heard about this renowned scenic spot. Liu Yong (fl. ca. 1045), the lyric writer of the Song dynasty (960–1279), extolled it as an opulent place populated by a hundred thousand families.[152] Just imagine how pompous it had already been a thousand years ago! Now, what would it look like? And so it was with these endless ruminations that Ma started the journey to Hangzhou. When he got there, although Ma noticed that certain ancient sites had fallen into ruin, he was completely bowled over by the charming scenery of the West Lake and the customs of the Jiangnan region.

As they walked on the Bai Embankment, enjoying the magnificent colorful view, they could not help recalling the great Tang poet Bai Juyi's (772–846) famous poem "Strolling in the Spring along the Qiantang Lake." They tried to locate the Solitary Hill Monastery (Gu Shan Si) and the Pavilion of Master Jia (Jiagong Ting). They noted that the chirping of the birds was just the way Bai Juyi had described it in the poem:

150. "Twice Entering the Palace" (*Er jingong*) is a play about two loyal officials who tried to avert the vicious plan of Li Liang, father of the Imperial Concubine Li, in usurping the throne of the young heir-apparent of Emperor Muzong (r. 1567–1572) of the Ming dynasty.

151. Xu Yanzhao was the descendant of Xu Da, one of the officials who had contributed to the founding of the Ming dynasty. Yang Bo was a Vice-President of War.

152. These descriptive lines are quoted from a lyric by Liu Yong, written to the tune of *Wanghaichao* (Viewing the Tidal Waves). See *Yuezhang ji, xiajuan*, p. 3a.

The scenes described seemed to reappear right before their eyes, one after the other. In fact, anybody who happened to be there in early spring would arouse a sentiment that echoed that of the poet and would want to recite his poem. Ma and his two sons chanted as they strolled along, all the while savoring the philosophical ideas hidden therein and praising the beautiful West Lake for its unique blessings.

Not only did they stroll on the embankment but they also went boating on the lake. Sometimes the weather was fine; other times it was cloudy and rainy. The poet Su Shi once commented that the West Lake looked its best on sunny days, but would become more intriguing in rainy weather. The Mas began to understand Su's poetic line, "[It] looked equally becoming whether wearing light or heavy makeup," as they observed the extraordinarily lovely scenery.[154] The colors of the hills and the water changed completely in different weather conditions. They might appear to be bright and clear; they might also change to sombre and misty. Transient as they were, however, each of the views had its own charm. Visitors to the West Lake often felt that they have been transported to a fairyland.

In the span of a few days the Mas paid their respects to the Lingyin Si (Divine Retreat Monastery) and the Yuewang Miao (Shrine of Duke Yue).[155] Undeterred by the weather conditions and unmindful whether it was day or night, they covered all the points of interest that appealed to them. In addition to enjoying the scenery, they were deeply moved by the historical events that had taken place in this very spot thousands of years ago. In those bygone days successes and failures had been repeated over and over again. The legacy was so rich that it could provoke endless reminiscences, inspirations, and feelings.

153. These lines are quoted from Bai Juyi's poem entitled "Taking a Stroll along the Qiantang Lake [i.e., the West Lake] in Spring." See *Baishi changqing ji, juan* 20, p. 109.

154. This line is quoted from Su Shi's poem entitled "Drinking on the [West] Lake on a Day with Showers Following a Sunny Period." See Wang Wengao, ed. and annot., *Su Shi shiji*, vol. 2, p. 430.

155. Built in the first year of the Xianhe period (326) of the Eastern Jin dynasaty, the Lingyan Si is not only the oldest and biggest monastery in the West Lake area but also counts among the most important monasteries in China. The Yuewang Miao, formerly known under the name of Baozhong Si (Shrine Honoring a Loyal Official), was built in the second year of the Longxing period (1164) to commemorate the Southern Song general, Yue Fei (1103–1142), who had been unjustly condemned to death for treason by the pacification faction in order to stop him from putting up a strong force resisting the invading Jin Tartars.

The Mas fell in love with the West Lake after they had toured it. However, they felt they had missed the elegant images of "the *guihua* (*Osmanthus fragrans*) which bloomed in the autumn and the patches of lotuses that extended ten *li*," and began to want to stay there longer.[156] They also came to understand why Bai Juyi was unwilling to leave the West Lake when he confessed in his poem: "[I] could not bear to part with Hangzhou, / Partly because [I] wanted to stay on this very lake."[157] How charming and alluring the West Lake was!

With a sigh, Ma Shaoxuan told his sons thus: "I came too late to the West Lake. If I had been able to come earlier, a lot more views of this lake would have been painted inside my bottles."

The weather became quite warm after the Mas had returned to Shanghai. A long-time resident of Beijing, Ma Shaoxuan found the muggy weather extremely unbearable. He soon took the whole group of travellers back to Beijing.

As soon as they arrived home and resumed their daily routines, they felt just fine. From then on, Ma began to get used to leading a leisurely life. He never left Beijing again.

LONGING SENTIMENTS

In his old age Ma Shaoxuan thought of his parents even more often than before. Every year, on the anniversary of the death of his father and mother, which took place in April and August respectively, he would visit the Ma clan's cemetery and pay his respects.

The Ma clan's cemetery is located at Sanlihe in the western suburbs of Beijing. It has three sections—old, middle, and new—in which were buried all members of the Ma clan ever since they had emigrated to Beijing. Nowadays, because of the availability of different means of transportation, one is hardly aware of the distance between Ox Street and Sanlihe, which is the same as the east side of the Yuyuantan (Jade Pool) Garden. Yet, fifty or sixty years ago, it was quite a different thing. In those days there was no public transportation service in this area. Sanlihe was a desolate farming village. Scattered about here and there were plots of cultivated land interspersed with large and small grave mounds criss-crossed by deeply-rutted mud paths. Whether rain

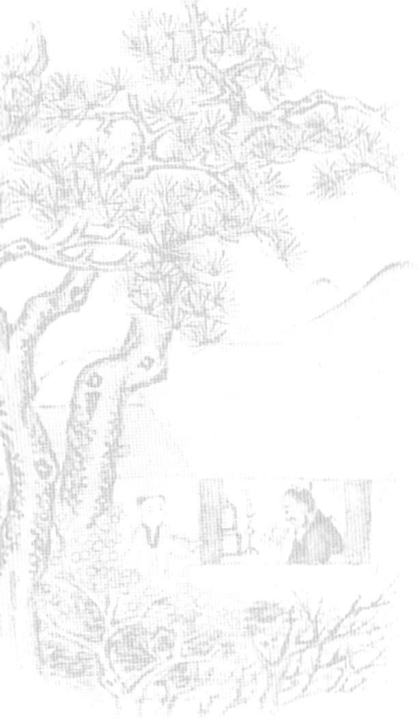

156. These phrases are also quoted from Liu Yong's lyric written to the tune of *Wanghaichao*. See *Yuezhang ji, xiajuan* p. 3b.

157. These are the last two lines from Bai Juyi's "A Poem Composed on the [West] Lake." See *Baishi changqing ji, juan* 53, p. 291.

or shine, it was quite taxing to walk on them. If one wanted to avoid treading on them, the only other alternative would be walking on the dikes. Therefore, a visit to the cemetery meant a long and strenuous trip.

Each year, as soon as spring arrived, Ma started to plan for a visit to the cemetery. For him, this was a very important thing, not just because he wanted to remember his forebears but also because he wanted to pass on to his descendants the notions of respect and remembrance one should cherish for one's ancestors. This was why he always took the whole family along if it was at all possible. His second son always went; so did the grandsons who could walk on their own. Old Mrs. Ma, however, joined them only infrequently. They would hire a few rickshaws. Yet these vehicles could only get them to the vicinity of the mosque at Sanlihe. After arriving, one of them would go to the mosque to get the imam, while the rest would follow the undulating dikes that wound about which would bring them to the graves after twenty or so minutes' walk. There, they would light incense sticks and kneel down on the grass to listen to the imam reciting verses from the Koran. In the new section were buried Ma Shaoxuan's grandparents, parents, and other relatives. At this time, Ma would half kneel and half sit on his heels, and with a most solemn and respectful heart, reminisced about the lives of his forebears, also praying to Allah on their behalf for forgiveness and happiness in heaven. Ma's son and grandsons would kneel behind him and do exactly what he did. Each time Ma visited the cemetery, he went with a heavy heart. He recalled the injunctions his father had given him and his parents' love for him. He also thought of himself and his offspring. . .

Before the Japanese occupation of Beijing, the Ma family undertook the cemetery visit year after year. This custom was changed after the occupation. Ma's second son took over the responsibility and went as his proxy.

DEATH

The Lugou Bridge incident took place on 7th July 1937. This led to the Japanese occupying Beijing. From then on denizens of Beijing entered a dark period: they were afflicted body and mind by the invaders. Under such circumstances, Ma Shaoxuan was constantly depressed. Within two years, he passed away in the autumn of 1939, at the age of seventy-three.

From childhood Ma was instilled with Confucian philosophy and Islamic teachings. A man of moral integrity, he was both responsible and strong-willed. When he was still a child and started to learn to write, his father already advised him that it would be all right to choose as his model any one of the masters like Zhong You, Wang Xizhi, Yan Zhenqing, Liu Gongquan, and Ouyang Xun, but that he should never emulate Zhao Mengfu. Ma kept this admonition in his mind throughout his life. He even conveyed the message to his progeny. Among the celebrated calligraphers who flourished during the Ming and Qing periods Ma was fond of Fu Shan, mainly on the ground that Fu had an upright and loyal character. In his autobiographical poem he had alluded to Fu who, as a remnant of the Ming dynasty, had adamantly refused to serve the new Manchu government, preferring instead to practise medicine for a living. In contrast, although Zhao Mengfu was a royal descendant of the Song dynasty, he served under the Mongol-ruled Yuan dynasty, for which conduct he had been despised ever since. This concept of national pride was deeply ingrained in Ma's heart.

At the time when Beijing was under Japanese occupation, other areas too suffered the same fate. The Chinese as a race were in great danger. Ma was therefore full of anxiety. Life under the aggressive invaders became more and more intolerable as all kinds of conflicts flared up.

> *Ominous clouds hung low,*
> *Rifles and swords pressed forward,*
> *The sky was about to collapse,*
> *The country was in dire straits.*
> *Where [could one find] a miracle whip?*
> *Who could fortify the strength of the nation?*
> *This hoary old man,*
> *Worried and depressed,*
> *How could he have fended for himself?*

Consumed by depression and anger, Ma fell sick suddenly. Though a healthy old man, he was never able to recover. His funeral was conducted in accordance with Islamic practices. It was a sorrowful yet dignified event in spite of the fact that it happened at the time of the Japanese occupation. Friends and relatives in Beijing were shocked by the news of Ma's sudden passing. All were saddened at the loss of this master of inside-painted snuff bottles. They attended the embalmment ceremony and the funeral. So numerous were the people that made up the funerary procession that many streets were blocked. Ma was buried in the clan cemetery at Sanlihe.

OLD MRS. MA

In looking back at the life of Ma Shaoxuan, a respectable elderly figure must be mentioned. That is Ma's wife, née Wang. She was good-natured, virtuous, sagacious, and generous to others. Supporting each other, she and Ma completed their journeys in life together. With infinite patience, she attended to Ma's daily needs and his artistic career. Without her, Ma could not have achieved such a phenomenal success. The following example, though small, is illuminating. Prior to painting the snuff bottles, the interior surfaces of each of them required to be treated. This task was at first undertaken by Mrs. Ma alone but later, after she had taught her second daughter-in-law, by both of them. Whenever they could snatch a moment they would fill a bottle with steel balls and, holding it in one hand, shake it back and forth steadily until the surfaces became evenly etched. It was only then that the ink and pigments could adhere and Ma could start to paint. Every piece in Ma's oeuvre therefore also embodied the labor of his family members, especially that of Mrs. Ma.

Mrs. Ma was brave and resolute. Whenever difficult situations arose she was always the first one to take charge. Protecting her family's safety and ensuring the proper upbringing of her children and grandchildren were her main concerns. As an example, on one autumn night when it was pouring rain, the gable wall in the inner room of the eastern chamber collapsed. Trapped inside were her two grandsons, fast asleep. Sensing that they might be in danger, Mrs. Ma rushed to the room to take them out single-handedly.

Another time, black smoke issued from the western chamber and a fire was imminent. Heedless of her own safety, Mrs. Ma dashed inside, found a smoldering old quilt cover, and quickly removed it. The cover lit up as soon as it was dragged outside. However, the fire was put out instantly.

Mrs. Ma was a devout Muslim. She obeyed strictly all religious commands. She was sincere, honest, and bounteous to those in distress. Every Friday, the day for special congregational prayers, she would put two packets of small change at the front entrance early in the morning. If any needy Hui compatriots came by to ask for help, she would take money from these packets to give to them. She did this every week. Never once did she stop.

She observed fasting strictly. As long as she was not sick, she would observe fasting for a whole month. Fasting is one of the Five Pillars of Islam.[158] Each year, during the month of Ramadan, she would neither eat nor drink in the daytime.[159] Only after sunset would she break her fast. At this time of the year a solemn air prevailed over the vicinity of Ox Street. At midnight of each day someone would go about the street sounding a watchman's rattle to summon people to partake of a meal, after which fasting would begin before sunrise. Then, after having endured a whole day without food, children would run over to the mosque as sunset approached to check out the red lamp mounted high up on the wall—the signal that marked the end of the fast. As soon as the lamp was lit, they would race back home, shouting, "The red lamp is on! The red lamp is on!" This would mean that the fasting was over for that day. Mrs. Ma would then share with her family a tasty meal which she had prepared. When the month of Ramadan came to an end, Mrs. Ma would celebrate by treating the family with an especially delicious meal which would include her specialty, a deep-fried donut called *youxiang*.

In her life as the wife of Ma Shaoxuan, Mrs. Ma shared with her husband all the joys and sorrows. She passed away in the sixth month of the lunar calendar, about a year or so after the death of her husband.

158. The Five Pillars of Islam are the profession of faith, prayer, the zakat—an obligatory tax, fasting, and the hajj—a pilgrimage to Mecca taken at least once in a lifetime.

159. Ramadan takes place in the ninth month of the Muslim lunar calendar.

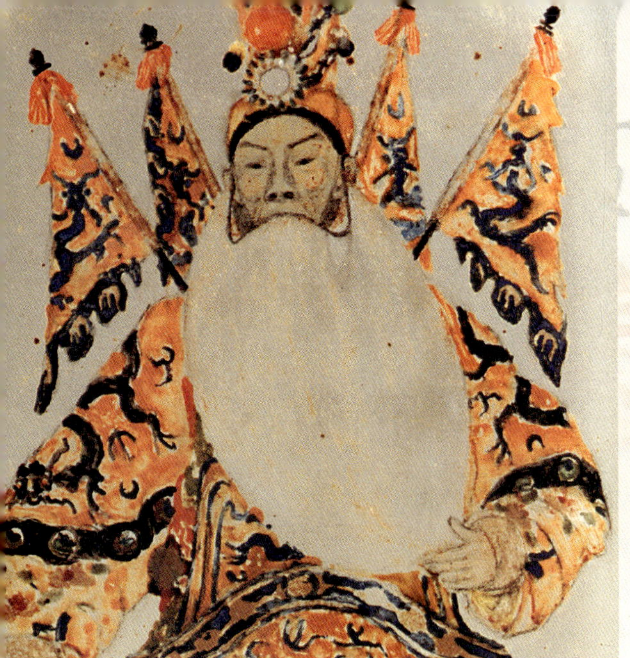

CHAPTER NINE
Ma's Roles and Contributions

Ma Shaoxuan left this world at the age of seventy-three, an all too brief span of life. Nothwithstanding, he had made the following contribution: during his lifetime he steadfastly put his heart and soul into the production of magnificent inside-painted snuff bottles. These works of art were not only sought after and treasured by his compatriots in China but also won worldwide esteem. Anyone who has a chance to see his works would marvel and extoll him unreservedly. This phenomenon is not unique to the present time. In the future, when people have an opportunity to enter the wonderful world opened up by him inside the snuff bottle, they will surely also heap praises on him.

Anyone who, at the end of his sojourn in this world, is able to leave his creations with a good name and inspire fond memories from future generations, his soul in heaven must be smiling with contentment!

Now, what we need to investigate are: what roles did Ma play and what contributions did he make in terms of the historical development of the inside-painted snuff bottle?

Before embarking on these objectives, however, we need to review the historical development of the snuff bottle, and in particular, that of the inside-painted snuff bottle. It is only when Ma is placed in the proper context that his role and contributions can be truly appreciated.

FROM THE SNUFF BOTTLE TO THE
INSIDE-PAINTED BOTTLE

With certain things, changes occur in quite an amusing way in their historical development. Nowadays people think it rather strange that at one time their forebears used the nose to inhale tobacco. Yet, it was not so long ago that in some places nearly all grown-ups, both men and women, took snuff. Today, we all know that smoking is harmful to our health and persuade smokers to quit; but not long ago people used to regard tobacco as a medication.

Snuff is a powder obtained by crushing the tobacco leaves, with aromatic ingredients added. When inhaled through the nostrils, it excites the senses and causes the taker to sneeze. It is also addictive.

Where did tobacco come from and when was it brought to China? It is believed that South America was the region where tobacco was first cultivated. It was after Columbus (1451–1506) had reached South America that he learned about the Indians' habit of snuff-taking. Afterwards, tobacco and the habit of snuff-taking spread to other parts of the world. The fad took Europe and Asia by storm. In Zhao Zhiqian's (1829–1884) *Yonglu xianjie*, it is recorded that "Matteo Ricci [1552–1610] arrived in China by sea in the ninth year of the Wanli period [1581]. He made his entry by way of Guangdong province. Not long after he went to Beijing to present gifts [to the emperor. It was at that time that tobacco] was first introduced into China."[160] Further on, Zhao also added that "it was toward the end of the Wanli period that a man surnamed Ma, a native of the area where the Zhang River and the Quan River converged, started a tobacco business."[161] It should be noted that Emperor Shenzong (r. 1573–1620) was on the throne for forty-eight years. The last year of the Wanli period was equivalent to 1620, about 130 years after Columbus had landed in South America.

China is a vast country. During the Ming dynasty communications with foreign countries were frequent and far reaching. There existed all sorts of possibilities for tobacco and its usage to be transmitted to China, whether by sea or by land, and whether from countries situated to the northeast or the south of

160. Zhao Zhiqian, *Yonglu xianjie*, p. 201. Zhao's epilogue was dated to the sixth year of the Guangxu period (1880). Yonglu is the name given to the god of the nose. The source of the term *xianjie* can be traced back to the Grand Historian Sima Qian who once remarked that when certain things lacked records, it would be the duty of the scholars to spend their spare time to look into these things and chronicle them. Heeding this ancient advice, this was exactly what Zhao Zhiqian did when he became aware of the growing popularity of the snuff bottle. For the English translation of Zhao's work, see Richard John Lynn, "Researches Done during Spare Time into the Realm of Yong Lu, God of the Nose: The *Yonglu Xianjie* of Zhao Zhiqian," *Journal of the International Chinese Snuff Bottle Society*, Autumn 1991, pp. 5–26.

161. Zhao Zhiqian, *Yonglu xianjie*, p. 203.

China. Matteo Ricci's gift presentation therefore, should not be regarded as the only way by which the Chinese came into contact with it. Once introduced, tobacco cultivation spread quickly. When the early Qing scholar, Wang Shizhen (1634–1711), a *jinshi* in the fifteenth year of the Shunzhi period (1658), wrote his *Xiangzu biji* (Jottings [Made in a Studio with] Orchids [Growing outside]), he mentioned that tobacco cultivation was already "all over the place."[162]

Both bottles and boxes have been used for storing snuff. However, the most suitable kind would be ones with large bodies and small mouths. Easy to carry would be another consideration. For this reason, there has always been a demand for dainty works produced with great workmanship. In the beginning the American Indians used animal bones, horns, and skins to make boxes or pouches. When the habit of snuffing was transmitted to Europe and certain monarchs became quite fond of it, much finer snuff boxes and bottles were manufactured. After the snuff habit was introduced to China, snuff bottles went through an extraordinary phase of development. As several Qing-dynasty emperors were exceedingly fond of the bottles and there was a large percentage of snuff-takers among the population, there was a great demand for snuff bottles. In addition, the Chinese have for centuries engaged themselves in the production of arts and crafts and during the course of time have acquired superb technical skills. As a result, they have used all kinds of materials and all sorts of techniques to produce the most diverse and beautiful snuff bottles to charm the world. Some extremely exquisite examples have been deemed to be rare treasures.

Over a period of more than two hundred years, the ten Qing-dynasty emperors not only frequently bestowed snuff bottles on their officials as esteemed gifts but also, from time to time, sent them along with other gift items to foreign emissaries and monarchs. The number of bottles used for these purposes was so great that according to Zhao Zhiqian, it was "impossible to have a full record."[163]

In addition, government officials of all ranks, nobles and successful merchants all liked to flaunt their wealth and status by using snuff bottles in their possession as indicators of their social

162. Wang Shizhen, *Xiangzu biji, juan* 3, p. 1b.

163. Zhao Zhiqian, *Yonglu xianjie*, p. 202.

standing. For this reason, they were constantly after bottles having new shapes and decorations, made from expensive or top-quality materials, and executed with superb workmanship.

Since the snuff bottle was so highly esteemed by the emperor as well as his subjects, it naturally became more and more valuable. Every imaginable artistic skill was lavished on its production. One innovative idea was put to the test after another in order to outdo the latest invention. There were bottles made of glass, jade, hardstones, agate, ivory, carved lacquer and cloisonné. They vied with one another in rarity and intricacy. Viewed individually however, they stood as gleaming beauties.

One thing should be pointed out, and that is no matter how the production methods have been improved upon, the bottles remained small—no bigger than what could be comfortably held in the hand. As to the mouths of the bottles, their sizes also tended to get smaller and smaller. At first, some bottles' diameters exceeded 0.4 cm. Later on, a lot were a good deal smaller. Such changes were made to ensure that the snuff did not lose its aroma through exposure to the air, thus better preserving its flavor.

As with everything, there is a limit to its development. The same is true with that of the snuff bottle. When all the new ideas of embellishment had been exhausted and a glut on the market had been reached, people tried to seek new ways to break through the conventional pattern in order to discover a turning point. It was at this stalemate stage that the inside-painted bottle was born. It permitted the depiction of a totally new realm inside the bottle through a tiny mouth. While it belonged to the snuff bottle family, in many respects, however, it departed from it. In the past, all snuff bottles were made to hold snuff and they were valued for this function. Yet, it is a different thing with the inside-painted bottle, for the main criterion for judging its value was based on the artistic quality of the painting and calligraphy executed inside the bottle. With a marvelous piece of work, who would want to put snuff in it? As a result, the inside-painted bottle no longer functioned as a container. From then on it was esteemed solely as a work of art having its own merits.

THE BEGINNING

The inside-painted bottle continued the bloodline of the Chinese handicraft profession and the traditions of painting and calligraphy. It was a new baby in the historical development of the snuff bottle, also a new invention in the history of the manufacture of the snuff bottle.

Who was the genius responsible for the invention of the inside-painted bottle? Who was that honorable ancestor who had given birth to this lovely baby? Although there exist all sorts of hypotheses and stories, this question remains to be investigated.

When did the inside-painted bottle first come into use? This also needs to be looked into. Several assertions prevail. According to one, it made its appearance during the Qianlong and Jiaqing periods. In other words, since the Qianlong period ended in 1795 and the Jiaqing period began in 1796, the inside-painted bottle first made its appearance in the late eighteenth century. Other people, however, believed that the time should have been a little later. Yet, how much later? Again opinions differ.

In 1884, when Ma Shaoxuan was eighteen years old, he had already seen inside-painted bottles. Attracted by the paintings depicted on them, he then and there decided to make producing similar works his life-long career. The importance of this fact cannot be underestimated.

Presently based on authenticated inside-painted bottles datable to the end of the nineteenth century, we could make the following assumptions: without scores of years for fermentation and development no bottle could have reached that level of quality; neither would it have been possible for so many artists to be engaged in inside-painting, nor would it have been possible for several among them to reach the status of a star.

Owing to insubstantial artifacts and information, if today we were to make a rough estimate of the beginning date of the inside-painted bottle, we should trace back several scores of years from the 1880s, and take the period spanning the late eighteenth century to the beginning of the nineteenth century as a more reasonable date. However, this assumption still awaits study for confirmation.

Since it is quite difficult to paint inside a glass bottle, it is understandable that the paintings and calligraphy embellishing works executed in the initial stage must have been relatively coarse. Before this "ugly duckling" was able to develop full-fledged plumes, its ungainly mien did not attract much attention. This is why nowdays very few pieces of information about it are available. Notwithstanding this fact, to show our deepest respect for the pioneers who opened up this area, we should emphasize in our writing their life histories and contributions to the historical development of the inside-painted bottle.

THE CALL OF HISTORY

In his *Yonglu xianjie* Zhao Zhiqian did not once mention the inside-painted bottle. Leaving aside the reason for this, this fact alone explains a social phenomenon: up to 1880, the inside-painted bottle did not exert much influence in the society of the capital. In other words, except for the few people who did inside-painting or who were art dealers, its influence was rather minimal.

Yet, when Ma Shaoxuan painted a portrait of Huang Zhong at the end of the last century, a matter of twenty years later, his work swept the capital off its feet. That such a big change could have occurred within a period of twenty years was of course due to Ma's successful inside-painting skills, the result of which not only hastened the pace of development of this particular genre but also garnered a positive response from society. Yet, these were not the only reasons. Underneath there were far-reaching historical considerations.

From its birth to its becoming the craze of the denizens of the capital, how many phases did the inside-painted bottle go through? This is a question that needs further research. However, by the time Ma Shaoxuan flourished, it is certain that the founding period must have been over. After several generations of painters searching for and introducing new techniques, a set of methods for doing artwork inside the bottle was now in place. The works produced, however, were not very fine; they were still artistically immature, lacking characteristics that could bowl people over. Nevertheless history had reached a turning point.

Several scores of years of hard work pumped in by the forerunners had paved the road to allow the new generation to innovate and push the art of inside-painting to a new height!

In this historical context, among the group of artists engaged in inside-painting emerging around the same time as Ma Shaoxuan were several masters with outstanding skills. They were Zhou Leyuan, Ding Erzhong and Ye Zhongsan (ca. 1868–1945).[164] All played important roles in history; all made significant contributions. In a matter of ten years or so, these superstars outshone their numerous colleagues in the field. This phenomenon was by no means a coincidence. It was a full-scale explosion of the energy accumulated bit by bit over a span of scores of years or even longer that preceded this period. Just like the growing of trees, it was the first bountiful harvest reaped from the forerunners' hard work involving seed-planting, caring for the saplings, watering and other chores. That the harvest was manifested in these superstars was again by no means a coincidence, for each had contributed his own share. Without these people, there would not have been a harvest. In view of this, their contributions cannot be underestimated.

CONTRIBUTIONS

Relying on their excellent command of technical skills, these masters created large quantities of inside-painted bottles. Their works embodied different styles and brushwork and were widely acclaimed for their artistic merits. Generally speaking, in the fifty years spanning the 1880s up to the 1930s, together with other inside-painted bottle artists, these masters forged ahead to make this period a time for the art of inside-painting to make progress by leaps and bounds.

In the history of this specialized profession what role did Ma Shaoxuan play and what position did he occupy? The following are some of the comments made by scholars and critics from China as well as overseas.

Zhao Ruzhen, the renowned art critic who published *Guwan zhinan xubian* (Handbook of Chinese Antiquity, Supplementary Volume) in 1943, had devoted Chapters 19 and 20 to the

164. See Bob C. Stevens, *The Collector's Book of Snuff Bottles* for information on these three inside-painted snuff bottle artists: Zhou Leyuan, pp. 249-250; Ding Erzhong, pp. 252-253; and Ye Zhongsan, pp. 253–255.

discussion of snuff and snuff bottles. Included in the text are these comments about the inside-painted bottle and Ma Shaoxuan:

> *Painting inside the bottle was invented towards the end of the Qing dynasty. The bottles used were either made of glass or white crystal. It is said that a specially designed pen with a bent tip would be needed to pass through the mouth of the bottle in order to write and paint. Best known among those who produced wonderful works were Ma Shaoxuan and Zhou Leyuan. Their calligraphic styles were derived from esteemed models. Their paintings too perpetuated the styles of various schools. So splendid were their creations that even if they were executed [in the normal manner] on the outside of the bottles they would stand as marvelous pieces of work. Now since they were executed on the reverse inside face and yet the quality achieved was so exquisite, surely such a feat must be described as a manifestation of supernatural workmanship.*[165]

Jin Shoushen was an ethnologist. During the 1930s and 1940s he published numerous articles on customs that prevailed in Beijing in a column entitled *Beijing tong* (Beijing Expert) in *Liyan huakan* (Establishing One's Words Pictorial). In 1989 these were collected by Beijing Publishing Company and reprinted in a book called *Lao Beijing de shenghuo* (Life in Old Beijing). In it are a few words about the inside-painted bottle:

> *There was nothing very attractive about the crystal bottle other than its clear and sparkling qualities. However, later when people were able to paint and inscribe compositions inside and called it an "inside-painted bottle," this special type of bottle gained an exalted status. The most celebrated artist was Ma Shaoxuan.*[166]

Bob C. Stevens, an American snuff bottle expert who published *The Collector's Book of Snuff Bottles* had this to say in Chapter 9 where the inside-painted bottles are discussed:

165. Zhao Ruzhen, *Guwan zhinan xubian*, Ch. 20, p. 13.

166. Jin Shoushen, *Lao Beijing de shenghuo*, p. 226.

For me, Ma Shao-hsüan is the Picasso of inside-painted bottle artists. I must add quickly that while Picasso's style is not as agreeable to my own taste as is that of Ma Shao-hsüan, their success, popularity, and productivity during the course of their lives make the two men somewhat comparable.[167]

Other critics also extolled Ma highly. They all concurred that Ma had played an outstanding role in this flourishing period; he was undoubtedly the leader.

In assessing the contributions Ma made during the course of development of the inside-painted bottle, at least three facts must be taken into account. These are:

1. Inside-painted portraits and inside-written calligraphy were Ma's forte. They were unique expressions of his individual artistic qualities and were representative of the highest level of excellence among works of similar nature produced by his contemporaries. His skills in these two areas had surpassed traditional techniques, thereby pushing these special art forms to new heights. Immensely creative, he had broadened the subjects to be illustrated on the bottles.

   Yang Boda, the former Deputy Director of the Palace Museum in Beijing, says in the preface he wrote for *A New Look of Chinese Inside Painted Snuff Bottles*:

   Of all the snuff bottles in the late Qing dynasty, the most important achievement was the development of inside-painted snuff bottles, especially the portrait snuff bottle. Many noblemen and distinguished personages desired to have their portraits made to order. This formed the last climax of snuff bottle art during the Qing dynasty and was a shining page in the history of snuff bottle techniques which was only 200 to 300 years old.[168]

   Ma Shaoxuan was of course not the only inside-painted portrait artist included on that glorious page; but he was certainly the chief representative.

2. In the historical development of the inside-painted bottle Ma was the first person to make known this art form on the international arts and crafts scene; he was also the first one to

167. Bob C. Stevens, *The Collector's Book of Snuff Bottles*, p. 250.

168. See J.H. Leung, *A New Look of Chinese Inside Painted Snuff Bottles*, p. 1.

win an important international award. In 1915 he submitted a number of inside-painted bottles to the Panama-Pacific International Exposition held in the United States and won high-ranking recognition. The honor of winning a gold medal for the inside-painted bottle for the first time in history belonged to Ma. Through his brilliant performance this art form stood side by side with other arts and crafts of the world. In this sense he made a major contribution.

3. In the historical development of the inside-painted bottle Ma and his colleagues successfully played their parts as perpetuators and innovators. They inherited the achievements of the vanguards of the founding period and pushed these a step forward, leaving behind a wealth of experience in artistic creation, large quantities of exquisite works which inspired followers to develop further this unique branch of Chinese art with confidence, a sense of honor, and a sense of responsibility. We may imagine that without that climax in the inside-painted technique, how boring it would be for us to talk about inside-painted bottles and how insignificant their influence would be for the posterity. We may also imagine that if, in the future, another climax emerges in the art of inside-painting, how people will still cherish the precious inspiration they obtain from the first climax.

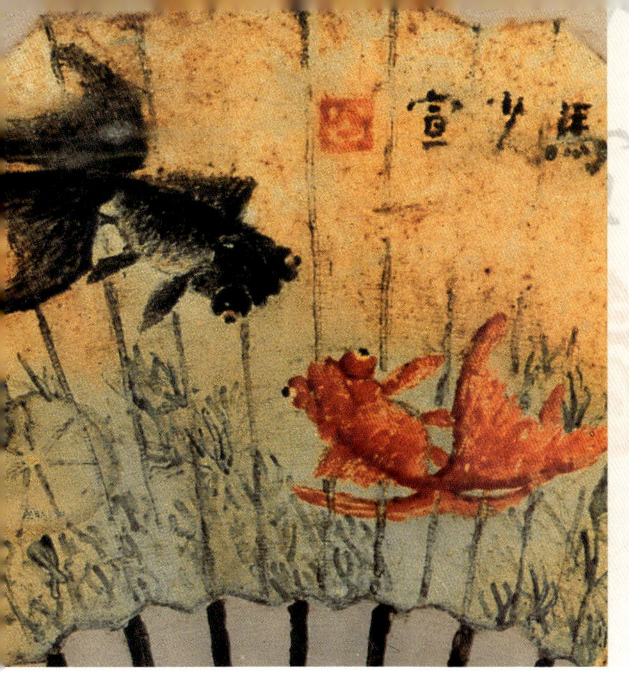

CHAPTER TEN

Spiritual Wealth

Ma Shaoxuan has passed away. His soul entered heaven more than fifty years ago when he left us. Yet, it seems that he has not departed, for he bequeathed to us many, many things which remind us of him all the time. It is not only because the numerous inside-painted bottles that he left behind continue to shine but also because he passed on to us a very beneficial legacy of spiritual wealth. His life was a book about a success story. If we read this book carefully, we will surely obtain nourishment and benefit from it.

Therefore, it would appear that an investigation into the substance and significance of Ma's legacy of spiritual wealth would be a subject of originality and interest. However, as with any book, reactions to it might vary from one person to the other. Here, the present writer would like to offer three observations.

NATURAL ENDOWMENTS PLUS DILIGENCE

On the whole achievers are very talented people. However, not all talented people are necessarily achievers. Ma Shaoxuan was blessed with these natural dispositions: an intelligent mind, dexterous hands, sharp observation, excellent memory and comprehension. Yet, good natural endowments are only inborn assets. They may not have decisive functions. The critical point depends on whether the natural endowments are permitted to develop fully. That Ma Shaoxuan was able to make good use of his natural endowments was because he had chosen painting inside the snuff bottle as his career, one that allowed him to do so.

Painting inside the snuff bottle is a highly skilled profession that requires a person with great intelligence and superb technical skills to work solely on his own. It is one of the specialized professions that lets gifted people utilize their talents fully. Ma made the right choice when he decided to undertake this vocation as his life-long career as it suited his personality, his interest and his specialty. However, even so, it did not guarantee his success. Of more importance was his untiring spirit of learning for self-improvement. Passionately in love with his chosen profession, he unrelentingly honed his skills to the point where he became oblivious to things that happened around him. It was after he had steadfastly overcome every conceivable difficulty that he finally embarked on the road to success.

In daily life we all have to face different kinds of obstacles. For example, money is a very tempting thing. We cannot do without it. Yet, we should not think too highly of it because many other things are far more important.

During the period spanning the late Qing dynasty and the early Republic the common people were destitute. As a result, the art market was sluggish. An ordinary inside-painted bottle artist might have to work for several days in order to produce a bottle. Yet, what it sold for was so minimal that he would find it difficult to feed his family. In the beginning years of his career Ma had hardly any income. It was the passion he had for his work that kept him going with an unflinching mind. Later, only after he had considerably polished his skills was he able to make a moderate living out of his production. His earning did not increase vastly until he had reached his forties and established a name. Without the hard work he had put in in his early years, he would not have been able to enjoy the sweetness of the fruit of his labor later in his life. Yet, if he had not been passionately in love with the art of inside-painting, he would not have been able to endure the hardship that he had to go through.

Ma loved the art of inside-painting fervently. From the time when he was a young man he already regarded it as a part of his life, not a means to make money. While it holds true that all living souls have to have some income to survive, it is also true that without any assurance of a livelihood, it would be impossible for anyone to dedicate his life to the creation of art. However, for Ma, the desire to devote himself to artistic creation took priority over the consideration of providing for his family. In any case, if a person paints for the sake of supporting his family, he will probably never produce anything of high quality. This has been a proven fact. Lü Fengzi (1885–1959), an art educator, includes a poem that says the same thing in his *Zhongguo huafa yanjiu* (A Study of Chinese Painting Methods):

> *We should not paint with the intent to*
> *   make profits.*
> *Before beginning to paint we should forget*
> *   ourselves.*
> *Having forgotten ourselves, we would be able to*
> *   become one with the objects [we want to depict].*
> *[It is only then that] we will understand why they*
> *   look the way they are.*[169]

Ma regarded the art of inside-painting with great respect. He would never produce a sloppy work. Even after he had become famous and orders kept pouring in, he still did each bottle with concentration and meticulous care. If he happened to be particularly busy, he would rather decline taking in new orders than to accommodate them by doing his work hastily. For him, art and the way one carried oneself were far more important than money.

Ma loved the art of inside-painting passionately. For him, painting and doing calligraphy inside bottles was hard work, but he thoroughly enjoyed these artistic endeavors. That is why he could devote his whole life to this pursuit. Over a period of forty to fifty years he worked at it with resolution, never succumbing to the temptation of monetary gain or the fear of leading a life of deprivation. Although he could also do painting and calligraphy on paper, he never sold such works. True to his chosen profession, throughout his life he preferred to make a living out of doing artwork inside a bottle.

Anyone who spends his whole life doing just one thing should be able to achieve something. This is similar to water dripping from the eaves. If it hits the same spot, in time it will bore a hole in the ground. One of the shortcomings of

169. Lü Fengzi, *Zhongguo huafa yanjiu*, p. 21.

humankind is the lack of persistence. A person who gets training in one skill one day and another skill another day will never be good at anything. Likewise, if fate ordains a person to engage himself in one type of work one day and another type of work another day, throughout his life he will always be a new hand. If, however, a person abides by a work requiring specialized skill and spends his whole life acquiring proficiency in it, even if he is not particularly gifted or if he has to cope with unfavorable situations, he is likely to attain some achievement. Seen in this light, how much more would a person be able to achieve if he happened to be blessed with excellent natural dispositions and favorable surroundings!

The story of Ma Shaoxuan tells us that after choosing a profession that allows him to fully utilize his forte, if a gifted person concentrates his energy on developing a passion for it, studies hard at it, and overcomes all the difficulties inherent with it, he will eventually win recognition. This is one aspect of his success that is worth noting.

FOUNDATION AND TRAINING

If we say a hardworking person with natural endowments is likely to succeed, in the field of inside-painted snuff bottles there is another consideration to be desired: the practitioner must start at a very young age. If a person has already reached mid-life and wants to start to learn the technique of inside-painting, even though he is talented and diligent, it will be hard for him to attain outstanding achievements. This is because human life is limited. Although the upper age limit for an inside-painted bottle artist varies from one person to another, on the whole a person would begin to encounter difficulty in his fifties. Since it takes a long time to polish the skills of inside-painting and the uppermost age limit is fixed, it means that one would have to push the starting point forward in order to lengthen this period of improvement. It is only by beginning at an early age that one can hope to achieve excellence by the time he reaches forty or fifty years of age.

What does early training mean? It entails a child receiving primary school education be given instruction in traditional

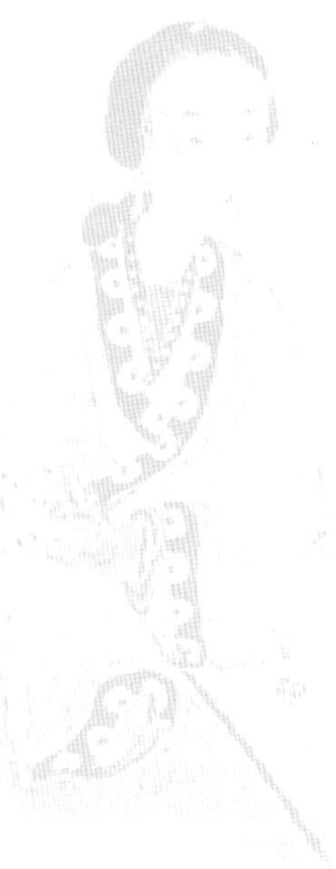

painting and calligraphy at the same time in order to build up a sound foundation. Ma Shaoxuan's father recognized Ma's potential at a very early stage. In addition to sending him to school, he personally taught the young Ma painting and calligraphy. Before Ma reached the age of eighteen, he was already equipped with a vast literary knowledge and had mastered the basic techniques of painting and calligraphy. In other words, he had already established a solid foundation for elevating the literary and artistic qualities of his work, a quest he pursued throughout his life.

At eighteen Ma started to learn the basics of doing artwork inside bottles. He applied the painting and calligraphic skills he had mastered to this new art form. By the time he reached his forties and fifties he still worked hard to improve his technique, enlarge the repertoire of his subject matter, and enhance the artistic quality of his output.

The nurturing of an inside-painted bottle artist is akin to constructing a house in that the foundation work cannot be neglected. The nature of the foundation has a direct bearing on the kind of house that can be built on it. A shallow foundation is only suitable for building a bungalow, whereas a deep and solid foundation can support a multi-storied mansion.

Yet, the nurturing of an inside-painted bottle artist also differs from the construction of a house. The foundation of a house is laid down in one operation. It is distinct from the architecture built on top of it. How would the foundation of an inside-painted bottle artist be viewed in relation to the architecture built on top of it? If his production is regarded as the architecture, then his proficiency in traditional painting and calligraphy, as well as in doing artwork inside the bottles should be viewed as the foundation. The laying of this foundation is not a one-time operation. It requires a life-long commitment to gaining more knowledge, striving for perfection and consolidating skills. In a word, he can never hope to learn enough. While it is true that the knowledge and techniques acquired during one's youth become the foundation, this foundation, however, is not strong enough. For the rest of one's life one should continue to reinforce one's foundation by acquiring more knowledge and upgrading one's skills. This was exactly what Ma Shaoxuan did. After he had turned thirty-five, that is, after he had gained recognition for painting the portrait of Tan Xinpei in the role of General Huang Zhong, he stopped doing this popular subject, and for several years kept very much to himself in order to attack the new subject of painting portraits of his contemporaries inside the bottles. This shows how much he valued the improvement of basic skills. Then, in the case of calligraphy, from youth to old age Ma insisted on practising the regular script in small size throughout his entire life. Even in practice he always wrote with meticulous care. Never would he write one stroke hastily. If he was dissatisfied with the composition of a certain character, he would repeat writing this character many times until he was happy with its form. It was this foundation that enabled him to write high-quality calligraphy inside the bottles from the very beginning of his career and make big strides to attain greater refinement in the later stage.

The course of development of Ma's art, whether in calligraphy, painting, poetry or seal design, makes it clear that his solid foundation was built on a thorough training in youthful years coupled with a constant effort made at advancing knowledge and techniques in later life. Because of this sound foundation, he was able to produce fabulous bottles one after another in all stages of his career. Similar to a large tree, only when it has developed far-reaching roots to take in abundant nourishment can it give flourishing flowers and foliage. As well, similar to architecture of great splendor, only when it has a firm foundation can it stand majestically.

Ma's life-long endeavors make clear that one of the principal factors for success is to first acquire a basic skill and then perfect it throughout one's lifetime. As the life and energy of an artist are limited, he should make good use of his valuable time span. Practising and improving his basic skills should be his priorities.

In the following we will examine the cornerstones that made up the foundation of Ma's grandiose hall—the art of his inside-painted bottles.

1. In knowledge Ma was erudite. He was well-versed in general history and history of literature, calligraphy and painting. Not only did he comprehend the significance of numerous famous poetic compositions, he also knew them by heart. Analogous to bricks, his cultural knowledge constituted the first type of material needed for the building of the foundation of his hall.

2. In technique Ma demonstrated excellence in penmanship and draughtsmanship. He also mastered the special skill of writing and painting on the interior walls of snuff bottles. Similar to steel rods, this ability constituted the second type of construction material.

3. In terms of an ideal state of mind, an inside-painted bottle artist not only requires strong physique, he should have, in addition, good psychological qualities such as calmness, meticulousness, patience, persistence and so on. A person lacking any of these qualities is not likely to become a good inside-painted bottle artist. Akin to concrete, developing and nurturing beneficial psychological qualities from an early age is the third type of construction material.

Ma lived in a period when the modern notion of an educational system comprised of a primary school, a middle school and a university was still non-existent. From an early age he received tuition from his father and his teacher. In reviewing his life, it was mainly family upbringing, old-fashioned tutoring, and self-education that prepared him to gradually gain his knowledge and skills, as well as to develop good psychological qualities. The three aspects outlined above are inter-related. They also complement one another. Therefore none can be left out. It is thanks to these foundation stones that Ma was able to produce many magnificent inside-painted bottles.

INHERITANCE AND INNOVATION

Having good basic skills enables one to do good artwork inside the bottles. However, if an artist wants to achieve excellence in his production, he still needs to handle correctly the relationship between inheritance and innovation. Ma Shaoxuan inherited with veneration his legacy of traditional culture, traditional art—in particular painting and calligraphy, and inside-painting techniques developed by his forerunners. He studied these subjects wholeheartedly, learning everything that needed to be learned. However, he did not follow traditions blindly. In his quest for excellence in the art of inside-painting he was never satisfied with what he had attained. He always wanted to stretch his limits. His whole life was spent in the perpetuation of the past while at the same time striving for innovation. At that time, there were indeed many blank areas in the field of inside-painting waiting to be explored and new ideas to be worked out. Ma boldly took on his shoulders these challenges imposed by history. In matters such as painting, calligraphy, inscription, and the use of seal images he made numerous innovative contributions to the development of the art of inside-painted snuff bottles.

The result of Ma's endeavor tells us that innovation is the fruit of intense labor. After innovative ideas have been tried and accepted, the happiness engendered belongs to no one but the creator who dares to take a bold step. When Ma first crossed the threshold of the art of inside-painting, he already demonstrated these desirable qualities: an active mind, keen judgment, creative thinking, and an exploratory spirit. When opportunity knocked on his door, he was always quick to respond. No matter how unheard of, how serious, and how difficult to resolve the problems history imposed on him were, he would face them squarely, showing neither fear nor any inclination to back off. Relying on his astute mental faculty, he tackled them unrelentingly. In the end he was able to produce not only satisfactory but often quite startling answers. At the same time, while trying to solve problems never encountered by his forerunners, he began to nurture a desire to innovate. From his rendition of "Boundless Joy" to his portrait of Tan Xinpei in the role of General Huang Zhong, and from his emulation of the "Lanting Preface" to his portrait of the Xuantong emperor, he was brave enough to handle each situation head-on, rising to the challenge single-handedly. As a result, he was able to reap the fruit of innovation, attaining an unprecedented high level of achievement. If, on encountering difficulties Ma felt that he could never overcome them and opted to back off because there were no precedents to follow, he would not have been able to try out new ideas; neither would his inside-painting techniques show any improvement nor would there be any significant works by him.

Innovation is not a fantasy. There is an idiomatic expression: *yigao ren danda* (A talented person is always ready to take risks). Being talented provides one with the foundation for being undaunted by risks. Likewise, that Ma was able to carry out his innovations was the product of solid skills to back them up. If Ma had not had superb technical skills and the will to pursue perfection, and hoped to become a winner by relying on vague notions of determination and courage, it would never have worked. This is why it has been said: having the fortitude to face challenges, one should set his artistic goal on a higher plane in order to achieve best results.

Some men tend to become conservative after they have entered their middle age. Others no longer want to take risks after they have won public recognition. At such a time they stop making further progress. However, it was a different thing with Ma. At forty-four he was already quite well-known in the field of inside-painted bottles. Yet, during this time he still forged ahead, experimenting with new techniques and new subjects. As an example, when he was commissioned to do a portrait of the German monarch, Kaiser Wilhelm II, on a bottle, his client specified that the inscription written on the reverse should be in German. Ma had never studied any foreign language. Neither had he ever attempted to write in any foreign hand. For him, therefore, writing this German inscription inside a bottle of some importance was no easy task. It was also a risky undertaking. A less adventurous man would have chosen a safer way out by insisting on inscribing in Chinese. But Ma remained undaunted. After serious preparation, he managed to write the German inscription in a flourishing manner and the result was actually quite magnificent!

An innovative artist is a treasure. Ma was an extraordinary case. Though he received instruction from the *Four Books* and *Five Classics* prescribed in traditional China, it was truly amazing that he could nurture such a forceful creative drive and an adventurous spirit. This might be due directly to the certain degree of freedom permitted in his family in his early years and to the self-satisfaction he derived from years of practising the special art form of inside-painting and the successes gained after overcoming its inherent difficulties.

In conservative traditional China Ma Shaoxuan was a rare talent. In the historical context of the transitional period between the late Qing dynasty and the early Republic he achieved many outstanding results. As the common saying goes: "When a man fulfills a task, he will be known for his accomplishment." However, the fulfillment of a task depends on the doer, and it is the abilities and qualities of this person that decide whether or not his mission will be accomplished.

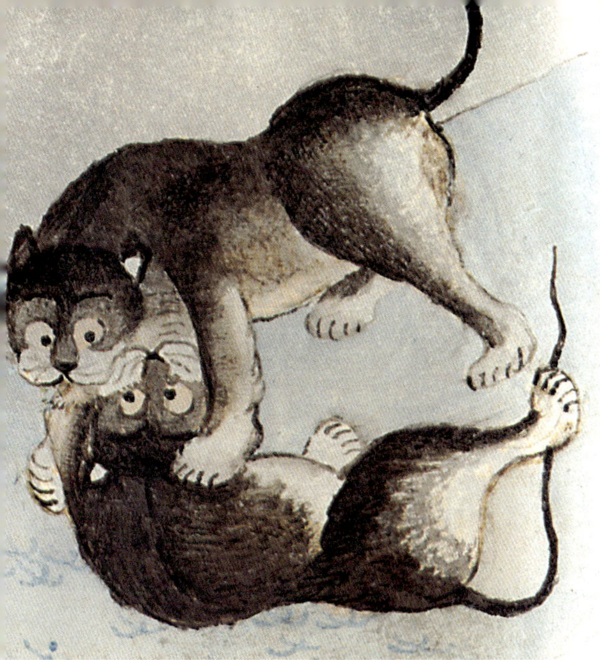

CHAPTER ELEVEN

Protect Precious Works and Boycott the Forgeries

For a long time two phenonmena have been detrimental to the image of Ma Shaoxuan and his oeuvre; they are equally harmful to collectors of his works. One is forgery. It affects Ma's reputation adversely and causes distress for collectors, researchers, as well as admirers. The other is the problem of damage sustained by the bottles which can totally ruin them. If we treasure Ma Shaoxuan's inside-painted bottles, we should think of ways to prevent these things from happening.

FORGERIES

By forgeries we mean the low-quality imitations made by people who assumed Ma Shaoxuan's name. There is enough evidence pointing to the fact that fakes exist in large numbers, that they are circulated widely, are extremely deceptive, and produce serious injurious effects. Many people have fallen victim to such works. Occasionally even renowned collectors regard forgeries as genuine pieces. Faked Ma bottles were produced in the following two periods:

1. Early fakes were made during the period starting from the beginning of the century to the 1940s. While counted among them were many poor quality works that have deceived quite a few people, there were also some productions whose high level of workmanship made it quite impossible to distinguish them from Ma's genuine works.

2. Recent fakes were made approximately after the mid-1980s up to the present day, that is, after the Chinese government had reset economic objectives and put into effect more relaxed policies. These productions are characterized by poor workmanship. The forgers and their agents went all out to make big profits, cheating unwary customers unscrupulously.

On a certain day in the autumn of 1991 the present writer saw with his own eyes a caseful of brand new fake Ma bottles displayed in an art dealer's shop in Beijing. Among these were works depicting the themes of "The Two Qiao Sisters," "Searching for the Plum Blossom in the Snow," "Leaping Fish," and "Picture of Longevity," and so forth. There were altogether sixteen bottles in the case, each selling at the price of RMB $600. In exasperation I asked the shop assistant, "Are you aware that your shop is blatantly deceiving customers by selling these low quality fakes?" To this question he responded by saying, "They are just imitations, not fakes." However, after I discussed with them the distinction between the principles of forgery and imitation, they became wordless. I then went on to find out more about the market for such bottles. On being questioned they said that "these are mainly sold to visitors to China," adding that "after special treatment to age them, such pieces can be made to look like artifacts and they will be worth a lot more." Seeing and hearing such things infuriates me, for they not only damage Ma Shaoxuan's reputation but also tarnish the credibility of Chinese businessmen. Shame on those who engage in the production and sale of forgeries! They should be brought to justice!

SUGGESTIONS

One of the effective ways of boycotting forgeries would be to publish a catalog of inside-painted snuff bottles by Ma Shaoxuan.

The total number of works counted in Ma's oeuvre was never huge to start with. Due to social upheavals and accidental damage sustained over the years, there exist at the present time even fewer bottles. They probably total not more than a few hundred. These treasured pieces are now scattered in China and throughout the world. Access to them is next to impossible. Thus far nobody has seen them all. Then added to this is also the problem of forgery, which has created a lot of trouble in art appreciation and academic research.

It would be of untold benefit to all if museums and private collectors throughout the world were to join together to carry out one project. This would involve gathering photographs of bottles bearing Ma Shaoxuan's signatures and information pertaining to their materials, sizes, and present condition. After examination and elimination of faked pieces, only authentic bottles would be published in a catalog complete with illustrations and detailed descriptions.

If this catalog could be published, it would present a complete record of Ma's genuine inside-painted bottles. It would also make appreciating and studying the Ma bottles a lot easier. Such a record would be circulated widely. It could also be preserved for a long time.

The standards set by the authentic pieces illustrated in this catalog would elevate people's level of appreciation and authentication. Whenever they encounter an inside-painted bottle attributed to Ma, they could compare it with the illustrations in the catalog. No matter how cleverly a fake is made, it is quite certain that it will reveal its deficiencies. Thus people will avoid being cheated.

Moreover, the catalog would set a parameter. On encountering an example attributed to Ma, people could first check the catalog to ascertain whether or not it had already been included. In the case that it was unrecorded, they should then proceed to seek an expert's opinion. If nobody purchases unauthenticated bottles, it will put a stop to forgery and the value of the bottles in private and public collections will be better protected.

COLLECTING AND SAFEKEEPING

Ma Shaoxuan's early works date back to a hundred years ago. Even his late works are at least sixty to seventy years old. Over this long period his oeuvre has undergone societal disasters and natural damage. As a result, a number of bottles have disappeared, making what still survives even more valuable. Yet, the treatment each bottle receives varies. While fortunate pieces may be preserved in perfect condition in storage with climate control, unfortunate ones often sustain damage because their owners do not care enough for them. They may be left in the cold or conversely in steaming heat. They may also be rubbed against rough surfaces. The artwork on some of the bottles may have become blurred because humid air has been permitted to enter. On others it may have been marred by specks of adhering particles of tobacco or dust. In still other circumstances, it may have sustained scratch marks induced by all-too-late-to-repent owners using small slivers to remove unclean spots. Some bottles may have developed crackles on their bodies as a result of exposure to extremely hot or cold conditions. Subjected to similar trying conditions, others may have simply disintegrated. In view of these casualties, safekeeping inside-painted bottles is an issue that really needs to be addressed.

The Chinese have a long history of glassmaking. Their glass snuff bottles are characterized by elegant shapes and a high degree of transparency. However, prior to 1949 glass products did not stand up well to drastic changes in temperature and humidity. This was especially the case with glass snuff bottles as they were small and thus even more delicate. Now, based on years of experience in the safekeeping of Ma Shaoxuan's inside-painted bottles, which also include the lessons learned from breaking and damaging a number of fine specimens, I would like to offer the following few points for consideration:

1. Each bottle should be stored in a padded case. It should never be stored without any protective measure. The solid structure of the case protects it from being bumped against, crushed, or shaken. The padding, whether made of cotton wool or foam, allows the bottle to nestle comfortably in the case, never to risk the danger of being abraded. Generally speaking, the bottle should not be taken out of its case. Even when it is being viewed, it should still stay in the padded case.

2. A bottle must be fitted with a stopper so that humidity and dirt cannot enter. In the case where humidity or dust has already made its way into the bottle, refrain from sticking any tool inside the bottle to remove the foreign agent.

3. Never examine an inside-painted bottle with bare hands. If it must be handled, gloves should be worn.

4. The room where inside-painted bottles are stored should be clean, dry, and well insulated against the heat or the cold. Ideally its temperature and humidity should be kept at a constant level. If it is not possible to do so, at least the temperature and humidity should be regulated to their optimum levels throughout the year.

5. Do not take inside-painted bottles out of the house on rainy or snowy days. The same prohibition also applies to extremely hot or cold seasons. If they must be taken outdoors, extreme precautionary measures should be taken.

6. Crackled inside-painted bottles by Ma still have high values in matters concerning appreciation, collecting and resale. Therefore they should still be carefully preserved to prevent them from sustaining further damage.

As time passes by, inside-painted bottles by Ma will become more and more precious. Let us preserve them with painstaking care so that they may enjoy immeasurably long lives!

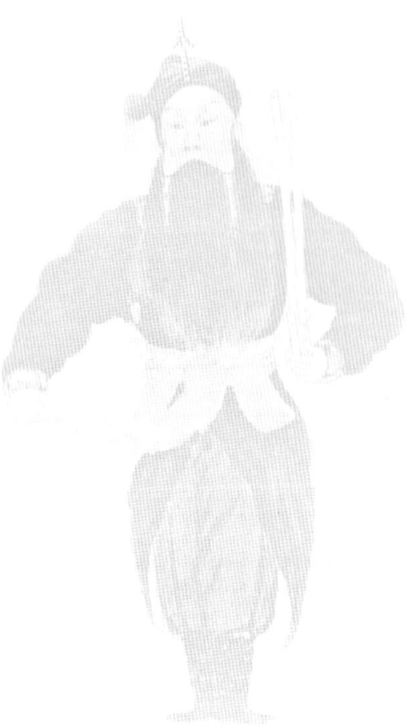

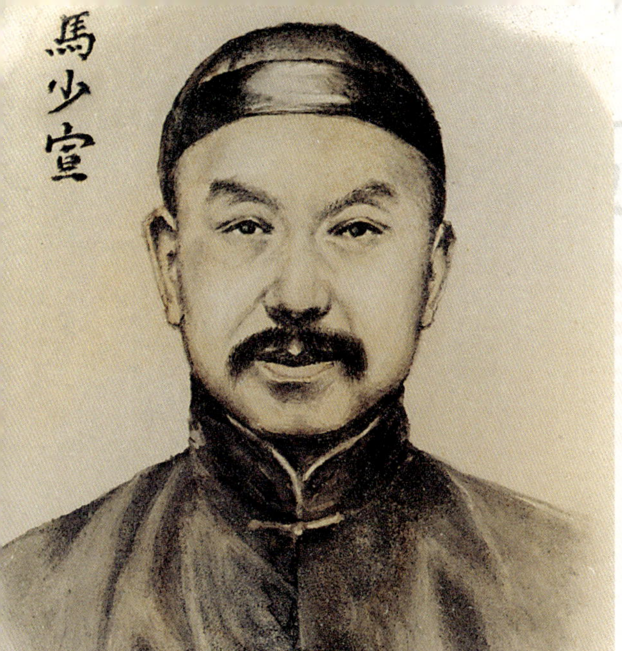

CHAPTER TWELVE

The Descendants of Ma Shaoxuan

Ma Shaoxuan had two sons and two daughters. The two daughters died at a tender age. His elder son was born in 1898. The name given to him at birth was Tong. His literary name was Zhenduo. He started his career as an employee of the Bank of China. When he was later transferred to Shanghai he stayed there until he retired and moved back to Beijing to live with Ma at number 53, Xizhuan Hutong. After Ma had passed away in 1939, he sold the property and divided the money earned from it with his younger brother. He then lived in Pan'er Hutong (Basin Alley) until he died in 1949. Married to a woman née Hei, he was survived by one son and one daughter. His son, Zengxiang, worked at the Beijing Railway Company and passed away in 1988. His daughter, Lifang, died in infancy. Zengxiang produced two sons and two daughters. They are all married and have different professions.

Ma's younger son was born in 1901. Called Zhong, his literary name was Zhensheng. Having received tutelage from Ma since childhood, he could already write beautifully in the style of Ouyang Xun by the time he became a young man. Although he also learned the technique of inside-painting from his father who would have liked to have him as his successor, because he was not truly interested in this skill, he did not make much out of it. At one time or another, he worked at the University of Communications, a government publisher, and the post office. He lived with his father when Ma was alive. After Ma's death, he moved to number 1, Menlou Hutong. After the liberation of Beijing he worked at the Beijing Post Office. At that time he lived in the employees' housing estate provided by the Post Office, located at number 4, Menggongfu. In 1953 he became ill and passed away.

Only two calligraphic works by Ma Zhensheng exist today. Both are executed in the folding fan format. One was written in the *wuyin* year (1938) for his wife Wang Peizhen. The text included two excerpts. One was quoted from *Bieji yicai yi* by Li Fu (1673–1750).[170] Li, a native of Linchuan in Jiangxi province, was also known under the names of Julai and Mutang. After attaining the *jinshi* degree in the Kangxi period (1662–1722), he served variously as the Governor of Guangxi province, Sub-Chancellor of the Grand Secretariat, and Vice-President of the Board of Revenue. *Bieji yicai yi* was a treatise about siblings living under one roof when they were of one mind and living apart when they no longer saw eye to eye with each other. The other was a poem written in ancient verse format with seven characters per line by Han Xia (fl. ca. 1644), entitled *Ji kanyu* (Satirizing the Geomancers).[171] The term *kanyu* originally connoted heaven and earth. Later on it was used to refer to geomancy and practitioners who made a living by giving advice on how *fengshui* affected daily life. These two literary works, one a prose and the other a poem, were copied onto the reverse side of a folding fan. The prose was made up of 379 characters; the poem consisted of sixteen lines and a total of 112 characters. Taking into account also the signature and date, the total number of characters written was 520. These were written in small-sized regular script. The calligraphy was neat and elegant.

The other work was an excerpt from *Huanggang zhulou ji* (An Account of the Bamboo House at Huanggang) by Wang Yucheng (954–1001), a renowned literary writer of the Song dynasty. In 1944 Ma Zhensheng copied the chosen passages on the reverse of a folding fan painted with birds and flowers in the meticulous style by Gao Houquan, a birthday gift presented to him by the painter in 1941 (fig. 103). The text was from the beginning to *jiangshan zhi wai, dijian fengfan shaniao yanyun zhushu eryi* (Beyond mountains and rivers there was nothing but sailboats, water birds, mists, wispy clouds and bamboo groves), totalling 194 characters (fig. 104).

170. For a sketch of Li Fu's life and achievements, see Tan Jiading, ed., *Zhongguo wenxuejia dacidian*, vol. 2, pp. 1473–1474.

171. For a biographical sketch of Han Xia, see *ibid.*, vol. 2, p. 1274.

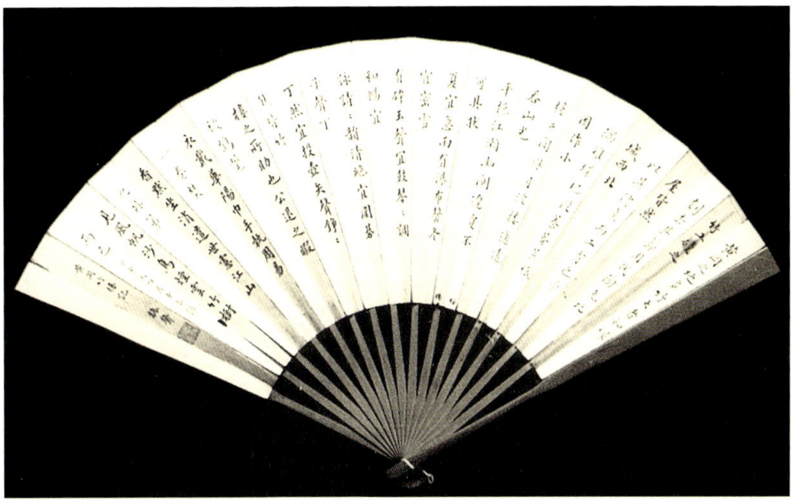

Fig. 103. Fan inscribed by Ma Zhensheng with the complete text of "An Account of the Bamboo House at Huanggang" by Wang Yucheng, dated 1944 (Ma Family Collection)

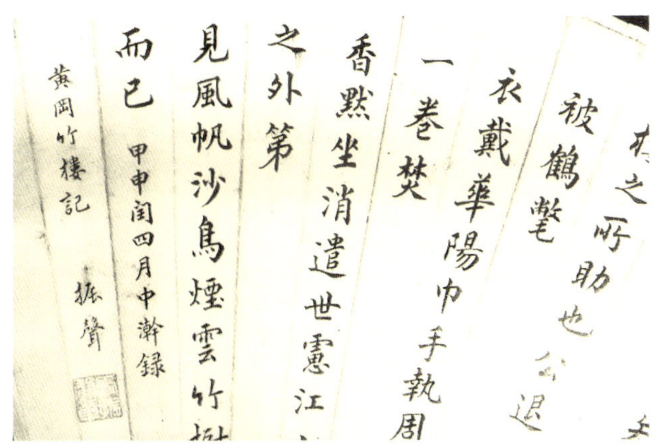

Fig. 104. Detail of fig. 103 (Ma Family Collection)

Ma Zhensheng's wife was born in the same year as her husband. She was a simple woman with an outgoing character, kind to people whether old or young, hard working, and quite devoted to the needs of everyone in the family. She bore four sons and three daughters. The sons are Zengrui, Zengshan, Zengqi, and Zengquan. The daughters are Lihua, Liyun, and Lizhuang. Among these seven offspring the eldest son became ill and passed away in 1991. The rest are in good health and still pursue their careers.

Ma Zengrui, known also under his studio names of Xueqiao and Yuqian, was born in 1924. As a youth, after graduating from the Northwest Middle School, he entered the North China Art Institute to study under Shen Tong and Gao Xinquan, two well-known metal and stone engravers. He eventually became an accomplished calligrapher, specializing also in seal-engraving and wood-carving. In the 1940s he had already exhibited his bamboo carvings and engraved seals jointly with his classmates in a waterside pavilion at the Zhongshan Park in Beijing. After working as a seal-engraver for eight years, he was assigned to do ethnic work. He stayed in that post for thirty-five years until he retired in 1985. However, still cherishing the skills he had learned when he was young, during these years he never stopped practising them. After he had retired he led a quiet life in Haidian in the northwestern part of Beijing, far away from the hubbub of the city. There, once again he relived an artistic life, busying himself with nothing but calligraphy, painting and seal-engraving.

Ma Zengrui was an outstanding carver of the endpieces of fan ribs. A folding fan is made up of a set of fan ribs and a decorated surface. Before it is opened the decorated surface is concealed; only the endpieces are visible. These endpieces are often carved with the works of famous calligraphers and painters. On hot summer days carrying such a sophisticated art object not only gives one a cultivated look but also serves a practical purpose. When Ma Zengrui did his carving, he had to first reduce the scale of the artwork of the chosen masters and transfer the images onto specially selected bamboo endpieces manufactured in the Jiangnan region. Then he had to decide which detail should be carved in relief and which should be carved in intaglio, as well as the most suitable treatment for the background.

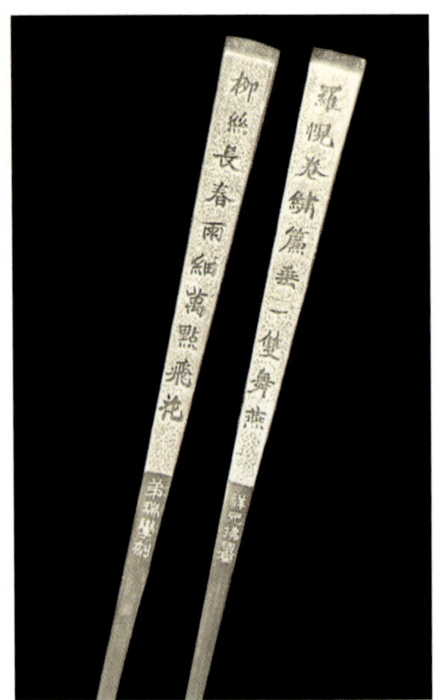

Fig. 105. Endpieces of a set of bamboo fan ribs carved by Ma Zengrui with a couplet written by Zhang Boying (Ma Family Collection)

The difficulty one encounters in bamboo carving, however, is that the fibres of the bamboo skin are very fine and strong, and cuts must be made at right angles to the natural vertical strands. One careless mistake would cause the fibres to fray and the carving would be completely ruined. Yet, Ma Zengrui could do extremely fine carving. He could also fully capture the spirit of the originals, whether paintings or calligraphic specimens. As an example, in his carving of a piece by the calligrapher Hua Rigui, he reproduced faithfully the varied thickness of each stroke, capturing the resilient quality of the

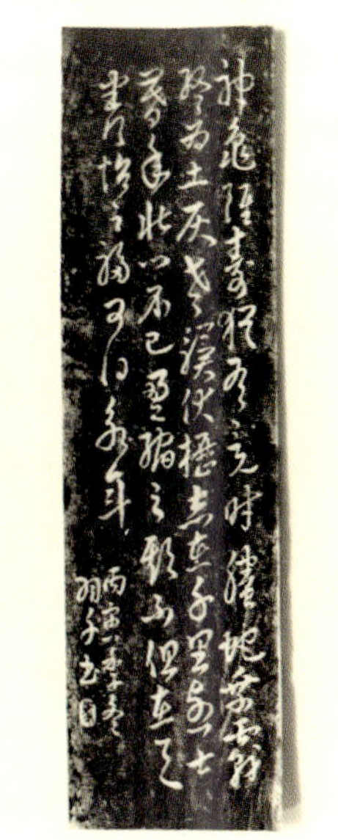

Fig. 106. Wrist-rest carved by Ma Zengrui with the poem "Although the Tortoise Has a Long Life" by Cao Cao, dated 1986 (Ma Family Collection)

brushwork even in the tiny characters. His carving of Chen Shizeng's (1876–1923) bamboo painting was another challenging endeavor.[172] Nevertheless his rendition was also true to the original. Although the foliage was sparse, it was no easy task to cut the slanting stems and perky leaves. Other fine works included the theme of depiction of antique objects and calligraphic couplets written by Zhang Boying (fig. 105).[173]

In addition, other examples of works by Ma Zengrui include several seal impressions, a wrist-rest and a carved wall hanging. The wrist-rest, made in 1986, measures 30 cm long and 8 cm wide. It is carved with Cao Cao's *Gui sui shou* (Although the Tortoise Has a Long Life), a poem included in *Buchu Xiamen xing* (Ballad of Strolling out of the Summer Gate) (fig. 106).[174] The wooden wall hanging is 120 cm long and 45 cm wide. It is carved with Su Shi's "Rhapsody on Red Cliff" and was a work completed in 1985.[175]

172. Chen Shizeng is the literary name of Chen Hengke, a celebrated child prodigy, calligrapher, painter, and art educator. See Yu Jianhua, ed., *Zhongguo meishujia renming cidian*, p. 1043.

173. Zhang Boying was a Ming painter from Jiaxing in Zhejiang province specializing bird-and-flower subjects. *Ibid.*, p. 823.

174. See Cao Cao, *Cao Cao ji*, p. 11.

175. See Su Shi, *Su Dongpo quanji*, *juan* 20, p. 268.

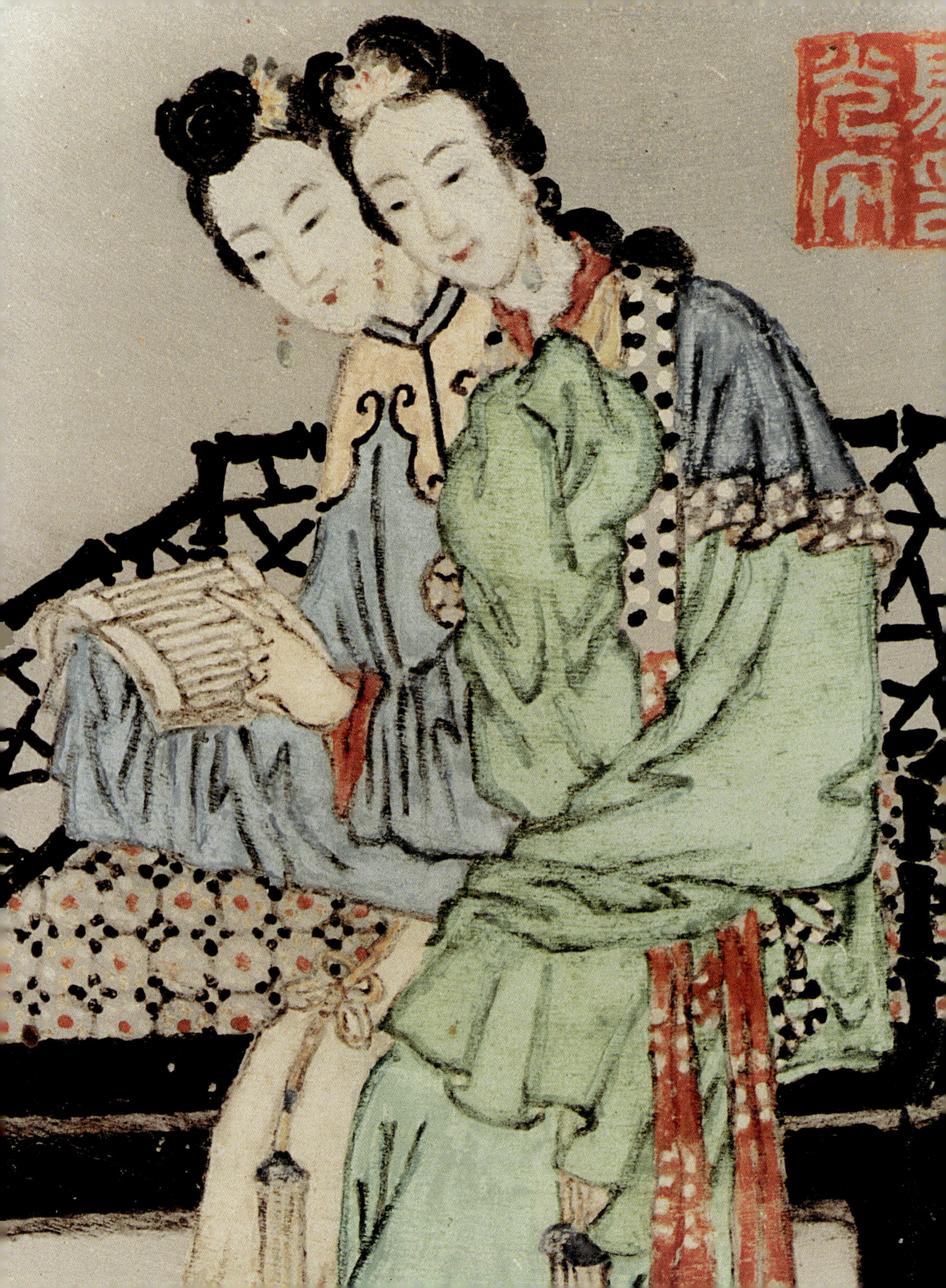

Bibliography

Bai, Juyi. *Baishi changqing ji*. Reprint, in *Baishi wenji*. Shanghai: Commercial Press, n.d.

Beurdeley, Cécile and Michel. *Giuseppe Castiglione: A Jesuit Painter at the Court of the Chinese Emperors*. Rutland and Tokyo: Charles E. Tuttle, 1971.

Billeter, Jean François. *The Chinese Art of Writing*. Geneva: Skira, 1990.

Boorman, Howard L., ed. *Biographical Dictionary of Republican China*. New York: Columbia University Press, 1967–79.

Bush, Susan. *The Chinese Literati on Painting: Su Shih (1037–1101) to Tung Ch'i-ch'ang (1555–1636)*. Cambridge: Harvard University Press, 1971.

Bush, Susan and Hsio-yen Shih. *Early Chinese Texts on Painting*. Cambridge: Harvard University Press, 1985.

Cao, Cao. *Cao Cao ji*. Reprint. Beijing: Zhonghua shuju, 1962.

Chen, Shou. *Sanguo zhi*. Reprint. Beijing: Zhonghua shuju, 1975.

[Chen Xixin] *The Fisherman's Revenge: a Peking Opera*, translated by Yang Hsien-yi and Gladys Yang. Peking: Foreign Languages Press, 1956.

Curtis, Emily Byrne. "China's Republican Period History as Mirrored in Portrait Bottles." *Journal of the International Chinese Snuff Bottle Society*, December 1978, pp. 5–16.

— *Reflected Glory in a Bottle: Chinese Snuff Bottle Portraits*. New York: Soho Bodhi, 1980.

— "Chinese Snuff Bottle Portraits: A Supplement." *Journal of the International Chinese Snuff Bottle Society*, Autumn 1985, pp. 131–133.

Daozang. Beijing: Wenwu chubanshe, 1987.

Du, Mu. *Fanchuan wenji*. Reprint. Shanghai: Commercial Press, 1965.

Egan, Ronald C. *The Literary Works of Ou-yang Hsiu (1007–72)*. Cambridge: Cambridge University Press, 1984.

Ford, John Gilmore. *Chinese Snuff Bottles: The Edward Choate O'Dell Collection*. Baltimore: The International Chinese Snuff Bottle Society, 1982.

Geng, Baochang and Zhao Binghua, ed. *Zhongguo biyanhu zhenshang*. Hong Kong: Joint Publishing and Taikong Culture Enterprise, 1992.

Guo, Weiqu, ed. *Song Yuan Ming Qing shuhuajia nianbiao*. Beijing: Renmin meishu chubanshe, 1982.

Hawkes, David. *Ch'u Tz'u: The Songs of the South*. Oxford: Clarendon Press, 1959.

Hummel, Arthur W., ed. *Eminent Chinese of the Ch'ing Period*. 2 vols. Washington, D.C.: Government Printing Office, 1943.

Jin, Shoushen. *Lao Beijing de shenghuo*. Beijing: Beijing chubanshe, 1989.

Kardos, Elisabeth. "Giuseppe Castiglione." *Journal of the International Chinese Snuff Bottle Society*, March 1978, pp. 3–16.

Knoblock, John, tran. *Xunzi: A Translation and Study of the Complete Works*. Volume I, Books 1–6. Stanford: Stanford University Press, 1988.

Lawrence, Clare. *Miniature Masterpieces from the Middle Kingdom: The Monimar Collection of Chinese Snuff Bottles*. London: Zhenliu Xuan, 1996.

Leung, J.H. *A New Look of Chinese Inside-Painted Snuff Bottles*. Hong Kong: Yang Xin Xuan Art Books, 1990.

Li, Zhuowu, annot. *Shishuo xinyu bu*. Reprint. Taipei: Guangwen shuju, 1980.

Little, Stephen L. and Joseph B. Silver. *The World in a Bottle: Chinese Inside-Painted Snuff Bottles from the Collection of Joseph Baruch Silver and Traditional Chinese Paintings*. Honolulu: Honolulu Academy of Art, 1994.

Liu, Yong. *Yuezhang ji*. Reprint. Taipei: Shijie shuju, 1965.

Lü, Fengzi. *Zhongguo huafa yanjiu*. Shanghai: Shanghai renmin meishu chubanshe, 1978.

Lu, Yitong. *Wang Youjun nianpu*. [China : s.n.], Xianfeng 5 [1855].

Lu, You. *Lu Fangweng quanji*. 2 vols. Reprint. Taipei: Wenyou shudian, 1959.

Luo, Guanzhong. *Sanguo yanyi*. Reprint. Taipei: Shijie shuju, 1954.

Lynn, Richard John, trans. "Researches Done During Spare Time into the Realm of Yong Lu, God of the Nose: The *Yonglu Xianjie* of Zhao Zhiqian." Annotated by the translator. *Journal of the International Chinese Snuff Bottle Society*, Autumn 1991, pp. 5–26.

Mackerras, Colin. *The Chinese Theatre in Modern Times: From 1840 to the Present Day*. London: Thames and Hudson, 1975.

Miyazaki, Ichisada. *China's Examination Hell: The Civil Service Examinations of Imperial China*, trans. Conrad Schirokauer. New York: Weatherhill, 1976.

Moss, Hugh. *Snuff Bottles of China*. London: Bibelot, 1971.

Moss, Hugh, Victor Graham and Ka Bo Tsang. *The Art of the Chinese Snuff Bottle: The J & J Collection*. 2 vols. New York: Weatherhill, 1993.

Ouyang, Xiu. *Ouyang Wenzhonggong wenji*. Reprint. Shanghai: Commercial Press, 1965.

Owen, Stephen. *Remembrances: The Experience of the Past in Classical Chinese Literature*. Cambridge: Harvard University Press, 1986.

Panama-Pacific International Exposition Official Catalogue: Department of Fine Arts. San Francisco: Wahlgreen Company, 1915.

Sikong, Tu. *Shipin ershisi ze*. Reprint. Changsha: Commercial Press, 1939.

Soothill, William Edward and Lewis Hodous. *A Dictionary of Chinese Buddhist Terms*. Revised edition. Taipei: Buddhist Culture Service, 1962.

Stevens, Bob. *The Collector's Book of Snuff Bottles*. New York and Tokyo: Weatherhill, 1976.

Su, Shi. *Su Dongpo quanji*. Reprint. Taipei: Shijie shuju, 1964.

Sullivan, Michael. *The Meeting of Eastern and Western Art*. Berkeley: University of California Press, 1989.

Sze, Mai-mai. *The Tao of Painting: A Study of the Ritual Disposition of Chinese Painting*. 2 vols. New York: Pantheon Books, 1956.

Tan, Jiading, ed. *Zhongguo wenxuejia dacidian*. 2 vols. Reprint. Taipei: Shijie shuju, 1967.

Waley, Arthur, trans., annot. *The Analects of Confucius*. London: George Allen & Unwin, 1938.

Wang, Fangyu and Richard M. Barnhart. *Master of the Lotus Garden: The Life and Art of Bada Shanren (1626–1705)*. New Haven: Yale University Art Gallery, 1990.

Wang, Qi, annot. *Li Taibai quanji*. Beijing: Zhonghua shuju, 1977.

Wang, Shizhen. *Xiangzu biji*. Reprint. Shanghai: Wenming shuju, 1936.

Wang, Su. *Kongzi jiayu*. Reprint. Taipei: Zhongguo zixue mingzhu jicheng bianyin jijinhui, 1978.

Wang, Wengao, ed., annot. *Shu Shi shiji*. 8 vols. Beijing: Zhonghua shuju, 1982.

Watson, Burton. *Chuang Tzu: Basic Writings*. New York: Columbia University Press, 1966.

Who's Who in China. 3rd ed. Shanghai: The China Weekly Review, 1925.

Ye, Ming. *Guang yinren zhuan*. Shanghai: Xiling yinshe, 1910.

Yu, Jianhua, ed. *Zhongguo meishujia renming cidian*. Shanghai: Shanghai renmin meishu chubanshe, 1981.

Zhang, Yanyuan. *Lidai minghua ji*. Reprint. Beijing: Renmin meishu chubanshe, 1963.

Zhao, Ersun *et al. Qingshi gao*. Beijing: Zhonghua shuju, 1977.

Zhao, Ruzhen. *Guwan zhinan xubian*. Reprint. Hong Kong: Zhongmei tushu gongsi, 1970.

Zhao, Zhiqian. *Yonglu xianjie*. In *Meishu congshu*, vol. 2, pp. 201–227. Taipei: Yiwen yinshuguan, 1963.

Zhu, Xi. *Shijing jizhu*. Reprint. Hong Kong: Guangzhi shuju, 1966.

費盡揣摩力翻成
書畫癡前賢應笑
我故爾覺支離題
博古圖於京師作
馬少宣